MAKING MEXICAN ROCK

Performing Latin American and Caribbean Identities

KATHRYN BISHOP-SANCHEZ, *series editor*

This series is a forum for scholarship that recognizes the critical role of performance in social, cultural, and political life. Geographically focused on the Caribbean and Latin America (including Latinidad in the United States) but wide-ranging in thematic scope, the series highlights how understandings of desire, gender, sexuality, race, the postcolonial, human rights, and citizenship, among other issues, have been explored and continue to evolve. Books in the series will examine performances by a variety of actors with under-represented and marginalized peoples getting particular (though not exclusive) focus. Studies of spectators or audiences are equally welcome as those of actors—whether literally performers or others whose behaviors can be interpreted that way. In order to create a rich dialogue, the series will include a variety of disciplinary approaches and methods as well as studies of diverse media, genres, and time periods.

Performing Latin American and Caribbean Identities is designed to appeal to scholars and students of these geographic regions who recognize that through the lens of performance (or what may alternatively be described as spectacle, ceremony, or collective ritual, among other descriptors) we can better understand pressing societal issues.

Other titles in the series:
  Creating Carmen Miranda: Race, Camp, and Transnational Stardom by
    Kathryn Bishop-Sanchez
  Atenco Lives!: Filmmaking and Popular Struggle in Mexico by Livia K. Stone
  *Living Quixote: Performative Activism in Contemporary Brazil and the
    Americas* by Rogelio Miñana
  Creating Worlds Otherwise: Art, Collective Action, and (Post)Extractivism by
    Paula Serafini
  Empathy and Performance: Enactments of Power in Latinx America by Laura
    V. Sández
  *Latin America and the Transports of Opera: Fragments of a Transatlantic
    Discourse* by Roberto Ignacio Díaz

Making Mexican Rock
*Censorship, Journalism,
and Popular Music after Avándaro*

ANDREW J. GREEN

VANDERBILT UNIVERSITY PRESS
Nashville, Tennessee

Copyright 2024 Vanderbilt University Press
All rights reserved
First printing 2024

This book will be made open access within three years of publication thanks to Path to Open, a program developed in partnership between JSTOR, the American Council of Learned Societies (ACLS), University of Michigan Press, and the University of North Carolina Press to bring about equitable access and impact for the entire scholarly community, including authors, researchers, libraries, and university presses around the world. Learn more at https://about.jstor.org/path-to-open.

Library of Congress Cataloging-in-Publication Data

Names: Green, Andrew, 1987- author.
Title: Making Mexican rock : censorship, journalism, and popular music after Avándaro / Andrew Green.
Description: Nashville : Vanderbilt University Press, 2024. | Series: Performing Latin American and Caribbean identities ; book 7 | Includes bibliographical references and index.
Identifiers: LCCN 2024018197 (print) | LCCN 2024018198 (ebook) | ISBN 9780826507280 (paperback) | ISBN 9780826507297 (hardcover) | ISBN 9780826507303 (epub) | ISBN 9780826507310 (pdf)
Subjects: LCSH: Rock music--Political aspects--Mexico--History. | Rock music--Mexico--History and criticism. | Music--Censorship--Mexico--History. | Musical criticism--Mexico--History. | Festival de Rock y Ruedas de Avándaro (1971 ; Valle de Bravo, Mexico)
Classification: LCC ML3917.M4 G74 2024 (print) | LCC ML3917.M4 (ebook) | DDC 781.660972--dc23/eng/20240426
LC record available at https://lccn.loc.gov/2024018197
LC ebook record available at https://lccn.loc.gov/2024018198

To my parents

CONTENTS

Acknowledgments ix

INTRODUCTION 1

1. After Avándaro: Censorship and Rock Journalism as Governmentality in the 1970s 27

2. Producing Independence: The Rock Boom and Commercial Censorship 53

3. The Monopolistic Ogre?: OCESA, Live Rock, and Enclosure 77

4. On Solidarity and Silence: Music Censorship, Open-Air Performance, and Zapatismo 96

5. Listening Down the Rabbit Hole: Independent Music Venues, Democratic Governance, and the Performance of Transition 113

6. *Foros culturales*, History, and the Right to Culture 141

7. Write for Your Right to Party: Rock Knowledge and the Opening of History 163

Notes 187
Bibliography 243
Index 257

ACKNOWLEDGMENTS

This book is a product of collaborative effort. While I alone am responsible for any errors or shortcomings it may contain, the fact that this book exists is testament to the support of many different people, who I wish to acknowledge here.

First, I am very grateful to all of the team at Vanderbilt University Press for supporting this project. I want to extend particular thanks to Gianna Mosser, and also to her predecessor, Zachary Gresham, who stuck with the book in its embryonic stages and provided encouragement as the ideas behind it began to take shape, even over a long period of time. I am also indebted to the two anonymous reviewers of the manuscript, whose insightful and thorough comments have improved this book immeasurably.

The origins of this book can be found in a pair of panels in which I participated, at the Latin American Studies Association conference in 2018, and at the American Anthropological Association conference in 2019. These panels brought me into contact with a group of inspiring scholars whose work engages with Latin American politics and culture from below: Kelley Tatro, Liv Stone, Michelle Tellez, José Martínez Reyes, Maurice Magaña, and finally Jeff Juris, who departed far too soon. This book is dedicated, in part, to Jeff; his scholarly legacy and his commitment to radical social movements worldwide. Of this group, Liv Stone also deserves particular thanks for supporting this project from the beginning and reading early drafts of what later became this book. The development of this project was also enriched by a number of conversations, virtual and in person, with Kelley Tatro.

In Mexico, I am grateful to everyone who took their time to participate in this project. Several people made especially important contributions to its development. David Cortés Arce generously gave his time to read several chapter drafts in their later stages, and we shared a number of particularly enjoyable, in-depth, fun chats over coffee about the history of Mexican rock. I am especially grateful to David for his continual insistence that I stop worrying and send off the manuscript. Javier Hernández "Chelico" invited me to participate in his workshop on rock journalism at the Faro de Oriente, and later presented me with the invaluable opportunity to present some of the reflections contained in this book to his "Rock Con Filo" group. José Riwes Cruz read through some of the book's later drafts and made many informed, helpful comments. Rafael González was a wonderfully warm, encouraging, and supporting presence through the process of research and writing. I had a number of interesting conversations about the magazine *Sonido* with Walter Schmidt, who not only shared with me invaluable insights and experiences, but also generously allowed me to access his personal archive. I am grateful to Rafael Catana for a number of insightful chats over coffee, and for inviting me to visit him in his studio at Radio Educación. Finally, particular thanks to each member of the group ColectivaMente: their dedication to the living histories of Mexican rock is what makes other kinds of intervention, such as this one, possible.

I am also indebted to many other people who have accompanied me on what is now a seventeen-year journey through Mexico. In Valle de Chalco, the Palacios family first helped me to experience Mexico with clear eyes, and with compassion, joy, and positivity. Thanks to all of you, but especially Teo, Angélica, Arcelia, and Alejandro. This book is partly dedicated to the memory of Tito Palacios: he might not have known it, but his example motivated my teenage self to want to be better. In Mexico City, to Ixel, Abi and Sergio, Karen and Rodrigo, Nicole and Roberto, Claudio and Sian, Sarahi, Benny and Janice, and Laura.

As the above suggests, soon after the idea for it was conceived this book quickly became a pandemic project. A number of people helped me to maintain my sanity during the pandemic. Most important of these is my brother David, who showed up at the train station with a crate full of trinkets, and a head full of ideas, about as soon as it was permitted to do so. I am very grateful to my parents for their constant encouragement, support, and belief in me, even in the hardest of times. My mother Sue takes both the credit and the blame for first suggesting that students might be interested in listening to me hold forth about music.

At the University of Glasgow, both Matt Brennan and John Williamson read through early drafts of chapters for this book, and provided invaluable guidance and encouragement. They also gave me the opportunity to work through some of the book's arguments in a pair of guest lectures on the Music Industries postgraduate course. I also discussed my ideas for the book at an early stage with Nathanial Gardner and Mike Gonzalez.

Since this is my first book, it marks a milestone in my personal journey as a scholar. Ever since my first steps in the world of academia as a doctoral student, I have been indebted to Henry Stobart, whose meticulous, patient, purposeful, and kind supervision opened the door to a scholarship that was in equal parts thorough, critical, intellectually curious, and essentially humane. I have been doing my best to walk through it ever since.

Besides those who have contributed directly to this book, I am grateful to many colleagues and fellow travelers who have supported me in various ways over the years. First, from the community of music scholars in the United Kingdom, I am grateful to Simran Singh, Cassandre Balosso-Bardin, Shzr Ee Tan, Tom Wagner, Fiorela Montero-Díaz, Hettie Malcomson, Laudan Nooshin, Byron Dueck, Katia Chornik, Hazel Marsh, Geoff Baker, Matthew Machin-Auchenreith, and Amanda Bayley. At the University of Glasgow, I would like to thank Bjorn Heile, Iain Findlay-Walsh, Louise Harris, Eva Moreda-Rodríguez, John Butt, Oscar Odeña, Phil Alexander, Jane Stanley, Drew Hammond, John Butt, and Valeria Carolina Gascón Grajales. At the University of Warsaw, many thanks are due to Dorota Łagodzka, Katarzyna Granicka, John Sullivan, Jack Harrison, Luis Javier Pentón Herrera, Julia Lewandowska, Tetyana Lewińska, and Ewa Jakubiec. In Warsaw, thanks to all of my fellow travelers at both Niewinność and Pardon To Tu, in hope that we'll meet again, someday. And thanks to Agata, whose name I got right, eventually.

The Leverhulme Trust supported this research with an Early Career Fellowship (ECF-2017-159), for which I am very grateful to them. The final stages of this book were completed while I was based at the University of Warsaw, carrying out a research project supported by the National Science Center, Poland, who I would also like to thank.

Introduction

In the run-up to Mexico's 2018 national elections, a rumor circulated online that Mikel Arriola, the Revolutionary Institutional Party (PRI) candidate for Mexico City mayor, was planning to ban rock in the capital. Apparently false, the rumor had Arriola blaming "the proliferation of rock concerts in the city" for young people having "fallen into drug addiction, homosexuality and atheism." This "proliferation," Arriola claimed, had occurred under the governments of Morena, the left-populist party that had governed Mexico City since 2015, and the Party of the Democratic Revolution (PRD), the center-left party that had governed Mexico City between 1997 and 2015. Arriola was rumored to have promised that under his administration, "there will no longer be rock concerts; so as to guarantee tranquility for your family there will be a firm hand against the companies that seek to attract these kinds of decadent spectacles."[1] Within an election campaign marred by disinformation, this piece of so-called fake news was especially pregnant with meaning. It painted Arriola as a holdover from the PRI's paternalistic and authoritarian past, as a remnant of the party responsible for more than seventy years of single-party rule in Mexico between 1929 and 2000. Indeed, it was not difficult to portray Arriola in this way: during the campaign, he had depicted himself as a social conservative and, in a widely mocked campaign ad, had blamed Morena for drug abuse in Mexico, despite the fact that the party held no seats at the federal level at that time. Crucially, this rumor also built on a history of music censorship that, by now, held an enduring place in the collective rock imaginary within Mexico. Sharing the rumor, some social media users linked it to a 2013 documentary entitled *El rock no tiene la culpa* (It's not rock's fault), which told a familiar narrative: that rock had been repressed by Mexico's single-party regime after 1971, when the first mass-scale rock festival in the country—informally called Avándaro—provoked scandal in the tabloid press.² The result was that rock in the capital was excluded from live venues, suppressed on the radio, and forced into informal venues colloquially termed *hoyos fonqui* (funky holes) on the city's margins.

The rumor about Arriola's plan to ban rock, and the reactions to it, were indicative of the ongoing power that stories about the historic censorship of rock in Mexico City possess. These stories, I want to show here, move people, provoke creative activity, and perform political work. They can, as in the case of this rumor, complicate narratives about democratic transition in Mexico, seeing continuities between single-party rule and electoral democracy; they can also draw a simpler narrative, based on a straightforward contrast between authoritarian oppression and democratic freedom. Their power reflects, in turn, the enduring popularity of rock in Mexico—a genre that has, through the period explored in this book, been referred to as *rock mexicano* (Mexican rock) and *rock nacional* (national rock).³ With the soaring popularity of Mexican regional music worldwide, and the enduring popularity of *banda* and *música norteña* among Mexican audiences, it is perhaps surprising that some surveys in recent years have indicated that rock is Mexican listeners' preferred musical genre.⁴

These stories are continually replayed within a vibrant, independent live music scene which has a certain literary identity. There is a vital, and unusually close, intertwining between music-making and the written word in this scene: many well-known musicians also have careers as journalists, writers, and radio presenters. Many event organizers, label owners, and other industry actors also write. Some resemble what journalist and organizer José Xavier Navar disparagingly termed "official Avandarologists" who (apparently because of their age) "are immune even to Carbon-14 dating," obsessed with this particular chapter in Mexican cultural history.⁵ Others write about a greater range of histories and experiences. What is common, however, is that actors within this scene intertwine music with other forms of knowledge production. This is the situation I intend to explore in this book.

Eric Zolov concludes the introduction to his 1999 book *Refried Elvis*—the first English-language scholarly tome on Mexican rock, and by far the most influential—with a call for "recovery" of the story of the repressed, forgotten and abandoned "Avándaro generation" of the 1970s.⁶ The context for *Making Mexican Rock*, researched and written decades later, is that much of this recovery has been carried out: scholars, documentary filmmakers, and journalists have worked to recover and popularize the music of the Avándaro generation, and to raise awareness of the ways this music has been historically subject to censorship. At an international level, the most high-profile fruit of these shared labors has been the 2020 Netflix docuseries *Break It All: The History of Rock in Latin America*, which focuses in particular on the histories of rock in Argentina and Mexico. The various intellectual activities, including the publication of several books, that coincided with the fiftieth anniversary of the Avándaro Festival in 2021 confirmed the canonical status of this history within Mexican alternative cultural movements. Alongside the research carried out for this book, I am invested in these efforts as a participant in an initiative to collect, digitize, and make public information about Mexican rock.

Equally, I am engaged with a different series of questions as a practitioner of ethnography who has been conducting research in Mexico City since 2012 with participants in what is known locally as the *escena independiente*, or "independent scene." The *escena independiente* comprises a number of small- and mid-sized venues, most of which are located in comparatively wealthy districts close to the center of the capital. Although this scene is complex and multifaceted, it is closely intertwined with the multiple subgenres that constitute rock; and it is informed by a pervasive sense of oppositionality and resistance. I use the term "scene" because it is used by my participants to describe their experiences, although I am aware of the scholarly debates that have surrounded this word.[7] Through my research, I have gained a perspective on the kinds of activities that help histories of censorship to live, and on the complex constitutive role played by narratives of censorship for action within this scene. I have also gained insights into how, within this scene, understandings about censorship continuously resist closure and escape easy definition. Many participants in this scene strenuously object to the idea that their histories should be marshaled in support of an "end-of-history" narrative—one in which their principal antagonist, in the form of Mexico's authoritarian single-party regime, is confined to the past.

Various kinds of questions have arisen through this research. What do these narratives about music censorship do? What are the different ways in which they are structured? How do these narratives relate to present-day experience and activity? And through what kinds of expressive activities are they popularized and perpetuated? In addition to being concerned about present-day experience, I am also interested in historical questions. How did these narratives arise, and which groups have organized to shape and disseminate them? Some stories about censorship are remembered widely, while others come to be forgotten. Why is this? What can such discrepant narratives tell us about how stories of censorship influence public discourse about the relationships between government, big business, and police? And what do they say about how people in Mexico think about the so-called democratic transition?

I contend that these are the right kinds of questions to ask if we are to deepen our understanding of the varied ways that music censorship may play out in practice and of the thorny, often divisive debates over Mexico's contemporary history. In the following section, I attempt to articulate why.

From Censorship to Governmentality

Conversations about music censorship in Mexico continuously raise questions related to political power and ideology. Which entities can be considered to exert censorship? Can private entities, as well as states, do so, and if so, under what circumstances?[8] In the terms of Isaiah Berlin, is what is described and understood as "censorship" strictly a question of the deprivation of preexisting negative liberties—for example, through direct prohibitions over certain kinds of speech—or may it be understood as the denial of positive liberties—through, say, a lack of financial support for certain forms of expression?[9]

The starting point for this book is that we can never enjoy an epistemologically straightforward perspective on censorship. To explore lived experiences of censorship is to engage with uncertainty and doubt. Censorship is characterized by a paradox: although the popular imaginary on censorship has long tended to focus on official bodies that openly prohibit certain kinds of expression, censorship is exerted implicitly or indirectly just as often as through official decree. Even totalitarian or tyrannical governments may reject accusations of censorship; and even here, the censorship of music can appear arbitrary, opaque, and inexplicable, typified—in the words of Nick Tochka—"less by its calculatedness than by its ugly triviality, its foul incoherence."[10] Indeed, certainty can often undermine the effectiveness of censorship, providing a clear pretext for mobilization against it. For these reasons, narratives about music censorship are often highly contested. Indeed, it is important to recognize that a given social actor's ability to deny having engaged in censorship is connected to their ability to influence media coverage and operate within the public sphere.

Until comparatively recently, scholars tended to understand censorship in relatively straightforward terms, as the prohibition of speech or expression by political power, especially the state.[11] Since the late twentieth century, however, scholarly accounts of censorship have vastly broadened, as part of what some have labeled "new censorship theory."[12] Where censorship was formerly associated almost exclusively with "direct forms of regulatory intervention by political authorities," poststructuralist thinkers have tended to perceive continuities between state censorship and broader "grammars of power" implicating a larger group of actors.[13] In turn, this creates a potential moral dilemma, since censorship may also be seen as a productive force, radically imbricated in the ways that subjects are formed.[14] For Butler, censorship may be understood simultaneously as "that which is directed against persons or against the content of their speech" and "a way of producing speech, constraining in advance what will and will not become acceptable speech."[15] Within this broadly poststructuralist frame, then, censorship is perceived as a basic condition of human social life, as well as an incursion by powerful entities into the same. A potential consequence is that the distinctive, aberrant moral weight of censorship may be diminished.[16]

At the same time that the "new censorship theory" has filtered through the humanities, there has emerged an increasingly complex and nuanced body of scholarship on censorship in the music industries.[17] The richness of this scholarly conversation is linked to transformations within this sector, especially as the power of music labels has given way to streaming platforms. Since the early 2000s, for example, scholars paid increasing attention to how corporate influence over musical expression overlapped with political power.[18] Widely noted is the case of a memo circulated within Clear Channel, a media company enjoying near-monopoly power within United States radio whose chief executive happened to be a member of the Republican Party, in the wake of the attacks in New York on September 11, 2001. The memo suggested a list of songs for Clear Channel's DJs to avoid, which happened to include the entire back catalog of Rage Against the Machine.[19] Music scholars have also considered coercive ways in which the music industries are structured, through onerous terms included within recording contracts.[20] In more recent scholarship, the transition to streaming raises concerns about the censorial implications of hidden algorithms—highlighting serious questions about methodology, opacity, and access.[21]

Evidently, it is increasingly taken for granted within this literature that music censorship may be exerted through market forces. John Street seeks to problematize this tendency, arguing that a definition of "commercial censorship" exercised through the "'normal' operation of the market" is "so broad as to be meaningless."[22] This response, in turn, clarifies the political ideologies underpinning distinct accounts of censorship: Street is writing from a liberal vantage point, characterized by a relatively untroubled distinction between public and private spheres. As Candea puts it, censorship has long been central to "a certain liberal democratic *mythos*," in which the censorship of speech is relegated to a "pre-democratic past."[23] At a time when the literature on music censorship has become increasingly decentered from the

United States and Europe—those global contexts in which liberal democracy is most culturally entrenched—it is vital that such work should avoid taking for granted the liberal-democratic teleology that Candea describes.[24]

Such a teleology was evidently at stake in the rumor about Mikel Arriola described above, in which the threat of censorship against rock functions as a synecdoche for the return of authoritarianism. Yet conversations about music censorship in Mexico are exceptionally complicated, not least because the recent political history of Mexico raises interesting questions about what it means to live in a democracy and what it means to transition to one. Constantly implicated in such conversations is the question: What kind of political system do we inhabit? Work discussing music censorship in Mexico has often emphasized acts of prohibition consistent with governance in established liberal democracies. For instance, multiple writers have explored the Mexican government's broadcast bans on narcocorridos, ballads glorifying the leaders of drug cartels.[25] These bans were enacted on a basis comparable to that used for the criminalization of drill music in the United Kingdom.[26] Yet to the extent that observers are willing to describe contemporary Mexico as a democracy, such descriptions are inevitably accompanied with one of several qualifiers—*authoritarian* democracy, *flawed* democracy, *limited* democracy, *violent* democracy. A similar ambiguity pertains to imaginaries of democratic transition in Mexico, something that may both be traced to a particular date—usually the first peaceful national transition of power in 2000—and be depicted as an ongoing, incomplete process of consolidation of democratic norms and institutions.[27]

Neither may we rely on past experience for clarity. Recent years have seen renewed debate about Mexico's single-party PRI regime: whether it constituted a perfect dictatorship, a hybrid regime or "*dictablanda*," or a violent militarized system comparable to the Southern Cone dictatorships.[28] Political power during the seventy-year single-party rule of the PRI was built on violence, but it was also predicated on a high degree of influence over the private sector and civil society, especially the press and labor unions, as well as prohibitions and restrictions on competing political parties. It is therefore generally impossible to disentangle government censorship from censorship exerted by other entities within the government's wide sphere of influence. PRI power was also built on clientelism, which extended to the cultural sphere, where public intellectuals were provided with implicitly conditional state support. This created what many understand to be a controlled public sphere, in which intellectuals supported by the government were given limited license to criticize the PRI. The very durability of single-party rule is also associated with a perception of Mexican society as especially quick to self-censor, based on an intuitive understanding of the kinds of ideas that one would face recriminations for expressing—especially direct criticism of the president and of the Catholic Church. This perception is often expressed with the phrase "inside every Mexican is a little *priista* [PRI politician]," which encapsulates a recognition both of the diffuse way that power operated under PRI rule, and of the ongoing legacy of authoritarianism in Mexico.

Both the authoritarian past and the ambiguous present are reflected in voices within Mexico City's independent music scene that conflate very fluidly what, in other cultural contexts, might be considered distinct forms of censorship. For instance, in an interview, the owner of one independent midsized venue in the center of Mexico City told me, "I don't believe in the democratic transition, not at all." Democracy could work, he said, "perhaps in Mexico City, in other places perhaps with other types of government"; in Mexico in general, however, the effects of the transition were "minimal." He concluded, bitterly: "So many people disappeared, incarcerated, killed. [. . . And] in the cultural sphere I haven't felt in these years any type of support from the authorities, never."[29] In a similar vein, an organizer of a venue based in Valle de Chalco, just outside Mexico City, told me that there existed "a censorship which is sometimes veiled, it seems it's not there. Often it seems there's a lot of openness, but it's not true. The fact that there isn't support for artists and venues, that's where censorship comes from."[30]

Both of these voices, then, identified censorship with a lack of government support. Yet in Mexico the waters are muddier still, due to a perception that funding originating from the political system limits political speech. It is relatively common for political parties to hire musicians to perform at their events, especially musicians with a large fan base; a common stipulation of such appearances, however, is that performers should not discuss politics or criticize political parties. Similar suspicions can also accumulate around arts funding, which some understand to be used by conservative politicians under single-party rule as a pretext to condition or restrict speech; although it was not a majority view, one radical hip-hop group I got to know believed that this situation continued until the present.[31]

In short, understandings of music censorship tend to intertwine with conceptualizations of political power, and this is true both of emic understandings of censorship within the scene studied here and of scholarly work. In *Refried Elvis*, Zolov argues that Mexican rock challenged a core mechanism of single-party rule: the so-called Revolutionary Family.[32] Presidential power, within this model, was diffused downward to family life: the *macho* figure of the *padre de familia* was expected to embody a society-wide model of paternalistic authority. The body politics of rock were therefore inherently subversive for mainstream, conservative Mexican society. It was in part because of this bodily subversion, as well as a broader fear of large-scale youth gatherings, that rock was subject to reprisals and censorship, principally by the state.

That Zolov's account of the subversive power of rock in Mexico fits within what may be understood as a broader "resistance paradigm" is clarified by the title of this book's Spanish-language translation, which translates into English as *Rebels with a Cause: Mexican Counterculture and the Crisis of the Patriarchal State*.[33] Musical subcultures have often been viewed by scholars as forms of resistance to political power.[34] The British tradition in cultural studies built on the "control/resistance paradigm" formulated by Hall.[35] This influenced many studies that perceived the symbolic systems created within subcultures as subversive of the mainstream symbolic order, and that understood subcultures as spaces of autonomy, in which the repressive power relations found outside them were challenged or suspended.[36]

In recent years, however, the resistance paradigm has also been critiqued. In focusing on resistance, it has been argued, we may ignore the more complex motivations people have for participating in subcultures. Critics have pointed out that accounts of subcultural resistance may misread the nature of political power, narrating the state as overly unified, all-powerful, and all-pervasive. These accounts may also misunderstand the intentions of subcultures' "others," such as government-sponsored musical cultures, and fail to do justice to the divisions and tensions that mark government policy in practice.[37] Equally, in reducing the symbolic production of subcultures to resistance against a monolithic external threat, we are applying a restrictive frame to the creativity of the artists that work in them and to the audiences that enjoy their work.[38] An overly monolithic account of state power, finally, may result in an unsatisfactorily straightforward and clear-cut account of democratic transition. Because change is associated with shifts in power between bounded fields (often the government versus civil society, or the government versus market forces), little room is left for the most common affects of transition: uncertainty, indeterminacy, and confusion.[39] The self-evident nature of "resistance against oppression" does not permit us to reckon with the intellectual conditions that underpin this narrative, with transition as an ideological process, as well as a political one.

The resistance paradigm, I suggest, is implicit within many histories of Mexican rock. Here, the Mexican rock subject often comes preformed: she is held to be always already *libertaria* (a term often rendered as "libertarian," but which I will translate here as "liberationist," to create some distance from the far-right authoritarian iteration of the term that has taken hold in the United States) and resistant to repression.[40] This is characteristic, for example, of Zolov's highly influential contributions, which replay the image of an inherently rebellious, antiauthoritarian rock gesture being "contained" by the single-party government.[41] Here, however, I want to move beyond the resistance paradigm. In doing so, I look to produce an account of music censorship in Mexico which cannot readily be contained within any straightforward historical narrative about transition. My aim is to explore how the censorship of popular music in Mexico relates to a peculiarly Mexican iteration of disciplinary governmentality. This disciplinary governmentality has pervaded many different activities in Mexico City rock; it relates most directly, however, to the challenges of ensuring the security of live music. Foucault sought to understand "government" as a practice that was dispersed throughout society, displaced from the apparent center of power in the administrative state. Governmentality denoted "the ensemble formed by institutions, procedures, analyses and reflections, calculations, and tactics" that permitted states to effect government, with "apparatuses of security as its essential technical instrument." Governmentality, then, was enacted through "governmental apparatuses (*appareils*)" accompanied by "a series of knowledges (*savoirs*)."[42] Governmentality is an especially useful concept for these purposes because it can help to elucidate how patterns of repression may be replicated, often under coercive conditions, within subcultures or countercultures themselves.

I say "the Mexican iteration," in turn, because this form of governmentality connects to national anxieties about the Mexican subject that traverse past and present. These highly classist anxieties present themselves in various forms, including the national inferiority complex known as Malinchismo and commonplace allusions to the "Third-Worldist" (Spanish: *tercermundista*) status of Mexico; they tend to reduce politics to "psychodrama," in which Mexico's problems are blamed on the allegedly defective, implicitly popular, Mexican subject.[43] Within the rock scene, the successive premises of this disciplinary governmentality were that the Mexican rock public was not correctly "educated" for live rock, unlike the apparently "educated" audiences of the United States and Western Europe; that they were incapable of self-governing; and that rock could therefore legitimately be suppressed or repressed by the paternalistic state.[44] This logic enjoyed support across wider society, including within the rock scene itself. It is evinced in community groups' complaints about rock venues as supposed threats to public security, but it is also demonstrated on the occasions that rock writers took it upon themselves to discipline the rock public, or when they bemoaned the low level of "education" of rock audiences in the wake of riots or disturbances. It is also shown in defenses of live rock on the grounds that Mexican rock publics had "reformed," learned to behave correctly, and become more docile. From an outsider perspective, this logic may appear curious: disturbances and (even fatal) violence had been present since the earliest rock festivals in the US, the UK, and elsewhere, and cultures of violence have prevailed at some such festivals until very recently.[45]

A key question for this book, therefore, is this: How did discourses relating to the repression of rock in Mexico become entangled with questions about safety within the entertainment industries? Here, it is vital to follow the astute observation made by several journalists I interviewed that the massification of Mexican rock occurred in a very idiosyncratic fashion, and at times happened very quickly. Mass-scale rock concerts were restricted in Mexico City in the wake of Avándaro, under a government worried about the political power of large crowds of young people. Riots and disturbances at rock events were commonplace throughout the genre's history in Mexico, and were topics of concern for musicians, organizers, and journalists. Questions were continually raised about the way that live rock was policed. During the 1980s, police commonly lined up, in a visibly threatening fashion, behind the stage, and members of the army were often present in large numbers outside venues. The approach used to police live rock in the present resembles somewhat of a compromise along neoliberal lines, in which public security is excluded from venues and private security operates within them. The repressive acts often committed by private security raise questions about security culture and training, and also about the ideological frame through which public entities such as the police may be accused of "repression" but subcontracted private security may not, despite the potentially similar role played by each.

Where Zolov sees rock as imbricated in a process of bodily liberation from the constraints of the PRI's "Revolutionary Family," I propose what might be considered a more pessimistic approach, emphasizing a more diffuse culture of governmentality that provides fewer possibilities for the closure of narratives about music censorship. This approach has the advantage of extending our understanding of the politics of expressive freedoms and nonfreedoms within Mexico beyond the PRI, and into the present era of multiparty democracy. It is also, I suggest, better able to account for repressive acts carried out by private companies and their representatives, and less forgiving of discourses equating growing corporate power in Mexico with liberation.

Censorship, Aporia, and Knowledge

Uncertainty is often understood within Mexico as a distinctive feature of acts of repression within the country's cultural sphere. As one musician put it to me in 2013, "They don't give you a piece of paper" to confirm that you've been censored. Thirteen years after Mexico's first nationwide democratic transition of power, this discourse replicated a long-standing trope relating to censorship under authoritarian rule. "Was it censorship?" asked one organizer in response to the abrupt change of venue for a cinema festival in 1990; "yes it was, but you know how it is in this country: there's never a way to prove it. Censorship in Mexico doesn't come accompanied with a birth certificate."[46] In other words, questions about censorship tend to suggest broader questions about how knowledge is shaped in and through society.

The accounts of music censorship that emerged from my conversations with participants in Mexico City's *escena independiente* are extremely broad in scope. It is not uncommon to hear that censorship in the music industries has been, by and large, consigned to the past by the transition away from authoritarian rule; yet one also hears that music censorship continues under new forms (for instance, through corporate control or through repressive acts by political parties) and that it has become increasingly subtle in recent decades. Equally complex are the different ways that censorship is conceptualized. Prior restraint is generally thought to be rare, but there is a tendency to focus on self-censorship—generally articulated as the counterfactual idea that musicians may be deterred from certain kinds of speech due to the threat of reprisals. While self-censorship is not necessarily connected to the state, it is often understood as a cultural legacy of seventy-one years of authoritarianism, during which survival often depended on knowing when to guard one's tongue. It is also seen as a longer-term cultural condition that has marked Mexico since the colonial era. Along with Claudio Lomnitz, respondents often understand self-censorship in Mexico as part of a broader socialization into politeness and obsequiousness, driven by the long-standing reliance on personal relations for access to precious public resources.[47] Participants also alluded to the notion of *ninguneo*—nobodying—the idea that criticism of powerful entities would lead to one's effective elimination from the mediated public sphere. Of course, the spectacular violence that has been unleashed since the end of 2006, after the government declared war on organized crime, has led to new kinds of censorship: some artists who were vocally critical of Mexico's political system told me that they were fearful of criticizing drug cartels.

Music censorship in Mexico was also understood to be related to spaces—particularly the availability of live performance spaces and, to a lesser extent, access to media spaces such as radio and television programs. Thus, a common complaint—and one that traverses democratic and authoritarian rule—was the lack of adequate performance venues. Venue closures and the denial of permits for live events were frequently seen as examples of censorship. As seen above, participants' accounts of censorship also traverse apparently discrete regimes of value, such as Isaiah Berlin's discussion of "negative liberty" (freedom from) and "positive liberty" (freedom to): the same respondents denounce both censorship constituted by government obstruction or repression and censorship constituted by lack of government financial support. Much of this apparent ideological admixture relates to the experiences of live music venues, whose survival may depend on a combination of government permission, government financial support, and broader market factors such as the cost of rent and the demand for live music.

The breadth of these accounts is indicative of another feature of censorship: it is experienced as an aporia, a vortex of uncertainty or a productive lack of meaning that draws broader discourses and activities around it. In practice, censorship does not enjoy an easily identifiable existence, partly because powerful bodies rarely admit openly to having been the author of acts of censorship and instead often create euphemisms to cover for them. Censorship therefore has to be intuited and interpreted through acts of knowledge work, one of which is musical performance itself. Revealing episodes of censorship and understanding them as such requires effort, resources, and collective action. Thus, the ability to express that one has been censored is the sign of a certain empowerment; on the other hand, when censorship is complete it is also almost impossible to identify. John Street astutely observes that "the story of censorship is not, for the most part (if ever), the story of images or words that offended, but of the political interests that articulate and respond to the 'offence.'"[48] Therefore, stories about censorship are also necessarily about the ways in which people come to articulate these stories themselves; they are about the production of certain kinds of knowledge. This book tells the story of the groups—principally musicians and journalists—that act together to carry out this labor, construct voice, and empower themselves.

We may note here Street's choice of the phrase "political interests." The fact that censorship is revealed through concerted action by such political interests means that it is never "disinterested." Studying censorship draws us into the intersubjective life of language and the imbrication of language with power. Narrating instances of music censorship is always already a political question, as well as an empirical one. Like other kinds of history, histories of music censorship tend to respond to the needs of the present. This is, in part, because they wouldn't exist if they didn't: present-day groups would have little incentive to marshal the resources necessary to produce and perform these histories.

There is also, then, an inherently productive and performative aspect to censorship. Actors within the scene I have studied continuously negotiate highly complex accounts and experiences of censorship in affective and aesthetic ways through the act of performing itself. Censorship's performative element has become especially apparent in recent years. It is seen, in particular, in the tactics of far-right political actors who intentionally cause offense in order to provoke outrage, censure, and "de-platforming," in this way claiming victimhood. The claim to having been censored thus serves to protect purposively harmful speech from criticism. Similar tactics have also been used in Mexican popular music. For instance, in the 1990s, the rock band Molotov began to combine forthright criticism of Mexico's media and political system with broader bad-taste humor. For example, they mixed attacks on politicians and media figures with homophobic and misogynistic language, particularly on the song "Puto" (Fag). Subverting the title of an album by Mexican stadium rock band Maná, their 1997 debut album was titled ¿Donde jugarán las niñas? (Where will the little girls play?) and featured an image of an apparently underage girl lying in a car with her underwear pulled down. Retailers boycotted the album, which only gave it greater attention and sales; in the words of a member of the band, "censorship has worked for us as free publicity."[49]

While scholars working within the "new censorship" paradigm have long engaged with censorship as productive or constitutive of certain kinds of activities and subjectivities, I focus on the possibility for experiences of censorship to be intertwined with the production of collectivities: shared identities; solidarity, what Mattern terms "acting in concert"; and social life, experience and meaning in common.[50] Music is engaged in these patterns as a target of censorship, but it is also one of the most important expressive media through which experiences of censorship become translated into shared meaning. At the same time, it would be a mistake to speak of censorship as somehow empowering. Something bleakly predictable is revealed about music censorship here: it tends to exacerbate broader forms of disempowerment—economic marginalization, lack of status, and lack of voice.

The legacy of music censorship in Mexico City informs and motivates many forms of action in the present: the organizing of venues, the fomenting of collective action, and the production of knowledge through the labor of musicians and journalists. Indeed, journalists are a continuous presence at some of this scene's most prestigious venues. These journalists do not simply review live and recorded music; they order and communicate the values and ideas that underpin action within this scene. In fact, there is a rich, decades-long history of rock journalists also participating as organizers and performers—thus constituting a hybrid figure, the journalist-musician—suggesting an intuitive recognition of the link between power and knowledge. In this way, the generative nature of stories about music censorship is directly reflected in the ways that the people who write these stories organize their lives.

It is widely known that some of Mexico's most prestigious twentieth-century writers, such as José Agustín, Carlos Monsiváis, and Parmenides García Saldaña, cut their teeth writing about rock in the 1960s. From a very early stage, rock in Mexico formed part of a wider transdisciplinary counter-cultural movement colloquially known as La Onda, which also incorporated literature, film, and visual arts. It was therefore, as Zolov and others pointed out, a literary scene from the beginning.[51] Not only was the literature of La Onda influenced by the Beat Generation in the United States, it also constituted an indispensable means through which rock was evaluated, framed, and understood, amid the challenges of adapting the genre to a Mexican setting. Unlike other transnational popular genres that have swept Mexico since—notably hip-hop—rock rarely told the hearer what it was. Thus, writing about rock constituted an indispensable resource allowing the Mexican public to position rock, responding to the immediate challenge of interpretation posed by the genre. In turn, the early decades of Mexican rock saw those writing about La Onda taking up roles between public intellectual and movement insider.

Although scholarship on the topic has overwhelmingly fixated on the contributions of public intellectuals such as the writers mentioned above, the less celebrated figures who published in rock magazines at this time were also concerned with articulating the value of rock. These magazines, it will be argued here, played a vital role within the rock scene in Mexico: not only did they help to coordinate activities among musicians and organizers, but they also helped to shape and articulate narratives about experiences of marginalization, repression, and censorship within this scene. Rock magazines did not only focus on music; they also dedicated a great deal of their contents to reviews of literature and film, and they repeatedly exhorted readers to become more widely read and "cultured."[52] This connection to the literary continues in the present: many contemporary rock journalists also publish fiction and poetry.[53] The current status of rock journalism as a straightforward "insider voice" has also become complicated and contested. As already noted, many of those who have written about rock in Mexico, especially since the 1970s, are also musicians. Yet in recent years rock journalists increasingly self-identify as "professional," write in a more formal register, and cultivate greater neutrality and distance from rock artists themselves. Even this claim to objectivity, however, has masked the reality that rock journalists often act as allies of and advocates for venues within the *escena independiente* within Mexico City, often using their labor to draw attention to venue closures, framing these closures as acts of repressive governmental overreach.

In traversing these connecting pathways between writing and musicianship, this book contributes to a wave of recent English-language scholarship on Mexican history that emphasizes journalism.[54] Above all, it explores symbioses between histories of censorship within the *escena independiente* and the ways that this scene is, and has been, made. I am interested, then, not only in the stories that are told about censorship, but also in how these stories have developed and what these stories *do*. I contend that only if we address censorship's abstract lives alongside its embodied, practical effects, affects, and affordances can we reach a satisfactory account of how and why certain stories about censorship survive and others fall by the wayside. And, finally, I argue that this has consequences for how we understand the Mexican state's changing relationships with big business and other entities within its sphere of influence.

Censorship and Transition

As described above, I am interested in how narratives about censorship advanced by scholars and participants in Mexico's rock scene draw around them broader metanarratives about transition. Critical scholarship on people's felt experiences is especially important at a time when stable, teleological accounts of transition to liberal democracy look increasingly weak. In recent years, the global stage has witnessed the emergence of an unprecedented number of formal democracies, and a rising number of poor-quality ones. This reflects a number of interlapping processes, including the oligarchization of economies in formal democracies; an increase in technocratic and neoliberal rule, which constrains the limits of possible political speech;[55] increasingly concentrated media ownership; authoritarian practices among police forces under formal democracies, especially toward ethnic minority groups;

and states of exception related to conflict under which democratically elected governments may assume executive power and remove individual rights.[56]

Revisionist histories of liberal thought have flourished through this time, showing how liberalism is founded on exclusion and highlighting the liberal "ideological containment" of colonial violence.[57] From the radical anarchist perspective common within the *escena independiente*, these developments are no surprise. Anarchists have long perceived continuities between liberal-democratic systems and authoritarian ones, which may often employ forms of statecraft and governmentalities that are similar to those in authoritarian systems. James C. Scott, for instance, has argued that state power depends on the imposition of a relatively consistent form of legibility and that modern states, "communist or neoliberal, populist or authoritarian," have implemented a similar "project of rule," summarized as the establishing of a praxis of enclosure across multiple spheres of human existence.[58]

Mexico, where political parties under multiparty democracy deploy many of the same techniques for maintaining power as the ruling party under the single-party system (such as clientelism, co-option of civil society groups, and vote-buying), is an especially interesting case in which to trace such continuities.[59] Polling data after the end of authoritarian rule has consistently shown that more Mexicans are dissatisfied than satisfied with the quality of democracy in Mexico, and that less than a majority of Mexicans consider that they live in a democracy.[60] Uncertainty concerning Mexico's democratic status can be discussed in the context of other experiences of democratic transition, but it may also be connected to the country's recent history.[61] Unlike the dictatorships of the Southern Cone in the second half of the twentieth century, Mexico enjoyed no single moment of liberation from tyranny; its seventy-one years of single-party rule occurred under the illusion of democracy. The transition to democracy in Mexico, perhaps to a greater degree than any other large country in the Americas, creates epistemic challenges for those living through it. Further, Mexico's democratic transition has been complicated by the patterns of spectacular violence that have characterized the war on drugs since 2007—and especially by increasing threats against the lives of journalists and politicians, which has undermined the ability to conduct open political discourse. Thus Smith warns, on the basis of a comparison between contemporary and past journalism in Mexico, of "the dangers of applying democratization theory, with its assumptions linking electoral freedom, press liberalization, and declining violence."[62]

Narratives about music censorship have often become intertwined with the complexities of such political transitions. This is true in the case of

Afghanistan, where the Taliban's ban on instrumental music was invoked as part of the justification for the invasion of the country in 2001, and of the former Soviet bloc, where journalists and scholars have argued both that rock served to resist communism and that rock was occasionally complicit in repression by communist regimes.[63] Similar stories have been told about the role of rock in the restoration of democracy after military dictatorship in Latin America. The edited volume *Rockin' las Americas: The Global Politics of Rock in Latin/o America* opens by gesturing toward varied ways rock has been repressed across the region—including direct military repression, social marginalization, and censorship within civil society and the press. This implies, as the book's introduction states, attention to repression against rock "under all forms of government—from Castro's Cuba to Pinochet's Chile."[64] Yet it is arguable that this aim is not entirely followed through; the book occasionally suggests an overly straightforward distinction between dictatorship/nonfreedom and democracy/freedom, and often implies a narrative with democracy as its point of closure. The introduction itself concludes, for instance, by juxtaposing twentieth-century Latin American nationalist projects, associated with dictatorship, with a neoliberal economics heralding the end of dictatorship, stating that "radical economic transition was accompanied by the return, after decades of military rule, of democratically elected governments all across Latin America." In this context, we are told that rock "thrived" amid increasing social acceptance, especially on the Left, and that through this period rock was "decriminalized."[65] Nonetheless, for some places, this summary presents somewhat of a historical reversal: neoliberal economic policy was introduced to the region by two of the most tyrannical regimes of the twentieth-century Americas: first by the Pinochet dictatorship in Chile and then through neoliberal reforms undertaken, but only partially implemented, by the Argentine military junta of 1976–1983.[66] Most important is the recognition that a straightforward opposition between neoliberalism and dictatorship imputes to regional democratization undue evenness and clarity. There exists the danger that rock is drawn into the frame as an inherently democratic practice, always-already resistant to dictatorship and freely expressed only under (neoliberal) democracy.

In a similar vein to Smith, quoted above, I am concerned that discourses about democratization may obscure the failings of posttransition politics in Mexico. In this book, I am committed to recognizing episodes of music censorship after the country's transition to multiparty democracy in 2000, since they can tell us much about its failings. In turn, I maintain that no grand narrative of music censorship can take into account all of the varied forms music censorship has assumed since the arrival of the rock 'n' roll dance craze to Mexico in the late 1950s. At the heart of this issue is the aporetic nature of censorship itself, its condition as a locus of the unknown and uncertain. Even during the 1970s, a period that saw a backlash against rock by the government and press, the status and meaning of rock censorship was contested within the rock counterculture itself. While the narrative about this period has become more settled in the decades since, present-day contestations of this narrative hold the potential to illuminate contemporary patterns of music censorship, silencing, and marginalization.

What stands out about these histories, then, is the ongoing need to retell and rework them. It is not simply the case that already-established narratives of historical censorship have been adapted to contemporary needs; these narratives were never fixed, always precarious, malleable, and uncertain. They were also ideological, imbricated in shifting discourses around democracy and freedom, and tied to the rapid ascendancy of neoliberalism, privatization, and corporate power since the 1980s. Indeed, one of the characteristics of allegations of censorship that is revealed in this book is their ability to reveal tensions within shared political worldviews. Such a history, then, not only speaks to the extent of state repression within society, but also tells of changing definitions of the political within society and shifts in complexly textured spaces for political engagement. As Claude Lefort states, "The fact that something like politics should have been circumscribed within social life at a given time has in itself a political meaning."[67] Narratives about censorship tell us about the patterns of speech and silencing they intend to address, but they also tell us about particular ideological orderings of spaces and times, the most recent of which has accompanied Mexico's transition to both a multiparty democratic system and a neoliberal economic consensus.

This is a potentially troubling situation for participants in the independent scene, which is founded on oppositional ideas about censorship and autonomy; the value of this scene for its participants pertains to its identity as something like a "shatter zone" in which the repressive power relations found outside it are suspended.[68] In turn, to characterize the actions of an individual, group, or entity as one of censorship is always an ideological act. Stories of music censorship are, inevitably, stories about something else as well, be it governments, socialism, corporate corruption, neoliberalism, or the Mexican "Revolutionary Family"; and this something else tells us about people and the filters through which they view the world.

Finally, as indicated above, given the symbiotic relationship between censorship and its mythology, accounting for stories of Mexican rock censorship implicates local actors in music scenes, such as musicians, event organizers, and owners of autonomous venues, as well as "knowledge brokers," such as local intellectuals, documentary filmmakers, journalists, and academics based overseas who invest in the continuous remediation of histories of Mexican rock. I assume here a broad, open-ended definition of "knowledge." Histories of rock censorship circulate across multiple registers: oral and written, linguistic and extralinguistic. I am interested in how these narratives emerge through performance and how agents in Mexico's independent music scene fashion knowledge about censorship in Mexico through acts such as playing live music, organizing events, working to maintain live spaces for performance, and writing and publishing books about the history of rock. Narratives of censorship are negotiated and retold in onstage performances, occasionally in ways that complicate straightforward narratives about the country's post-2000 democratic transition. In this book I consider such local, musically embedded, affectively rich forms of knowledge creation alongside narratives within international academic discourse and music journalism. At stake in these histories, I suggest, are possibilities to critique simultaneously single-party rule, the flawed multiparty system of contemporary Mexico, and the effects of neoliberalism in the country.

Methodology and Approach

Censorship tends to have an affective and aesthetic component. This is often linked to its overdetermined nature: because words fail to account for the complex interaction of factors through which people are denied voice, people often reach for nonlinguistic forms of expression to process experiences of repression and censorship. As such, music censorship is challenging to study. The overdetermined nature of censorship is also connected to the fact that censorship is *longue durée*. Narratives about censorship can have an impact long after the event; they can lose nuance and texture with the passage of time; they are also frequently reworked and adapted to suit the present.

For these reasons, I have found it especially fruitful to combine historiography with ethnography. The ethnography for this book took place in Mexico City and, to a lesser extent, Estado de México, mostly between 2017 and 2022, when I spent twelve months in total in Mexico City. This ethnographic research builds on fieldwork carried out since 2012 in Mexico City that centered on the work of activist musicians affiliated with the Zapatista movement. I carried out participant observation in several sites, principal among which were Multiforo Cultural Alicia, Tianguis Cultural del Chopo, Foro El Mictlán, Multiforo 246, Bajo Circuito, and El Faro de Oriente. I also carried out eighty in-depth interviews with rock journalists, musicians, policymakers, and organizers. These interviews have produced a rich set of data.

Archival research took place through personal collecting of magazines and publications, as well as consultation with publicly accessible archives, especially the Hemeroteca Nacional de México. (The collection at the Hemeroteca is extensive due to the legal obligation imposed on magazine and newspaper editors to submit two copies of each edition they publish—although they do not always comply.) I was also allowed access to the personal collection of a journalist and musician, Walter Schmidt; I am very thankful to him for this access. I read publications from what may be described as the "specialized rock press," as well as publications with a more general audience, especially the culture and entertainment pages of newspapers. In the former category, I consulted *Pop*, *México Canta*, *Conecte*, *Sonido*, *Discothéque Rock-Pop*, *Acústica*, *Etcétera*, and *La Banda Rockera*; I also consulted the fanzines available in Museo Universitario del Chopo's *fanzineoteca*. In the latter category, I used as sources *La Jornada*, *Proceso*, and *Unomásuno*, and to a lesser extent others. I also consulted personal memoirs of individual musicians, journalists, and organizers, and individual publications that are difficult to access but highly significant, such as the tomes *Nosotros* and *Avándaro: ¿Aliviane o movida?*, both published just after the Avándaro Festival in 1971.

Not all of this work took place simultaneously. I opened by carrying out ethnography, before going on to conduct archival research in the summer of 2019. This raised new questions that I sought to address through additional ethnography that I conducted toward the end of the research for the book. This combination of archival and ethnographic research has helped to unravel some of the nuances of histories that are unexpectedly contested, such as that of Avándaro and post-Avándaro repression, and the influence of the entertainment company OCESA over the press starting in the 1990s. It also drew attention to episodes of censorship or repression that scholars have given almost no attention. I would include here the repressive acts carried out by OCESA's security apparatus, the almost complete media silence that followed four deaths at a concert given by Televisa-backed artists in 1987, and the deaths of thirteen young people after a police raid on the venue New's Divine in 2008. This book represents, in part, an attempt to recuperate some of these under-discussed histories and to reflect on why they are so comparatively unknown to begin with.

As explored by Eric Zolov, José Agustín, and Maritza Urteaga, among many other writers, rock 'n' roll (often written as *rocanrol*) was first imported to

Mexico as a new dance craze in the 1950s. The genre was first incorporated into the repertoires of dance orchestras, such as that fronted by singer Gloria Ríos, before a number of dedicated rock groups such as Los Locos del Ritmo and Los Rebeldes del Rock were formed.[69] As their names indicate, such groups took on some of the imagery of the "rebel without a cause," playing mostly covers of English-language songs and releasing music with mostly Mexico-based labels, especially Orfeón. These groups performed in what were known as *cafés cantantes*—effectively, juice bars where live rock was performed.[70] While the *cafés cantantes* were somewhat innocuous venues, they were targeted on multiple occasions by the Mexican police, especially under the authoritarian regime of Gustavo Díaz Ordaz (1964–1970), with an especially widespread wave of closures occurring in 1965. In the background of these repressive acts was the specter of the so-called "Revolutionary Family": the idea, emerging in the wake of the chaotic, bloody Mexican Revolution (1910–1920), that societal order ought to be sustained hierarchically, with the nuclear family serving as a microcosm of society as a whole, led by the intolerant, authoritarian masculine head (the president/father/*macho*). Rock 'n' roll at this time presented two implicit challenges to societal hierarchies: first, it challenged traditional forms of masculinity, especially in its exuberant dancing; second, it was built around a life stage (that is, youth) that had no place within the Revolutionary Family.

Toward the end of the 1960s, the cultural movement known as La Onda was formed, influenced by the hippie movement in the United States. Within this movement, rock was more explicitly politicized and aestheticized, with greater emphasis placed on original composition, and La Onda grew in popularity and reach at the turn of the decade. As a youth movement, rock found some common ground with the leftist, pro-democracy student movement, although it tended to be dismissed as "cultural imperialism" by leftist student activists; activist musicians such as Oscar Chávez and Leon Chávez Teixeiro, whose work bore traces of the rock influence, did not participate in the rock movement. The repression of student activists under the authoritarian governments of Díaz Ordaz (1964–1970) and Luis Echeverría (1970–1976), which manifested in massacres of protesters in 1968 and 1971, affected rock vicariously, since the authorities occasionally grouped rock together with the wider youth movement. This was the background against which the negative reaction to the 1971 Avándaro Festival among government, press, and mainstream society—discussed in Chapter 1—has generally been understood.

The repression of the post-Avándaro period, and the debates around it, form the context for the opening of this book. In the first chapter I begin by recognizing that this history is more contested than is often recognized; while the 1970s are often remembered as an era of blanket "prohibition," many participants in the rock scene at the time produced a more nuanced and specific account of government repression against rock. The chapter focuses, then, on the ways that narratives about post-Avándaro repression developed within the specialized rock press, in response to the fierce and baseless criticism that had been leveled against rock in the mainstream press in the wake of the Avándaro Festival. I look, in particular, at the magazine *Conecte*—an underused source of information about this period, and one that continues to provoke controversy. *Conecte* was the closest thing, within the 1970s rock scene, to a publication of record: it documented activities in this scene in some detail, had a wide (even international) reach, and was important for coordinating action. Yet its contents occasionally make uncomfortable reading today: *Conecte* writers often endorsed censorship of unfavorable musical expressions and fiercely criticized rock audiences acting in ways they considered harmful. The contents of *Conecte*, I argue, are testament to a rock scene that was far from straightforwardly antiauthoritarian, as many influential voices saw their role as disciplining rock audiences.

The second chapter focuses on the 1987 BMG-Arriola-funded publicity campaign *Rock en tu idioma*, widely seen as a breakthrough point for Mexican rock, as transnational corporate backing catalyzed the sudden explosion of the genre into the mainstream often referred to as the rock "boom." This breakthrough was grounded on a long lineage of less well-capitalized organizations within Mexican rock and responded to preexisting debates about commercial censorship. I show that *Rock en tu idioma* built on a series of projects for "independent" production developed by rock bands since the period immediately following Avándaro, when music labels in Mexico stopped signing rock acts. This chapter offers a genealogy of rock "independence" from the late 1970s to the late 1980s. Early uses of the term saw "independence" in positive terms, as a means to an end—an expansion of rock "communication" that could be facilitated by companies of any size. Musical production was understood as the result of the collective labor of many different actors—musicians, producers, organizers, journalists—who saw their role as shaping, channeling, and directing impulses and energies associated with youth. Later iterations of rock "independence," however, suggested a more stratified imaginary in which transnational labels and large media companies such as Televisa were seen to threaten musical freedom of expression, producing a more sanitized, light, or *fresa* (literally: strawberry) sound. Understandings of rock "independence" thus raised questions about commercial censorship—and especially about the intertwining of private and official censorship under single-party rule. Recognition of this reality, I argue, is vital to understanding the ways that the acts associated with *Rock en tu idioma* sought to portray themselves in the press.

The book's third chapter takes up the growth of the live music industry in the 1990s, looking at the case of the entertainment company OCESA, whose offering in the first years of its existence was centered on rock, and which rapidly grew into a vertically integrated monopoly in the Mexican entertainment sector. This has often been described as a moment of "opening" (*apertura*) for rock, but I demonstrate that OCESA's growth—occurring during a time of widespread privatization—may be understood instead as an expanding set of enclosures. Most consequentially, the expansion of OCESA was built on the privatization of security at live events, often with repressive consequences. The company faced the frequent possibility of scandal, as attendee injuries (and in some cases deaths) at OCESA events undermined the commoditization of the live rock event through security. In this context, the organization gave significant support to a press department that leveraged the company's monopoly in order to influence the work of the journalists covering their events. Partly on the basis of this press influence, OCESA exploited histories of rock censorship in order to gain legitimacy for its otherwise controversial commercial expansion.

Chapter 4 discusses what may be seen as the other side of the coin: OCESA's growth was facilitated not only by extensive government help but also by governmental repression. In the mid-1990s, a large group of rock bands embarked on a complex and fascinating entanglement with the movement of solidarity with the EZLN, which launched an uprising against the government in the southern state of Chiapas in 1994. This association with radical activism was partly curtailed, and partly stimulated, by a prohibition against live open-air rock issued by the city government, which was provoked by riots at a Caifanes concert. The series of live rock events that followed, mostly held on the campus of the National Autonomous University of Mexico (UNAM)—a location at least nominally outside of government control—challenged both misinformation about conflict in Chiapas and government prohibition against open-air rock. In this way, live rock came to fulfill some of the tasks attributed to journalists. This account complicates any attempt to straightforwardly distinguish between public and commercial censorship. In fact, the expansion of a live music industry, based on the enclosure of large-scale live rock, benefited from government censorship in other areas—especially in the capital's public spaces. Nonetheless, the ban was eventually lifted in 1997 by the first democratically elected Mexico City government, pointing to one reason that this particular history of censorship is commemorated so little in the present: it found lasting closure through the democratic process.

Chapter 5 turns to the experience of *foros culturales*—small-scale music venues whose offerings have tended to center on rock—since the election of the Party of the Democratic Revolution (PRD) to office in Mexico City in 1997. By exploring the relationship between these small-scale venues and local governments, the chapter shows how *foros culturales* are subject to a grinding, everyday, and bureaucratic pattern of repression. Many of the challenges for this scene remain the same as those of previous eras: participants complain of clientelism, excessive regulation, police repression, and corruption within local government. In responding to this situation, small-scale venues become active participants in a collective knowledge-fashioning enterprise, both within the live music performed at *foros culturales* and in the labor of journalists who frequent these spaces. The image of Mexico's state and establishment that is produced in this scene is often one of tyranny, hierarchy, and repression—a depiction that responds to the repressive acts of Mexico's transitioning government and the challenges of grounding a shared set of oppositional identities. This image, I show, becomes especially prominent during moments in which *foros culturales* come under threat from local government; here, they exert a degree of media power, maneuvering conversations about venue safety into discourse about tyranny, governmental repression, and freedom. Building on ethnographic research carried out with musicians performing in these venues, this chapter shows how this task is effected aesthetically, as well as through journalistic practice. At the same time, it points out that the musical and journalistic portrayals of these venues—portrayals that emphasize the way that the venues suspend outside hierarchies and exclusion perpetuated by government and the mainstream cultural industries—obscure the unequal power relations which can often occur within them.

Chapter 6 closely examines the politics of these venues amid a drive for their legal recognition as "independent cultural spaces." Ever since the PRD came to power in Mexico City in 1997, these spaces have come to symbolize the progressive cultural policies the city government has sought to implement, based on ideas about cultural freedom forged in the rock movement. The PRD, and Morena after it, invested in networks of state-run cultural spaces to serve a "democratic," community-led vision of culture that contrasted with the PRI's clientelistic uses of cultural spending. While the PRD has avoided the perception that these networks are motivated by the party's self-interest, their expansion must be understood alongside efforts to co-opt and formalize independent cultural spaces, efforts that often impose a punitive administrative burden. In response to these issues and broader experiences of repression, a group of Mexico City music venues have organized a lobbying group to demand the establishing in law of a "right to culture" and legally codify "independent cultural spaces." Beginning in 2017, the newly elected Morena administration in the capital made efforts to pass such a law. This legislative project used histories of repression of culture in Mexico to work in support of an expansion of "culture" in its broad anthropological sense. Nonetheless, it is unclear whether the "right to culture" will protect rock venues from the myriad ways in which rock is subject to repression and marginalization in Mexico, especially given the new administration's austerity program, the ongoing administrative dysfunctionality of the city government, and the history in Mexico of invoking "rights" as a prelude to state intervention.

All of this points toward a deeper reflection on the ways that knowledge flows across borders and is translated and transformed as it negotiates different sets of hierarchies. Chapter 7 builds on ethnography carried out with rock journalists to explore the role of knowledge production—both that embedded locally and that rooted in international scholarly exchanges—within the rock scene. Rock journalism may serve, vicariously or implicitly, as a repository (if not a vitrine) for a set of journalistic principles and subjectivities under threat in one of the most dangerous countries in the world to practice journalism. Equally, rock journalism is often structured and understood as a form of documentary labor rather than labor to shape "history" as such. Rock journalism in this context provokes questions about the purpose and value of history, and about the experiences and musical expressions that rock history may obscure. Chapter 7 concludes with a critical reflection on the acts of translating knowledge carried out by scholars seeking to produce "history" rather than simply to document the past. It calls for a revaluing of the locally relevant, documentary labor of journalists—work that undergirds vibrant, local musical and extramusical activities but registers only very rarely outside of this local context. This is, in part, because the claims made for purportedly universalizable scholarship are increasingly untenable.

Let me conclude with a few words about myself and my motivations for writing. I have been traveling to Mexico under various auspices—as a volunteer, researcher, teacher, and partner—since a four-month trip to Valle de Chalco, on the southwest edge of Mexico State, as a volunteer in 2007. During this trip, I worked (mostly teaching English and music, and working in a nursery) in a community on the very fringes of the city, formed a couple of years earlier by rural-to-urban migrants and constructed of informal houses with corrugated iron roofs built on insecurely owned terrain. There were social problems of almost every kind in this community, and many basic needs—such as access to water, electricity, transport infrastructure, education, and health services—were met only very partially. This experience bore witness to the troubling legacies of neoliberalism in Mexico.[71]

I vividly remember the experience of traveling with a group by car from the center of the city—with its comparative wealth, green spaces, cafés, and bars—to the marginalized and rapidly expanding outskirts of Estado de México, full of dry, dusty air, concrete edifices, and dirt roads. Another vivid experience from this time relates to the aftermath of the 2006 national elections. One of the daughters in the family I was staying with had been working for a radio station as a researcher. However, for most of the four months that I spent living in Valle de Chalco, she went without pay, as the radio station was experiencing financial difficulties. Only later did I discover that these difficulties had been caused by the punitive withdrawal of government funding after the radio station backed the wrong horse, the center-left PRD, in the 2006 elections.

Experiences such as this one served as an early initiation into the complexities of Mexico's posttransition political system—in particular, the chilling of free speech that can sometimes accumulate around electoral democracy through a winner-takes-all clientelism constituting an ongoing legacy of authoritarianism. It threw me, a middle-class teenager from the east of England, headlong into an affectively complex political transition that I struggled to understand. In many ways, this book represents a still-partial attempt to address the same questions that arose from these early, bewildering, experiences.

CHAPTER 1

After Avándaro

Censorship and Rock Journalism as Governmentality in the 1970s

The 2020 Netflix docuseries *Break It All: The History of Rock in Latin America* provoked intense controversy among rock aficionados in Mexico.[1] Some highlighted the partial nature of the series; most of the artists featured had ties to its Argentinian producer, Gustavo Santaolalla. Many notable Mexican rock artists, such as Panteón Rococó and Cecilia Toussaint, were conspicuously absent.[2] Amid conflicts over the exclusion of certain bands, a more latent controversy emerged about the political status that the docuseries claimed for rock. *Break It All* depicts rock in Latin America as an inherently subversive practice that, even when not explicitly political, inevitably made its practitioners a target of censorship and repression: "We were enemies of the state," said Santaolalla in an interview held with the *New York Times* to promote the docuseries.[3] Specifically in relation to Mexico, the docuseries uses the voice of Maldita Vecindad y los Hijos del Quinto Patio singer Roco Pachukote to claim that rock in 1970s Mexico was prohibited "by law" by the single-party regime of the Institutional Revolutionary Party (PRI). This occurred, the documentary stated, in the wake of the Festival de Rock y Ruedas (Festival of Rock and Wheels—colloquially simplified to Avándaro after the site at which it took place), in September 1971. The festival sparked outrage in the tabloid press and led to a government crackdown. Mexico would not open up to rock, the docuseries states, until the mid-1980s.

This narrative about rock censorship is hardly controversial—indeed, it has achieved a certain dominance within the discourse concerning Mexican rock. Writers have tended to place post-Avándaro repression in continuity with the Tlatelolco massacre of October 1968 and the Corpus Christi massacre of June 1971, both of which targeted the student movement. On both occasions, state-linked armed forces opened fire on crowds of protesting students, leaving hundreds dead. These atrocities, which cast a shadow over all youth mobilization, occurred as part of the Mexican Dirty War, a campaign of vicious state repression against leftist student and guerrilla groups in the 1960s and 1970s involving kidnappings, torture, and assassination.[4] Such a context of atrocity amplifies particular details about Avándaro: above all, that there was a highly visible presence at the festival of the army and armed federal police, and that organizers, desperate to show that they could organize security independently, created their own volunteer security force for the festival whose status was marked by red bracelets bearing the word "order" in white letters. Avándaro also tells us about a state that was modernizing "its mechanisms of political repression and intelligence surveillance," since we now know that the festival was attended by government spies.[5] It also tells us about the changing boundaries of the political: the student movement that was violently repressed in 1968 enacted a "radical transformation of the horizon of politics" to include the everyday and personal as well as the institutional, thus establishing a frame through which Avándaro could be seen to assume wider significance.[6]

Given this context, it is notable that *Break It All*'s by now-familiar account of post-Avándaro censorship was challenged by some commentators. One, taking on "the myth of the censorship of rock," criticized commercially successful Mexican acts from the 1980s and 1990s for airing "the myth that they suffered censorship," when in fact they were embraced by the transnational music industries.[7] Another commentator, the rock journalist and scholar Julián Woodside, alleged a narrative of "victimization" underlying claims about post-Avándaro censorship.[8] Where *Break It All* depicted the 1970s as a period of heavy state repression against rock in Mexico, levied as a consequence of the controversy that followed Avándaro in September 1971, Woodside argued that this narrative was overplayed. Unlike practitioners of politically engaged genres such as *nueva canción*, rockers had not been assassinated, kidnapped, or tortured during the Dirty War; their complaints about being forced "underground" reflected, he contended, a middle-class disdain for unworthy venues. Yet this pushback invoked intergenerational tensions, since Woodside was a comparatively young contributor to these debates. One established, and much older, journalist later responded by telling me that repression against rock at this time could only be understood by those who experienced it, rather than by reading contemporaneous journalistic sources—a claim indicative of how most literature on post-Avándaro rock is based on oral history rather than archival research. Contemporary discourse about this scene, then, poses constant questions about which kinds of knowledge are credible; who is permitted to speak and through which forms of media; and—above all—which kinds of experiences give authority.

Many writers have sought to understand how repression against rock functioned during this period.[9] On the whole, accounts of post-Avándaro censorship may be grouped into "hard" and "soft" versions. In the former, rock is understood to have been subject to an explicit and official ban, emanating primarily from the state. Prohibition is generally seen to have been provoked by Avándaro and to have lasted throughout the 1970s. Many hold that it lasted until the mid-1980s, although this period is also subject to a shifting baseline: for instance, some writing in the early 1990s held that prohibition had lasted until the late 1980s.[10] This narrative—what Zolov calls the "myth of rock's total extinction" after Avándaro—does a disservice to the musical expressivity of this period, excluding the accomplished sounds of acts like Enigma, Chac Mool, Los Dug Dug's, Pájaro Alberto, Nahuatl, and Nuevo México from the story of *rock mexicano*, and also excluding from the picture more experimental acts influenced by progressive rock and jazz that often found refuge in universities.[11] I find the "softer" alternative more convincing.[12] This vision tends to paint antirock censorship as piecemeal—filtering in complex ways across distinct media spheres and different actors, only one of which was the government; geographically uneven, being most intensely experienced in the Mexico City metropolis; and existing in continuity with repression in earlier and later times, especially through venue closures and societal censure of rock primarily exerted through the institution of the nuclear family.

Reading the rock press from the post-Avándaro period (of which I provide an outline below) further points toward the latter, "soft" account of censorship. Mexican rock was subject to restrictions on the radio that resulted in part from government intervention and that were openly discussed in the rock press, although contemporaneous press accounts also show that these were by no means total.[13] Labels reduced their support for Mexican rock acts, although it is unclear the extent to which this was a result of government pressure or a consequence of diminished radio play.[14] The commonplace idea that "native rock was eliminated from the airwaves" in the 1970s applies only partially to television.[15] By 1975, for example, most well-known rock bands in Mexico had made appearances on the television show *Rock en la Cultura*.[16] The most important restrictions related to live rock. More live events were permitted than one might presume, and some took place in comparatively formal, respected venues such as the Teatro Ferrocarrilero, Sala Chopin, Teatro Manolo Fábregas, and the Poliforum by the Hotel de México, as well as official venues such as the Instituto Nacional de Bellas Artes and the Museo de Arte Moderno. Some descriptions of rock events entirely subvert the image of a rock scene forced into the inglorious margins.[17] Yet these events appear comparatively exceptional in light of consistent accounts throughout the 1970s, and into the early 1980s, of permits being refused or revoked, and of live rock events being subject to constant police raids.[18] Rock festivals also struggled—several were shut down after being linked to Avándaro by organizers or in press coverage—although festivals that eschewed such direct connections were permitted to take place, especially outside of the capital.[19] For example, festivals were held in Monterrey in 1972 and in Cuernavaca in 1973.[20] A one-day festival, which attracted a crowd of ten thousand, was even held in the Arena México in June 1975.[21] Finally, rock fans were subjected to continuous police harassment—including beatings and enforced head-shaving—ostensibly on the grounds of appearance (rock fans were frequently denigrated as *greñudos*, a word implying both a general disheveled appearance and tangled or matted hair), as described in vivid detail by Víctor Roura.[22] The combined effect of these sustained, but far from total forms of repression was that live rock became less attractive to the middle classes, so bands migrated toward so-called *hoyos fonqui* (funky holes)—squalid, densely packed, informal, clandestine, and generally unsanitary and unsafe venues, mostly on the outskirts of what was now a rapidly expanding metropolis.[23] Many of the bands that performed at Avándaro continued to play at *hoyos*, although they were often ill-at-ease in this performance context; many of these bands also performed at "nocturnal spaces" (*espacios nocturnos*), medium-size bars in need of background music.[24]

From this we can see that post-Avándaro censorship is best understood as uneven and incomplete. In marked contrast, *Break It All* exemplifies a tendency for accounts of censorship to become increasingly simplified, identified with the actions of governments and distanced from the influence of other entities that exert power, such as the mainstream press and conservative society. Over time, 1970s rock has come to be defined by its resistance to government power. Mexican rock culture has frequently been depicted as antiauthoritarian and "liberationist."[25] Represented by the gritty blues sound of Three Souls in My Mind, later to become El Tri, and the performing contexts of the *hoyos fonqui*, 1970s rock is seen to have defied the authoritarian nationalism of the PRI.[26] The characterization of Mexican rock in the 1970s as antiauthoritarian—a refuge from the repression of the outside world—has dovetailed with depictions of this scene as unified by shared social and ethnic marginalization. Thus for Moreno-Elizondo, the *hoyos fonqui* "facilitated the imagining of a sonic space in the dissidence typical of the memory of anti-authoritarian political culture, aware of its exclusion and class situation."[27]

By contrast, I am interested in challenging the notion that authoritarian or hierarchical power relations were suspended within this scene. This may be contextualized within a broader scholarly rethinking of the presumed antiauthoritarian tendencies of "countercultures" elsewhere, with some arguing, for instance, that the United States counterculture combined libertarian and communitarian influences.[28] To be sure, one finds an emphasis on individual (especially sexual) freedom throughout the music of La Onda. Yet I argue that reading post-Avándaro rock journalism in conjunction with interviews with musicians and journalists of the era, allows us to identify subtle intergenerational tensions, incommensuralities, and silencings that traverse these histories and the ways in which they are reproduced, and that complicate the straightforward portrayal of the 1970s rock scene as defined by antiauthoritarianism and resistance against the state.

This chapter thus focuses on an important but curiously neglected source: the magazine *Conecte*, strangely absent from many histories of Mexican rock.[29] Reading *Conecte* in continuity with its predecessors *México Canta* and *Pop* achieves two things. First, it situates rock's position at contemporaneous ideological interstices—something that may help us understand how ideas about Avándaro formed. By exploring the processes by which narratives concerning the Holocaust (as universal symbol of aberrant moral evil) and Watergate (as unprecedented political scandal) took shape over time, Jeffrey Alexander shows that shared traumatic events take time to coalesce and that their development is often imbricated with longer-run conceptual and ideological changes.[30] This idea has also informed rich historical accounts of the 1968 movement in Mexico.[31] The notion that the Avándaro narrative concretized over time as a story about state censorship was indicated to me by the journalist and editor Antonio Malacara Palacios, who wrote for *Conecte* beginning in the 1970s: "[We thought] the government hadn't done anything to us. We understood that [it had] only years later."[32] At the time, he told me, the rock scene's principal antagonist was understood to be the mainstream press.

Second, reading these publications can help us to understand the relation of the rock press to the broader rock scene and to political power. As Malacara Palacios indicated, many 1970s rock journalists defined their role as resisting the disinformation and moral panic about rock in the mainstream press that established a pretext for repression. This suggests a model of "insurgent journalism" existing in order to counter official hegemonies, but rock writers from this time did not only resist political power.[33] In fact, 1970s rock journalists—generally writing from a middle-class standpoint—often extended, rather than challenged, the disciplinary logic in which acts of public disorder at concerts could constitute a legitimate pretext for censorship levied against entire genres of music, and in which the main solution to authoritarian censorship was for audiences to reform their behavior. To understand rock censorship in the 1970s, it is vital to reckon with the role of knowledge-making practices in the complex diffusion of power throughout this scene.

Journalism, and Power, and the Emergence of the Rock Press

One of the first responses by rockers to the media onslaught that followed the Avándaro Festival was to publish. A number of books were produced by participants in the rock scene soon after the festival, including *Nosotros* (Us), published in early 1972, and *Avándaro: ¿Aliviane o movida?* (Avándaro: Good time, or happening?), published in October 1971. Reflecting on the festival itself, these publications documented the festival in different ways. For example, *Nosotros*, edited by the organizer and radio presenter Humberto Ruvalcaba, contained photographs from the festival alongside accounts written by journalists. Meanwhile, *Avándaro: ¿Aliviane o movida?* contained a detailed eyewitness account of the festival and several extensive interviews with attendees and organizers, as well as with traders and residents of the nearby town. These publications anticipated a desire to write about Avándaro that flourished in the years afterward, reflected in the development of specialized magazines focusing on rock culture—a media ecosystem I will describe here as "the rock press." These magazines included *Conecte*, *Rock Poster*, *México Canta*, and *Sonido*, as well as the preexisting *Pop* and *Piedra Rodante*.

Why this wave of new magazines? They responded, in part, to the hysterical mainstream press reaction to Avándaro, built around a series of fabrications about what had happened at the festival, which in turn served as a pretext for censorship against rock. By most eyewitness accounts, the reality of Avándaro was comparatively innocuous. The festival, with performances by twelve *rock nacional* bands, was oriented around a motor race that was eventually cancelled. Although the event attracted a crowd of somewhere between one hundred thousand and two hundred thousand attendees, no major disturbances were registered; most participants experienced Avándaro as a site of peaceful coexistence. A small number of incidents, however, were scandalous for the conservative mainstream of Mexican society, especially a photograph of a nude female attendee and the performance of the band Peace and Love, which contained a song about marijuana, onstage swearing that incited moral panic, and a song entitled "We Got the Power."[34] The latter song's titular refrain, sung repeatedly by the entire band during the chorus, has often been understood to have caught the attention of political leaders at a time when the power of large gatherings of young people was a source of anxiety for the authoritarian government. Yet post-Avándaro repression resulted not from the events actually recorded at the festival but from the exaggerated image of scandalous behavior at Avándaro presented by the press.[35] As a rock journalist put it in a later retrospective, the mainstream print media claimed that there were "orgies, with sex and drugs; that there were many deaths; that the youth had become unhinged."[36] The negative press coverage of Avándaro was a catalyst for repression against rock by the authorities, police, and conservative society in the years following the festival. In turn, the print media's operation as part of a mechanism for wielding authoritarian power—long established in other sectors and now unavoidable within popular culture—informed the rock journalism that emerged after Avándaro.

Nosotros, Avándaro: ¿Aliviane o movida?, and the new rock magazines that followed took ownership of narratives about rock as part of the scene's struggle to exist. "Avándaro was going to make, and be, history," boasted the introductory section to *Nosotros*, "and this time, nobody was going to tell it for us."[37] Some who attended Avándaro were rock journalists whose engagement with the festival was converted into long-standing journalistic projects. Víctor Manuel Alatorre attended Avándaro after his friend Arturo Castelazo—part of a journalistic dynasty including his father, a well-known entertainment journalist who helped to establish the National Circle of Journalists—proposed that the pair write a feature on it for the magazine *Figuras de la canción*. Alatorre described arriving to set up a makeshift tent, improvised from repurposed flour sacks, about fifty meters from the stage. There, the pair attempted to work, armed with only notebooks, press passes, and a camera they borrowed from a woman they met at the festival:

> We were there apparently to work, but we were also really excited to be at a concert that was, for the first time in Mexico, of that size and magnitude.... The night set in, and the fervor started. After dark we couldn't find our tent. People everywhere, it was dark, loads of bonfires, the only strong light came from the stage, but almost all the place was covered in bonfires, and some had torches, and it looked really weird, no?... So we started to work with whatever patience God had given us, and by midnight, I'll tell you, I don't even remember what state we were in, in truth. It was all so nice, the music, the people, all really switched on, some dancing, others meditating, others screwing, all good, all very good.... It was free, of our free will. We started walking around and now... I mean, we didn't even have a voice recorder. We were just writing down notes, and seeing how we could fit comments to the photos we'd taken. And that was it. The music was just like, we forgot about journalism, and it was "let's enjoy life, Daddy."
>
> I was there naked, bathing with everybody, carefree, and you know, hitting it off, haha. We were hippies! Long-haired ones. I remember, what I did was cover myself with mud, and got a few pictures of that, but I don't remember those photos, nor where they got to, nothing.[38]

Returning from Avándaro, the pair began to write for *Figuras de la canción* on a more consistent basis. Three years later, they joined the editorial team of *Conecte*, a publication established in 1974. Created when the magazine *Pop*—a publication founded in the 1960s that had increasingly focused on rock—had ceased to operate and when the rock-focused *México Canta* was in decline, *Conecte* was to be the most important publication in the rock scene for almost two decades. Building on the format and approach of *México Canta* (and indeed directly appropriating many of its writers after layoffs in 1975), *Conecte* became the closest thing to a publication of record within the rock scene in 1970s Mexico.

Conecte was distributed across Mexico, as well as in Latino communities in California, Arizona, and Texas. In a busy week, *Conecte* would sell twenty thousand copies in the capital alone.[39] Many of its readers bought the magazine for its posters, rather than for its content—something also true for *Conecte*'s competition, such as *Sonido* and *Rock Poster*. Yet *Conecte* was distinguished by the often serious tone of its editorials and features, and the role it sought to play in promoting and growing the rock scene. The magazine's name celebrated the link between rock and marijuana—a *conecte* was a colloquial term for a street-corner drug dealer—yet the term can be read as more than a flippant joke; *Conecte* intervened in many ways to articulate a scene. It provided a platform for musicians to contact one another to form groups, printed lyrics and chords from well-known English-language rock songs so that fans could perform them (in a context where LPs cost about US$12), conveyed information about performance venues and concerts, organized occasional concerts and rock competitions, and informed readers about how to record their own music and produce live events.

Conecte also, however, continues to attract a curious set of mixed feelings related to suspicions about government influence over the press. During the 1970s, the government exerted power over the press through controls on the price of paper distributed by the state-created paper monopoly PIPSA (Producer and Importer of Paper).[40] Indeed, an editorial in *Conecte*'s inaugural edition, in December 1974, blames the near disappearance of rock magazines on rising paper prices.[41] *Conecte* avoided such control, a former member of its editorial team claimed to me, by using "pirated" paper distributed outside of official state channels.[42] Correspondingly, journalists who wrote in *Conecte* and edited the magazine have insisted to me that they were free to publish what they wished, without interference or coercion by government.[43] Several alluded to the broader idea that *Conecte* and publications like it were seen by the government as marginal and unthreatening. "They didn't care about culture," claimed Alatorre, before ventriloquating the voice of authority as aloof, secure, and detached: "*Ay*, they're really out of control [*desmadrosos*], leave them there, they can continue with their rock and roll."[44]

Yet looking in from the outside, *Conecte*'s journalistic output appeared different—characterized by self-censorship and perhaps more. For the musician and journalist Walter Schmidt, who edited *Sonido* in the 1970s and 1980s, *Conecte*'s writers "kept themselves within certain limits. . . . There was an implicit ethic, there were things that they'd never mention."[45] Such self-censorship could be understood as self-preservation in response to repressive precedents, such as the famous example of the magazine *Piedra Rodante*, forced to close shortly after Avándaro. The magazine, which combined original content with republished stories from *Rolling Stone*, attracted scandal due to its publication of nude images, but it also openly discussed the massacres of October 2, 1968 and June 11, 1971; its eventual closure came after death threats were issued to the editor.[46] Some writers made a stronger claim:

that *Conecte* was actively complicit with the authorities. One well-known rock writer active since the 1960s described the magazine as "allied with the enemy—with the police, with power. . . . The idea was to have a telephone toward the underground, controlled by the government."[47]

Questions thus remain about how *Conecte* and similar publications from the same era may best be read: whether as victims of government-induced self-censorship, as complicit with government power, or as part of a genuine counter-public sphere. These questions underline an especially striking feature of *Conecte* when read from the vantage point of the present: the magazine often struck a moralistic, disciplinary tone when addressing its own readership. The magazine narrated post-Avándaro repression in changing ways, first producing a complex and open-ended account of censorship against rock, before increasingly identifying the government as the prime mover of censorship. As I argue in the next section, this shift in perspective reflected not only a comparative lifting of Echeverría-era censorship but changing ideological conditions at the interstices of Mexico's developmentalist and neoliberal eras.

Remembering Avándaro

It was no secret that rock slumped after Avándaro; yet while in the early 1970s the journalistic frames through which this slump was understood were varied and unstable, toward the end of the decade much of this variety had given way to a relatively consolidated account of government repression. While the contemporary rock press freely wrote about the "prohibition" of rock and criticized government refusals and revocations of licenses for rock events, the post-Avándaro slump was also explained in other ways, and occasionally mystified. As an event organizer put it in *Pop* in November 1972: "There don't exist centers where [rock] groups can work. Why? Nobody knows." The genre's ills were ascribed to a variety of factors, such as economic slowdown, a lack of work for rock musicians, insecurity, fraud and internal conflict, and a lack of a professional work ethic within the rock scene.[48] Editorials frequently denounced fraudulent or misleading promotion, disorderly behavior during live concerts, the curatorial processes and creative priorities of recording studios, corrupt business practices such as payola, and the unreliable behavior of rock bands and organizers.[49] Rock journalists directed ire toward the police for reprisals against rock fans, and also expressed anxieties about the quality of Mexican rock when compared to the standard set by artists from Europe and the United States.⁵⁰ Government censorship was, then, understood to be one of several causes of rock's era of crisis.

It is worth paying special attention to commemorations of Avándaro, since writers often used these events to reflect on the development of the rock scene. As the decade wore on, the festival was increasingly remembered as a harbinger of catastrophe. A *Conecte* editorial from 1981 titled "What has happened to rock ten years after Avándaro?" mocked "the entertaining stories told about it, what the media said about it and the scandalous moment it represented for all those people who had closed off their brains." "More noise was made after the Festival," the article concluded, "than at the Festival itself. . . . Ten years later we're still the same, both in repression, as in musical freedom," because rock was exiled from polite society "Because rock is colonizing, it makes us foreign [*extranjerizante*], it is alienating; because rock means excess, laziness, drugs, revolt; because the old don't understand rock, or simply don't want to. . . . Avándaro was not the beginning, nor the end. It's the same as always: Simply, in our country we don't want rock, true rock, the rock of big national and international groups."⁵¹

An unattributed article in the same issue, titled "Ten years later: 11 September 1971," put Avándaro in the context of a year that was "the pure effervescence of Mexican rock." At the festival, there were "people in their tents, talking, playing the guitar and dancing. By the river, there were nudists"; participants were "dreaming with nature, free from the reins of their parents, trying to imagine themselves hippies and releasing all the repression they carried around inside them." Yet tabloids twisted this innocent reality, accusing participants of taking drugs, participating in orgies, and causing deaths; "they caused controversy and sensationalism. . . . And, ten years later, we're still in the slow lane [*seguimos en la lenta*]."

Most importantly, from the late 1970s it became increasingly common for writers to understand the response to Avándaro as part of broader Dirty War repression by the government. Although the massacres of October 1968 and June 1971 were not mentioned at Avándaro, and rock musicians had tended to distance their music from the student movement, connections between the festival and student activism were occasionally made.⁵² Writing in the publication *Nosotros*, the Telesistema news anchor Jacobo Zabludowsky situated Avándaro as a response to the massacres of student protesters. Pushed by these experiences of repression, Zabludowsky wrote, youth went to Avándaro in search of "something more important than an *halcón* [the paramilitary group that perpetrated the Corpus Christi massacre]: something to believe in." Where Zabludowsky—writing in the immediate wake of the festival—saw Avándaro as an *antidote* to repression against young people, more catastrophic later accounts increasingly characterized the reaction to Avándaro as an extension of the Dirty War. Antonio Malacara Alonso, writing in *Conecte*, asked whether rock in the ten years since Avándaro had witnessed either "decadence or total ineptitude?" "After the Avandarazo," he wrote, "the second and most serious obstacle for national rock emerged: closure and prohibition of 80 percent of rock concerts, at least in the capital. As governmental aggression against rock developed, which had as its primary effect the closure of sources of work for the rock musicians, the genre . . . had to look for work in other places."

It is not clear when the phrase "Avandarazo" was first used, but it conveys two prominent aspects of this account: first, the idea of Avándaro as an aberrant, catastrophic event whose consequences were immediately apparent; second, in its similarity to "Halconazo" the term implied a connection between repression against rock and the government repression of the Dirty War.[53] A letter by a reader called Manuel García, published in *Conecte* in October 1981, made this link explicit, suggesting that the festival had given an outlet to "the energy of the youth, with it motivating the outrage of a society which, in reality, is tricked by the demagoguery of the government itself." The government's motivation for granting permission to the festival, García speculated, was "to make public opinion forget about what had happened a few months prior, that fateful 10th of June."[54]

This reader's hierarchy of repression—active government manipulating passive civil society—indicates how the "Avandarazo" narrative tended to simplify accounts of post-Avándaro censorship so as to make the state the prime mover of repression. It is possible to attribute this shift to a lifting of self-censorship after Echeverrían authoritarianism—writers at this time certainly skirted around the topic of state repression for the sake of self-preservation, and the closure of *Piedra Rodante* represented a chilling precedent for the rock press—yet it was also related to some journalists' changing ideological tendencies. In 1978 Carlos Baca—a journalist, ecologist, and mainstay of the rock press—published a *Conecte* feature titled "Can rock and the mixed economy coexist?," one of a series of articles in the late 1970s and 1980s in which Baca connected rock culture with capitalism.[55] In "free" countries dominated by capitalism, Baca wrote, "the youth [*los chavos*] have so many discos to go to . . . and all this because the government doesn't interfere in the lives of private citizens [*particulares*]." Mexico, as a mixed economy, enjoyed capitalist freedom incompletely, "since the government intervenes in various spheres, impeding private citizens' completely free expression." By contrast, Baca stated, communist countries left no room for rock expression, criminalizing the genre and its dissemination:

> Did you know that in Mexico we have far greater freedom than in other countries? Did you know that there are countries in which it is a crime to listen to and play Rock without government permission? Where not only are there no discotheques nor concerts, but where you can't get rock albums, and where radio stations do not play Rock because they consider it harmful for the youth? ... These countries in which freedom does not exist are communist countries. ... By contrast, in advanced capitalist countries, freedom of expression is complete, absolute, unrestricted. ... In our country we have less freedom [than capitalist countries]; but it's because of the same thing, we're not completely capitalist, but have a mixed economy.

Baca's ideological positioning had transformed dramatically over the course of the 1970s—from ecologically minded hippie to staunch procapitalist and antisocialist. This shift reflected Baca's evolving self-interest: during the same time, Baca opened a successful chain of health food stores, on the basis of which he became a wealthy businessman.[56] Yet it ought also to be understood in the context of broader ideological turmoil during momentous times for the Mexican economy. José López Portillo (1976–1982) was Mexico's last president before the shift to neoliberalism; he supported the economic path of the "Mexican Miracle," constructed around state investment and protection of industry. López Portillo responded to Mexico's debt crisis, provoked by the crash in oil prices at the end of the 1970s and an interest rate hike, by nationalizing Mexico's banks. He was succeeded by Miguel de la Madrid (1982–1988), who, under pressure from the International Monetary Fund, opted for neoliberal "structural adjustment" with its attendant cuts to public services and privatization of state-owned industries.[57]

Written at the dawn of neoliberalism in Mexico, "Can rock and the mixed economy coexist?" clarifies the ideological stakes of narratives about music censorship, which tended to attract around them broader sets of political ideas. Baca's writing was neither out-of-place nor uncontested within the pages of *Conecte*; some outraged readers wrote to the magazine to object that rock did indeed exist in socialist societies such as Cuba.[58] That Baca's antisocialist viewpoint took increasing prominence in this magazine toward the end of the decade is reflected in the following contrasting accounts of Avándaro: at the beginning of the 1970s, the festival was celebrated in *Piedra Rodante* as "the dawning of the socialism of love," a utopian alternative to Cold War–era political binaries.⁵⁹ By the end of the decade, however, one of the editors of *Conecte* blamed rock's woes on the left-wing politics implemented under Luis Echeverría (1970–1976): "We were living under a presidency of wasteful socialism [*socialismo despilfarrador*] and censorship turned its gaze toward rock."⁶⁰

To trace the emergence of the "hard" account of censorship found in *Break It All* is, emphatically, not to imply that repression of rock was somehow imaginary, constructed from the ground up, as Woodside seems to suggest at the beginning of this chapter. It is, instead, to reckon with the inherent complexity of experiences of censorship and with the perspectival nature of censorship, in which distinct frames and standpoints illuminate different patterns of silencing. It is also to engage ongoing debates about how political power was exerted under authoritarian rule—especially the extent to which PRI authoritarianism left open spaces for pleasure and creativity.⁶¹ Karush's description of post-Avándaro censorship is especially instructive here; he claims that "Mexico's one-party, authoritarian government repressed rock in the 1970s more effectively than the Argentine dictatorships."⁶² To the extent that this is true, we may observe that repression in Mexico was facilitated by doubt and uncertainty, and it was weakened when groups achieved sufficient shared epistemological clarity to produce organization. The ability to instill epistemological confusion within marginalized populations was fundamental to authoritarian rule in Mexico; this included the ability to extend disciplinary governmentalities into those populations themselves. As I explore in the following section, this governmental power was exercised in part through rock journalism.

Communication and Censorship

Although accounts of Mexican rock have overwhelmingly tended to emphasize its antiauthoritarian stance, the post-Avándaro rock movement was not straightforwardly a hotbed of resistance against restrictive, official cultural conservatism. In fact, rock journalists and musicians often endorsed the censorship of some forms of musical expression. This section explores how and advances a theory as to why.

The editorial team of *Conecte* consistently supported the repression against disco in the 1970s carried out by Venus Rey, the trombonist, bandleader, and head of the Unique Syndicate of Musical Workers (SUTM) in Mexico City. Rey was a conservative voice in the music scene, but his orchestra had been among the first in Mexico to perform rock and roll;⁶³ rockers thus viewed Rey as a natural ally. SUTM maintained a fiercely antidisco posture through the 1970s and 1980s, which was justified in economic terms by ideas about musical work and ensuring jobs for performers.[64] Indeed, there was continuity between SUTM's reaction to disco in the 1970s and their reaction to what were termed *sonideros* or *tibirís* from the late 1980s. SUTM had a great deal of power in the musical world—they often orchestrated strikes, and they demanded that all live musical events be registered with them—so they were often able to exert control over certain kinds of musical expression. With the arrival of New Wave in the 1980s, for instance, SUTM sought restrictions on the use of electronic instruments.

Rock journalists and musicians had often framed rock's post-Avándaro slump in terms of a lack of performance opportunities, and this drew many to engage both SUTM and the government. In 1972 and 1973, rockers' efforts to lobby for their interests included a project titled Rock Sobre Ruedas (Rock on Wheels), in which rock bands performed directly for the public from a converted truck traveling around Mexico City and to a lesser extent outside the capital, and a hunger strike. They also met on multiple occasions with Venus Rey and visited Los Pinos, the official presidential residency, to request help.[65] On these occasions, it was reported that rockers were requesting intervention in order to support their sources of musical work. As the band Tinta Blanca told *Pop* in 1973: "We went first to ask for the support of Venus Rey and he told us that he was going to help us. . . . We went to Los Pinos. And they told us yes, too, but we haven't seen anything yet. We trust that this trend [of lack of work] will ease."[66]

On what may be the same occasion, *México Canta* described how a group of rock musicians

> met outside the Musicians' Union to make Venus Rey hear them. For this they were playing for a long time and then they managed to get Venus to go down. . . . He was talking with them and among the problems that were raised was precisely that of sources of work for rock 'n roll fans. . . . They agreed that Venus would try to solve this problem for them. Let's see if these were more than just empty words, because this rock thing is not viewed positively by the other musicians of the union, who classify the rhythm and its interpreters as not worthwhile. This, in addition to the fact that they told me that Don Venus was not interested in anything related to rock.[67]

Despite such apparent rejections, the rock press could be highly supportive of Venus Rey. An editorial in the magazine in July 1976 hailed the fact that

Rey had been chosen as a PRI legislator in the Chamber of Deputies, praising the union leader's struggle "against 'discotheques,' where only recorded music is played. . . . He considers that this type of space displaces music." "Soon," the editorial says, "musicians will achieve a law protecting themselves against discotheques," which would involve prohibiting "the establishment of discotheque-bars." The editorial goes on to caution, nonetheless, that such censorship might not have the desired effect since "people from the capital often prefer to travel to Estado de México to listen to good albums to staying in a venue where rock bands perform live."[68] Here, *Conecte*'s editors assumed not a principled opposition to censorship but an ambivalence toward it on pragmatic grounds.

Conecte's support for Rey, in both his union leadership and his political career, hinged on optimism that the union leader would simultaneously support favored music venues and crack down on unfavored ones—especially the *hoyos fonqui*. In early 1977 the magazine's editors praised an initiative by SUTM to create a list of *hoyos* so that "the corresponding authorities refuse [them] licenses and permits." SUTM also promised to create a dance hall "in which exclusively rockers may work," which *Conecte* took as a move to coerce rockers into joining the union and paying its fees.[69] Later the same year, the magazine reported that amid a comparative relaxation of the government' restrictive stance toward live venues and radio, Rey had "started to twist arms so that discotheques would open in the city."[70] Such support for Rey's actions against the *hoyos fonqui* was not an outlier within the pages of *Conecte*; rock journalists had often called for censorship against these venues. In May 1976, Arturo Castelazo wrote in "Ahí se va," his regular column in *Conecte*, that Sunday afternoon *tardeadas* held in the *hoyos fonqui* should be banned: "Although I know that many will label me as corrupt, and perhaps in cahoots with the authorities, I won't tire of writing that the Sunday concerts are HARMFUL AND UNPRODUCTIVE, as well as fraudulent, and vehicles for incorporating vice into rock, and so on. I am of the opinion that their prohibition is necessary in order that national rock gain its true importance."

The previous year, the same writer had called for more government oversight, complaining that these venues had not been visited by government inspectors, nor had their licenses revoked, nor been fined.[71] This stance was still common in *Conecte* by the end of the decade, when the magazine—in the context of a conversation about SUTM and the *hoyos*—stated the need "to stop many dire routes [*trenes nefastos*] for rock in Mexico."[72]

What explains the prevalence of this anti-*hoyo* posture? Castelazo denounced fraud at the *hoyos*, in which bands were falsely advertised without having been booked, and venue organizers' unscrupulous business practices, which meant that events were expensive and held in inadequate venues, with small entrances "so that nobody slips through" without paying.[73] The *hoyos fonqui* had many other problems: bands frequently had equipment stolen, disturbances were often reported, and many venues were structurally unsound. Equally, this anti-*hoyo* attitude was intimately tied to what may be described as the politics of connection. The journalists working at *Conecte* saw rock as the epitome of individual expressive freedom, but they also emphasized values such as unity, communication, and identification. This was linked, in turn, to a utopian vision of progress that saw rock as a vehicle for connecting young people across national boundaries. Communication was a paramount virtue within the rock scene, alluded to in the titles of publications, the names of bands (including one called Comunicación), and the names of recurring columns in rock magazines (for instance, "Conexión" in *Pop*). Communication was associated with a particular iteration of cosmopolitan modernity facilitated by new media technologies; it was also the subject of conceptual exploration in rock journalism, often in ways that reflect the 1960s-era communication theory of thinkers such as Marshall McLuhan.[74] As Antonio Malacara Palacios recognized, communication was a topic for open, exploratory discussion in part because broadcast media were relatively novel.[75] Rock was valued as an ideal vehicle for communication because of its perceived status as culturally "universal": a mass-mediated practice that by the 1970s traversed most of the globe.[76] For this reason, communication was at the heart of debates over which language to use: for example, the band Tinta Blanca told *México Canta* that singing in Spanish "creates more communication" to their public, while the "sacred music" act La Verdad Desnuda chose English as "a language that the whole world accepts."[77] Armando Molina, meanwhile, wrote that many bands chose to employ "both languages, achieving more communication," although linguistic deficiencies often meant that the result "doesn't sound sufficiently harmonious."[78]

Communication became central to a certain ethical discourse within the 1970s scene; its antonym, alienation (*enajenación*), was an oft-denounced evil. The presence of "communication" characterized good social relations; it was seen as vital to the musically "good" at live events, within the studio, and elsewhere, and it affected judgments concerning musical style as well as evaluations of live music contexts.[79] "To communicate" was used as both a transitive and intransitive verb. Humberto Ruvalcaba, the radio presenter, journalist, and organizer of Rock Sobre Ruedas, told *Pop* in November 1972 that rock responded to "the needs of the youth to communicate" in ways not permitted through traditional media; true communication, he stated, "did exist in a festival like Avándaro." The key aim of Rock Sobre Ruedas was "communication" to the parents of participants in the rock movement, to the broadcast media, and to the authorities that "well, what we offer is GOOD."[80] Here, the communication of a message, and communication as a practice of social intimacy and co-presence, were intertwined.[81]

Rock magazines understood themselves to play an intrinsically "communicative" role in tying together, expanding, and empowering the rock scene. In February 1978, celebrating the fact that they now had distribution in Los Angeles, Chicago, and New York, an editorial in *Conecte* claimed, "Our work is starting to bear fruit.... Today communication has finally been achieved."[82] *Conecte* made constant efforts to directly engage readers and bring together participants in the rock scene by, for example, publishing contact details for venues, recording studios, and musicians seeking collaborators.[83] Good communication was seen to lead to "unity" or "union": a heightened sense of collective purpose or synchrony, being on the same wavelength (*onda*). In 1973, José Luis Pluma compared this process to "communicating vessels in physics.... Different glasses on different levels communicate and are placed on the same level."[84] A *Conecte* editorial from 1975 called for "harmony" and a "unification of judgement [*criterio*]," since "strength comes from union. ... We want the connection to cover all ideologies."[85] On the other hand, the failures described as a lack of "professionalism" among rock musicians and venue organizers were also characterized as a failure to communicate, to produce union.[86]

This ideological admixture is largely familiar from the United States hippie counterculture, but what may mark out the Mexican case are the specific ways that ideals of expressive freedom and communication came into conflict.[87] There was a certain ambiguity in the political implications of discourse about rock as communication. On the one hand, talk of "unity" had a distinctly Echeverrian taste. By contrast, although this link was rarely made explicit in the rock press, the valorization of rock as a vehicle for communication reflected what Draper calls the "desire for social connectivity" characteristic of the student movement.[88] Mexican rock journalists both associated their movement with "freedom" and called for censorship of genres or contexts perceived to impede "communication." *Hoyos fonqui* were disparaged because they failed to facilitate "true" communication, because audiences did not listen in the attentive manner that rock's "advancement" demanded. Thus, as Arturo Castelazo called for licenses to be denied to *hoyos fonqui*, he criticized these venues as poor listening environments in which "the vibe [*la onda*] is not to go to listen, nor to see entertainment. The point is to go to party."[89] In a similar vein, Vladimir Hernández criticized poor conditions and drug-taking in the *hoyos*, where "the organizers only want money, and don't care about rock."[90] "Communication" in the rock press implied a paternalistic gaze: good communication was associated with audience behavior, often denoting an attentive listening style characterized by physical passivity. Attentive listening practices served to distinguish rock from less esteemed genres, such as disco—good for dancing, but for "moments of listening . . . it's useless to play disco music."[91] The *hoyos* were also sometimes defended in the same terms, such as in one article that described the venues as "sacred temple[s] for all those who seek communion, liberation, and the channeling of all their problems, traumas, complexes, and loneliness."[92] When, in 1979, enduring blues guitarist Javier Bátiz played a *tardeada* in a gym after several months without performing, it was recounted like a miracle that the audience sat on the floor: "There were the youth, listening, listening! Javier couldn't believe it, the whole audience LISTENING in orderly fashion."[93] Communication and "attentive," physically passive listening were thus central to the hierarchy of values articulated in the rock press.[94]

Social class is, evidently, fundamental within such dynamics—these are middle-class voices speaking to, and on behalf of, mostly lower-class ones, and journalists' criticisms of rock audiences often had decidedly classist overtones. It is nevertheless important to allow these voices to speak on their own terms, as embedded within a certain ideological position through which music was given value and on the basis of which the censorship of music could be justified. Several present-day voices I spoke with put the willingness of writers within the 1970s rock scene to endorse the censorship of music down to a broad conservatism among some participants. Indeed, some gave the example of Javier Bátiz himself: in *Break It All* he had blamed post-Avándaro repression on the band Peace and Love for cursing onstage, rather than on the authorities for their repressive actions. Clearly, rock from the time sometimes evinces conservative perspectives; misogynistic attitudes, in particular, are heard in songs from La Onda such as La Revolución de Emiliano Zapata's 1971 hit "Nasty Sex" and El Ritual's "Easy Woman" (a song announced at Avándaro as "Prostituta"). Yet it would be unfair to categorize as conservative those contemporaneous writers willing on occasion to endorse censorship without recognizing the politics of connection underpinning such gestures, which put forward a utopian, positive, and imaginative vision of progress.

Disciplining the Rock Public

The politics of connection—especially toward the end of the 1970s and within *Conecte*—motivated continuous efforts on the part of journalists to discipline the rock public. Some rock journalism was engaged in what might be understood as a civilizing project, intended to encourage self-controlled, "educated" behavior among rock publics, especially in response to disorder at live concerts. One incident came to symbolize the apparently "disorderly" nature of rock publics. The rock band Chicago's November 1975 concert in the Auditorio Nacional took place at a moment of optimism: many rock journalists believed that the incoming government of José López Portillo would relax the restrictions placed on rock by the Echeverría government, describing excitement at the news that the family of the president-elect attended the concert.[95]

As it turned out, however, the Chicago concert was a disaster. Events were reported as follows by *Conecte*: the police were reselling tickets (even, one bemused journalist remarked, selling fakes), and evidently many fans felt excluded from the concert by the price and scarcity of tickets.[96] In response, rock fans staged a so-called *portazo*—an attempt to storm the venue in order to gain free entry. This provoked repression by riot police, to which some responded by throwing bottles and stones, and leaving one police vehicle "semi-burned."[97] Almost two hundred attendees and police were injured in the incident. *Conecte* criticized mainstream press coverage of the concert afterward, running a feature with a montage of outraged press headlines alongside a brief note contesting this coverage: "[The press gives] little importance to the vandalism that occurs in events of a sporting or social nature. We all know that wherever large crowds meet, there are riots, fights, and rampages: why then do they only fixate on rock events?"[98] Yet even within the rock press, this attempt to contest the grounds on which rock was repressed was drowned out by much more widespread moralistic admonishments of the rock public. In *Conecte*, Arturo Castelazo argued that the event ought to have been more forcefully policed: public security, he wrote, should have "analyzed the case and sent a squad of riot police, enough to control the people who arrived." Blame for the disturbances, he claimed, lay not with the police but with a few provocateurs who "honestly, did not look to us like youth," as he rebuked "the prehistoric and irresponsible attitude of [these] 'young people' [*chavos*] who went 'looking to disrupt everything.'" This event nonetheless revealed broader anxieties about Mexican rock publics. "Since we're not used to groups like Chicago coming," Castelazo said, "we all want to see them, but we belong to the most layabout and selfish [*golfa*] generation of recent times, we want everything for free."[99]

Within the rock press, the Chicago incident raised questions—also posed after similar episodes at concerts by Deep Purple and Johnny Winter in 1980—about security at live events. These questions, in turn, were folded into anxieties about the Mexican rock public itself. Rock writers aired frequent concerns about any behavior during live concerts that fell short of their idealized attentive, physically passive audience—often grouping together actions such as throwing objects at musicians, disturbances by groups aiming to gain free entry to events, and audience disquiet after discovering that events had been falsely advertised or were held in substandard conditions. This criticism of rock audiences sometimes slipped into an overt discourse of internalized colonization, in which rock's Mexican iteration fell short of the model of the "civilized countries" of the West.[100] Cancellations and revocations of licenses were often blamed on prior disturbances; most damaging were cancellations by international acts, which rock writers took to have been put off by the poor reputation of Mexican rock audiences.[101] These inverse-exceptionalist claims about Mexican audiences' poor behavior were reinforced by claims that these audiences had reformed, matured, or become more "civilized." In 1979, *Conecte* published a story championing the supposed "new behavior of the rock-listener" in the *hoyos fonqui*. Here, although there was "a lot of energy, whistles, shouts, lots of youth," this behavior was now "within the limits [*marco*] of not bothering the people next to you. . . . The kids [*chavos*] arrive with the main intention of listening to rock." Such controlled comportment represented, it was claimed, "new behavior for the Sunday afternoon gigs: the kids arrive, listen, dance, get along together and then go back home." This concern with fan behavior was related to security: "We must respect the individual rights of each person, and if not there are the security guards for those who want to spoil the party."[102]

The term here translated as "security guards," *chavos de seguridad*, implies that these individuals were participants in the movement itself; thus, the policing of rock was taken as a constitutive part of the genre's advancement rather than an external imposition to be resisted. Indeed, *Conecte*'s moralizing discourse was converted into a mandate for the rock press to discipline audiences. In January 1978, Antonio Malacara Alonso wrote a series of articles in *Conecte* that critiqued other writers, apparently in response to debates occurring both in person and in other publications. He sought to move Mexican rock on from what he saw as the antiestablishment attitudes of the past, in which "everything was *reventón*" (a spontaneous, uncontrolled "outburst" of rock expression). With the arrival of the hippie influence, he wrote, "rock in Mexico should have shifted its mentality in definitive fashion," but this shift was interrupted by Avándaro, leading to "disintegration once more due to immaturity" rather than the promised "union."[103] Malacara Alonso called on other journalists, several by name, to be more proactive in advancing the rock scene, criticizing *Sonido*—*Conecte*'s closest market rival—for having "stuck with only color photos . . . and advertisements," rather than investing in valuable intellectual labor.[104] "If the rock magazines in Mexico, with their writers, had had the capacity and sufficient sense of responsibility to try to instruct the entire *raza* and make them see their—our—obligations as rock 'n' roll fans and what they represent in a new society," Malacara Alonso wrote, "the rock atmosphere that we are living in our country would be completely different. . . . Is it enough to report, document, and analyze records? I don't think so."[105]

This writer's sentiments were commonplace in *Conecte*, which constantly advocated for rock to "advance" musically, become more "progressive" (*progresista*), increase in professionalism, and transcend "mediocrity."[106] In the late 1970s and early 1980s, the publication began to intervene in the rock movement to encourage greater professionalism and invention, especially by organizing a series of competitions in which progressive rock values could be inculcated. In 1978 the Medalla Phonos awards were established by the youth division of the National Circuit of Entertainment Journalists. It was followed by a series of Competitions of New Values of National Rock, established in 1979 by *Conecte*, and another competition supported by the Museo Universitario del Chopo (Chopo University Museum), titled El Rock Del Chopo, in 1980. For the Competition of New Values, bands competed in a series of preliminary rounds, each judged by a panel of experts, before passing to the high-profile final, held in a formal venue. The first final of the latter competition was held in April 1979, with a jury including Alejandro Lora, Javier Bátiz, Carlos Mata, and Carlos Baca; the second took place in June of the same year. Contestants from across Mexico without recording contracts were allowed to participate; they had to perform original compositions of under six minutes each, and the organizers could refuse entry to groups judged to lack "artistic or musical quality."[107]

This allusion to "values" correctly suggests a competition that was simultaneously moral, disciplinary, and aesthetic in nature. The first Competition of New Values was described in a *Conecte* editorial as a way to support and promote the rock movement, to "discover and encourage new musicians," and to encourage "healthy competition."[108] This issue, and the one following it, ran a feature intending to provide guidance to new artists, which broke down success in performance into five elements: communication, technique, change, expressivity, and creativity.[109] In the third such element, the writer (again, Antonio Malacara Alonso) locates a political and ethical discourse:

> Ideologically, rock was born from a youth desiring of a social change. That was reflected in music which sounded new, and which would bring, musically and artistically, true changes.... Change is an element, or factor, of great value. It implies new ideas which enrich the great personality of rock, and principally, which reinforce their principles with more fruits. This is the result of talent, dedication, and true professionalism (ETHICS); inventing new ideas—giving it a meaning—is no trivial thing. It's the first moral obligation of every new rock group.[110]

Malacara Alonso nonetheless warns that excessive stylistic innovation could put effective communication with one's audience at risk; "[change] should be introduced with much care," he concluded, and "combined with musical techniques of communication so as to not suffer a complete rupture with the audience, and they think you're crazy."[111]

The concern that bands behave "professionally"—that they work diligently, dress well, bring their own equipment, write original music rather than pass off English-language songs as their own—and anxieties about audience behavior were recurring themes through these competitions. During the second Medalla Phonos award held at the Teatro Insurgentes in 1979, *Conecte* reported that a group of a hundred *mugrosos*—a classist term denoting "dirty" fans, implicitly from poor backgrounds—demanded free entry into "that historic and important venue"; once permitted entry, they started to "smoke joints, inhale thinner [*cementear*], stand up on the seats, [and] bother people." According to the magazine, the venue owner swore never to host a rock event again, and blamed the incident on "self-destruction, unawareness, lack of awareness, education, and principles," leading the editor of *Conecte* to attack rock audiences.[112] At the 1979 Competition of New Values of National Rock, meanwhile, controversy broke out over the competition's eventual winner, Jorge Trevilla, a pianist with conservatory training and grand ambitions who proved to be a somewhat graceless victor. After the competition he boasted that "musically I knew I had no rival.... I don't want to say that I'm the best, or that there aren't good musicians in Mexico, because clearly there are... but they play in commercial or classical bands and orchestras."[113] Trevilla's victory was not universally accepted; Arturo Castelazo reported that some participants "left unhappy and, in one or another way, wanted to vent their 'anger.' Some had the idea of taking the odd amplifier, others the certificates and trophies."[114] Castelazo's disappointment in participants' apparent inability to lose this competition with grace—in other words, to participate in "healthy competition"—reflected long-standing anxieties among *Conecte* writers concerning the behavior of fans and musicians. In different ways, both cases—a victor whose success was steeped in familiar musical hierarchies with Western art music at the top, and condemnation of fan behavior that employed classist language—revealed internal class divisions within the rock scene.

It is worth pointing out that these competitions frequently attracted suspicions about corruption: for instance, in April 1980 the journalist Víctor Roura accused the organizing committee of the Competition of New Values of National Rock of promising eventual victors Azzor that they would win the prize that year.[115] The organizer of the competition Rock en El Chopo responded to suspicions of nepotism by outlining, in a *Conecte* interview, who the judges were and the criteria for evaluation.[116] Such controversies were indicative of a broader sense in which the scene had failed to become "professional." These competitions, whether organized directly by *Conecte* or covered assiduously by it, thus intervened in *rock nacional* in order to encourage a series of "professional" values, to embed a project of social change, and to establish certain principles about musical creativity and language.

Conclusion: Disciplining Journalism

This chapter has complicated enduring but simplistic "hard" accounts of post-Avándaro censorship, in which rock is held to have been "outlawed" or subject to official "prohibition." The example of *Break It All*, which focuses on the Mexican and Argentinian cases but claims to concern Latin America in general, suggests that part of the ongoing appeal of this narrative is the facility with which it may be incorporated into a regional metanarrative of struggle against despotism. This metanarrative may nonetheless obscure the nuanced, varied, and specific ways that rock was repressed in Mexico, where it was subject to a complex mixture of censorship, clientelism, coercion, and uncertainty diffused throughout society. I have explored this point by showing how the contemporary rock press perpetuated such governmentalist logic. While Moreno-Elizondo claimed that *hoyos fonqui* were "spaces outside government surveillance or control where the regulations of daily life tended to disappear, be redefined or negotiated," I suggest instead that rock journalism often extended the "regulations of daily life" into such spaces.[117] Although they depicted themselves as resisting mainstream press conservatism, rock journalists were surprisingly willing to support censorship in certain scenarios; some not only openly endorsed forms of prohibition against *hoyos fonqui* but also actively supported institutions such as SUTM who promised to enact them. This support did not straightforwardly reflect the impact of government control over the press but related to a complex of values explored here as the "politics of connection," which complicated rock's association with expressive freedom and antiauthoritarianism. Further, rock journalists often accepted key premises of the censorship of rock: that Mexican rock audiences were too immature to appreciate the genre and that audience behavior needed to reform as a prerequisite for the lifting of prohibitions. Some rock journalists took on a kind of civilizing project with respect to rock audiences and musicians, enacted in part through competitions established by rock magazines in the late 1970s and early 1980s.

Accounts of censorship depend, here, on a set of complex and challenging conceptual disentanglements. Reading 1970s rock journalism tells us, for instance, something that has remained relevant throughout the history of rock in Mexico: it is not always easy to distinguish authoritarian government repression against live music from legitimate actions to protect people from harm, such as crowd control. Attitudes toward censorship in the rock press were also entangled with contemporary ideological debates in ways that made some kinds of censorship more recognizable than others. (This is especially apparent from the feminist account given in Estrada's *Sirenas al ataque* of the continuous censorship of women in rock, even during less repressive eras: the official narrative of post-Avándaro repression is thoroughly androcentric.) Further, such complex textures of censorship changed with the times. The "hard" narrative about censorship, in which rock all but disappeared after 1971 as a result of government intervention, itself came to prominence over time, slowly. It was at the dawn of neoliberal Mexico, in the late 1970s and early 1980s, that this account took precedence, over and above earlier versions in which rock was censored through a subtle combination of factors of which the print media were the key catalysts.

To engage with music censorship is always to engage with the question of which voices are permitted to speak and which are not. In this sense, alongside recovery of the music of La Onda, it is important to revisit the contributions of the journalists who made sense of it at the time and to understand these contributions on their own terms. Yet a documentary such as *Break It All* indicates, instead, how some of the most prominent contemporaneous voices in the post-Avándaro rock press have fallen out of time since the end of the developmentalist era in Mexico. *Break It All*'s version of events is, arguably, that of a later generation of writers, situated on the right side of history, who came to understand 1970s cultural history from a posttransition vantage point defined by antiauthoritarian resistance against the state.

CHAPTER 2

Producing Independence

The Rock Boom and Commercial Censorship

In 1988, a competition organized at the open-air theatre Teatro Ángela Peralta under the aegis of BMG-Ariola's publicity campaign *Rock en tu idioma* (Rock in your language) had its license revoked at the last minute by the authorities of the Miguel Hidalgo district of Mexico City. It was then moved to another open-air venue to the west of the capital, Foro Felipe Villanueva in Estado de México, with the same outcome: the state government canceled the event's license "when the stage was already set" with neither "apologies nor official explanations." Speaking to the magazine *Proceso*, BMG-Ariola's artistic director Herbe Pompeyo took on the task of interceding with the official, censorial state gaze:

> The authorities continue to identify rock with sex and drugs, when the real causes for youth disorder are different. They have not perceived that rock has expressions that encourage life. Young people are naturally irreverent and unrestrained, and this annoys some of the authorities, who are solemn people. In general, the groups that we have heard are optimistic, they ask to be allowed to communicate with their generation, they bring great energy to do things. They are all anti-drugs, anti-violence. There is social criticism, but it is not what prevails. They care about love.

Pompeyo, however, sounded an optimistic note: while the authorities were intolerant of rock in Spanish, "no longer will this music be stopped by anyone."[1]

Today, *Rock en tu idioma* is often celebrated as the catalyst for the so-called rock boom in Mexico, a glimmer of cultural dynamism in the midst of the economic disaster known as the "Lost Decade."[2] In the 1980s, a wave of Spanish-language rock from Spain and Argentina hit Mexico before major labels began to invest heavily in Mexican bands. BMG-Ariola's *Rock en tu idioma* took place across Spain, Argentina, and Mexico, investing in a series of well-publicized albums and hosting live competitions featuring rock artists. Several of the rock acts with the most enduring fame in Mexico were promoted through this project, such as Maldita Vecindad, Los Amantes de Lola, and Caifanes. Pompeyo's confidence, then, was rooted in the genre's newfound corporate backing. Yet within Mexico, anxieties swirled around *Rock en tu idioma* concerning a feared loss of social criticism within rock expression. A contrast was often made between rock with *filo* ("teeth" or "edge") and rock that was *fresa* (literally "strawberry," but connoting a middle- and upper-class lightness, sweetness, and lack of substance). These fears concerned something more complex than "selling out" to commerce: as Pompeyo's quote above suggests, an apparent softening of rock's oppositional posture not only was conceived in terms of corporate power but was explicitly depicted by commercial operatives as a concession to authoritarianism in government.

Pompeyo combined his work for music labels with rock journalism; since the late 1970s he had pushed for more support for Mexican rock bands. He did this while simultaneously working for the transnational labels WEA and Polydor and writing for specialized rock magazines such as *Sonido*. His ability to ventriloquate state authority was thus built on an extensive network of media connections. More marginalized contemporaneous groups organized around rock, such as the *chavos banda*—working-class youth from the outskirts of the capital who increasingly favored punk—were both excluded from the mainstream press and frequently invoked as a source of middle- and upper-class anxiety. These groups were subject to much more violent forms of police repression, including a continuous pattern of physical violence and occasional extrajudicial killings, which is difficult to uncover outside of informal fanzines published by these groups themselves.[3] It is in fanzines that one reads about the unprovoked March 1988 police raid on an open-air concert in Querétaro in which fifty-four *chavos banda* were arrested, with many beaten and robbed by police, despite the fact that the concert was organized by a government agency.[4] These fanzines are testament to a fiercely antiauthoritarian, oppositional culture informed by anarchism and punk, and conceptually centered around resistance against systemic oppression that was seen to be spearheaded by government and extended by corporate capitalism.

The rock movement of the 1970s and early 1980s thus produced two contrasting tendencies: middle-class rock that increasingly gained corporate backing and the punk-influenced musical movement in the margins. Both reflected government repression; one was seen to resist it, and the other could at times reproduce and redirect it. It is important to recognize that the oft-repeated narrative about the flight of the middle classes from rock during this period is highly exaggerated.[5] Recent research conducted within Mexico has sought to recover the rich histories of Mexican post-punk or New Wave acts (such as Size, Syntoma, Volti, Alquimia, Pedro y las Tortugas, and Escuadrón del Ritmo) and venues (such as Hip-70 and Rockola) in the late 1970s and early 1980s that appealed specifically to the middle classes.[6] Many present-day voices within the *escena independiente* blame the erasure of these bands from history on the corporate influence of *Rock en tu idioma*, which constructed an artificially "hard" version of post-Avándaro censorship in order to portray its own offering as a form of *rescate* (rescuing) of rock. In reality, there were strong continuities between *Rock en tu idioma* and other, similar projects with less financial backing; many previous efforts had been made to organize independent labels and develop independent recording studios. In turn, rock organizers' search for alternatives to mainstream production led them to articulate varying understandings of "independence" reflecting, among other influences, discourses from the transnational punk movement.[7] The oppositional sense of "independence" that is foundational to the *escena independiente* in the present may be traced back to this point.

Later discourse on Mexican rock has tended to read present-day definitions of the term "independence" into the past. So, for instance, Paredes Pacho describes the rise of "independent" organizations in the 1980s rock scene but does not address how the activities these terms describe were conceptualized at the time.[8] Urteaga states that Mexican rock "independence" emerged in the mid-1980s as a response "to the alienation and homogenization of mass musical taste effected by transnational labels," which necessitated the creation of "another market . . . that would permit and receive creative experimentation," rather than compete directly with the transnationals. As a result, "a precarious and still fragile field of independent production" emerged, comprised of "young amateur musicians who produced in artisanal technical and financial conditions, and under highly adverse political circumstances," but whose legitimacy was predicated on a shared "series of liberationist attitudes and values" forged in post-Avándaro repression.[9] These conceptions are reflected in foundational definitions of Mexico City's *escena independiente*, in which the creative freedoms of the scene are established as acts of resistance against transnational labels and corporate mass entertainment companies.

Yet such contributions overlook ways that the notion of "independence" may transform in meaning.[10] Uses of this term in the Mexican rock press were scarce until the late 1970s and early 1980s.[11] Early uses of the word—often interchanged with the term "alternatives"—to describe music production, distribution, and performance did not necessarily refer to opposition to powerful entities, such as the government or transnational labels. Participants in the rock scene during this period often put forward an inclusive vision in which "independent" activities constituted practical stepping-stones toward the advancement of the rock movement. For instance, when it was put to the New Wave band Syntoma in 1984 that venturing to create "independent productions" had been "a truly important step," the band responded in the affirmative: "Perhaps it took a few years to happen, because it was a brave and risky enterprise. Nevertheless, right now the only step remaining is that big companies throw themselves into promoting a few groups."[12] It was only later that "independence" took on the oppositional meaning assumed in the present, based on a conceptual stratification between the "authentic" underground and the "inauthentic" mainstream. This stratification built on a notion of commercial censorship resembling a form of governmentality: an extension of the PRI's authoritarian gaze into rock.

The cultural formation described above by Urteaga thus both took time to emerge, and raised new questions about censorship, commerce, and the "mainstream." Within scholarly debates about popular music censorship, the notion of "commercial censorship" is highly contested, and some call into question the meaning of the term; after all, private companies are not obliged to provide anyone a platform.[13] In turn, discourses around commercial censorship raise dilemmas concerning the designation of the political which are especially complex in Mexico, where the authoritarian single-party regime of the PRI extended government power through business and civil society. I engage these questions here by addressing the question of "production," mostly in the narrow sense of producing studio recordings, but also in the broader sense of the cultural production of a music scene. I show how the emergence of practices for producing recorded and live rock that were understood as "independent" invoked broader questions about censorship, expressive freedom, and systemic repression; I also explore the role played by the specialized rock press in constructing the changing meanings and affordances of the term "independence." I note how the wave of late-1980s bands promoted by *Rock en tu idioma* pushed back against prevalent but constraining discourses in which mainstream labels were seen to threaten the expressive freedom of their artists. The popularity of these artists, I argue, was contingent on an effort to reshape and retexture received ideas about censorship.

Production and Self-Organization after Avándaro

Mexican rockers in the 1970s frequently complained of a production crisis, consisting of a dip in the number of rock recordings, a decline in their quality, and a drop in distribution. Bands, one writer wrote in 1979, "hardly exceed ten thousand copies sold," and many struggled to attain "very poor sales of 20 thousand LPs sold in four years," meaning that self-respecting producers "flatly refuse to record rock."[14] To be sure, Zolov's claim that post-Avándaro repression "halted the flow of recordings" is an evident exaggeration: a number of accomplished Mexican rock LPs were released and circulated during this period, especially Pájaro Alberto's *Viaje fantástico* (RCA-Camden, 1974), a self-titled LP by Nahuatl (Raff, 1974), and Los Dug Dug's' *Cambia, cambia* (RCA-Camden, 1975).[15] At the same time, documenting rock from the 1970s continues to present a challenge since many notable bands recorded little of their work. This situation has typically been attributed to record labels dropping support after Avándaro, partly under direct pressure from government and partly as an indirect result of decreased demand resulting from diminished radio play. However, it can also be understood in an international context in which rock producers had developed innovative multitrack studio techniques.[16]

Rockers responded by creating their own studios and organizations, with some degree of independence from labels.[17] In 1975 Carlos Mata, of the band Nuevo México, produced the band's LP *Hecho en casa* (Made at home) himself, although the album was released with established national rock label Orfeón. Responding to the unreliable and exploitative nature of concerts in the *hoyos fonqui*, Mata also declared his plans to "invest the little money I have" in self-organized concerts—since "myself as a rocker, I know what you need for everything to be done well"—and create Arco Iris, a promotional company.[18] Other groups had similar ideas: José Luis Pluma in March 1975 reported that the band Nahuatl was creating its "own organization with offices, secretaries, an agent, and who knows what else"; in 1973, newly created act La Raza stated their goal that the band should be run "like a company"; and it was reported in November 1976 that part-band, part-commune La Semilla del Amor was to form a business to tour Mexico.[19]

Self-organized rock recordings were facilitated by two twenty-four-track studios. One was established by Américo and Waldo Tena, two of the founders of 1950s rock outfit Los Rebeldes del Rock, and the other by two members of Los Locos del Ritmo, who had formed Mister Loco, a new outfit with a style mixing rock, pop, and folklore. Indeed, the latter studio was created as a rehearsal and recording space for Mister Loco. Once the band opened their studio for outside hire it proved a commercial success; Mister Loco found that the studio was so overbooked they were forced to rehearse in the early hours of the morning. They subsequently opened a second recording studio (with an eight-track recorder only) in early 1978.[20] The high demand for Mister Loco's studio anticipated a proliferation of new recording studios at the turn of the decade. Rock magazines frequently supported new recording ventures by running features describing these initiatives and including their address and contact details. A growing concern for the technical aspects of rock production during this period is witnessed in the contents of the preestablished rock press and in the emergence of new industry-linked publications, such as *Estéreo*, which promoted specialized equipment for sound engineering, recording, and high-fidelity domestic sound systems.

Issues of *Conecte* in the early 1980s ran continuous stories on a new studio, Studio 88, which had—as one brief feature put it—an "open-door" approach to new bands "who feel sufficiently capable to forge their ideas on a disc" and "are already tired of struggling, for years, for a recording contract that won't leave them more than frustrations and wastes of their irrecuperable time." This policy, the feature continued, resulted from

> a firm conviction that the best way to foment rock music in Mexico is precisely to leave the vicious circle representing by the market of the commercial industry, and looking for alternatives, at an independent level ... alternatives in which there do not exist restrictions of creativity and musical development; alternatives in which groups may simply record what they want, without their music being censored by people who, most of the time, do not even have any idea about what rock is and totally ignore the great demand that this music has, and saturating the media with the customary alienating monotony.[21]

"Let's take advantage of this opportunity!" the article concluded. "Let's give Mexican rock a long life!" As well as promoting such "alternative" enterprises,

Conecte ran features on self-organized event organization and recording, such as a 1979 multipart series titled "Producing Albums Oneself: The Only Alternative for Mexican Bands," authored by journalist and musician Jorge Reyes. The series highlighted instances of independent labels overseas, such as Schneeball (formerly April) in Germany and Virgin Records in the United Kingdom, which (allegedly) provided greater creative autonomy than the major labels, where "he who adapts and accepts cliché" was rewarded. "The musician has the choice in his hands," writes Reyes, "either he plays what and how the company wants and takes the leap to stardom, or plays what he wants and remains faithful to his own music."[22] Readers were then exhorted to create their own, similar independent labels: "Although VIRGIN RECORDS is not exactly a radical alternative to commerce, it is so within the world of commerce. The great freedom given to artists during production of their work comes to demonstrate clearly that it is possible to leave the vicious circle of 'musical prostitution.' . . . The idea of all of this is that you will become aware that alternative companies are a reality, not a simple utopia."[23]

The series concludes with a practical and technical guide to recording.[24] Reyes advises bands to arrive thirty minutes prior to recording; describes the spatial ordering of the studio into different sections for "loud percussive sounds" and for "long or prolonged sounds" such as voices, strings, and brass; suggests the creation of a backing track over which vocalists may later sing, while admitting that many singers prefer to record with their band "to preserve an exciting and spontaneous atmosphere"; details various functions of a sound desk; and outlines how microphones should be used for multitrack recording.[25]

As the 1970s gave way to the 1980s, the language of "alternatives" was first complemented, and eventually substituted, by that of "independence." In 1979 Arturo Castelazo praised "the production of discs in an independent fashion" as "the only alternative for Mexican rockers, whatever we call it." It praised the efforts of many, who had "awakened," for creating a patchwork of "small recording studios, scattered here and there," mentioning an eight-track setup run by Alfonso González and the twenty-four-track setup of the studios of Hermanos Tena and Mister Loco. "Independence is the solution," Castelazo wrote, "because those who continue to wait for a big company to call them will grow old during the wait."[26] Independence also came to describe the activities of well-established bands. A 1980 article by Antonio Malacara Palacios entitled "Dug Dug's: An Independent Production" noted the long-standing rock band's recent decline in activity—including the fact that they now had to hire a bassist to perform live—and described their efforts to record their fifth album after their contract with RCA expired. The band planned to record a self-funded album in a studio in Los Angeles, aiming to release it in 1981. "All of [their previous albums] have been worth it," Malacara Palacios concluded. "Let's hope the next one is even better."[27] This allusion to "independence" served to place a positive spin on a story that otherwise reflects a well-known band's declining reach and influence.

While "independence" was occasionally depicted as a bulwark protecting rock from the "cliché" of the mainstream music industries, as we have already seen, the discourse of independence occasionally invoked altogether more complicated accounts of expressive freedom. Here, I describe in depth a two-page *Conecte* feature from 1981 titled "How to Make an Album . . . of Independent Rock?," written as a practical guide to recording by producer and radio presenter Jorge Álvarez Estudillo, who had organized a compilation album titled *Rock Nacional 1981*, featuring original tracks by twenty-nine artists.[28] The feature broke down the production process for this album into seven steps: curating groups to record a track for the album, choosing a suitable studio for recording, choosing an order for tracks, hiring a designer to make the cover art and an artist for the typography, cutting a master of the disc, and pressing the disc. Álvarez Estudillo explains the mechanics of reproducing discs from the master, the ways that a front and back cover are put together, the need for bands to rehearse before entering the recording studio, and the need to verify recording studios' availability in advance.

The curatorial process described by Álvarez Estudillo is of particular interest. This writer is, first and foremost, concerned with a judgment about the "quality" of the material; thus he recommends "listening to and choosing which groups—among those that don't have a contract with a given label—have the potential to sound high-quality in a recording studio." The other criteria involve regulation of content: organizers should ensure that material is "not so 'strong' that censorship might prohibit it," that songs address "the type of themes which, due to their originality, might be of interest for the public, and that their message may contribute something to the youth culture of the age."

Thus "independence" is not presented here as a means of establishing artistic autonomy from conservative society, government institutions, or the aesthetic judgments of the mainstream. Strikingly, it serves instead to enforce the imagined priorities of a conservative general public and extend official censorship. The legitimacy of censorship-through-curation is not questioned or interrogated; the "independent" curator instead imposes values guarding "proper" musical expression and establishing norms of originality and creative advancement. Such paternalism extended beyond the curatorial process: Álvarez Estudillo also criticized "envious creatures" who "without knowing how the LP turned out, are attacking it." He criticized bands—one, the blues rock act Stray Cat, by name—for withdrawing from the album after recording and for being "incurably egocentric." Given that Álvarez Estudillo describes eliminating some eighteen "negative" acts from the album, it is evident that this project served to discipline rockers: weeding out individuals with insufficient professionalism, irrespective of their musical contributions.

Equally as significant are those processes that might otherwise be related to a praxis of "independence," but which are *not* explained in this feature. Álvarez Estudillo mentions signing contracts for album distribution and cover art, but does not discuss contracts with the contributing artists, nor agreements concerning intellectual property ownership.[29] The feature describes the process of hiring professional designers to create album art but provides readers no information about how to carry out these activities themselves. Similarly, it discusses the process of hiring a studio and an engineer but is somewhat light on the technical details of recording. *Rock Nacional 1981* was produced in an austere manner; since the project required sixty hours or more of studio time, its organizers elected to record in Audio Producciones Sitar, a cheap independent studio equipped only with a four-track mixing desk. While this approach excluded the possibility of using "special effects," Álvarez Estudillo writes, "we could achieve our base objective, to record the groups with a basic sound which presents a real reflection of the group's potential." After all, this was a new experience for many members of the participating bands, who "had never set foot in a recording studio." While this comment attributed inherent value to familiarity with the recording process over and above its outcomes, Álvarez Estudillo's denunciations of "egocentrism" suggests that the bands participating may have felt otherwise. Notably, nowhere does Álvarez Estudillo present a stripped-down approach to recording as an aesthetic choice signifying subcultural authenticity; the limited studio possibilities provided by the project are instead seen as inherently negative. This article accounts for "independence" mainly in organizational terms, as a decentralized and outsourced production practice, inasmuch as almost all of the tasks performed were completed by private individuals or companies, and as the product of discrete, mundane forms of labor.

By the beginning of the 1980s, self-organized production practices described as "independent" had reached a certain prominence, but they were not necessarily viewed as antagonistic to the creatively limited "mainstream" or as a bulwark of expressive freedom resisting commercial censorship. In fact, the censorial gaze of government and society could be extended without apology or explanation into these practices. Even as rock embraced independent production, writers in the rock scene were calling for deeper engagement with mass-scale events.[30] It is most appropriate to understand self-organized production practices at this time as an apolitical response to a practical challenge—a loss of access to recording opportunities with established labels—which emphasized technological achievement and discrete forms of labor as a means to advance rock "communication" at mass-scale *and* small-scale levels. As a *Conecte* editorial put it in October 1979, "To lift up [the rock scene] will take work, work, and more work."[31]

Venues, Labels

Self-organization was not only related to the production of recorded music, but also seen as a solution to problems within the live music scene. As described above, *hoyos fonqui* tended to be run by unscrupulous businessmen who failed to manage their spaces safely, and often provoked unrest by defrauding audiences. Musicians frequently had their equipment stolen in such venues, and they could also be unsafe places for women.[32] In response, one journalist in 1975 recommended that bands "promote themselves and organize their own concerts, since otherwise they're exposed to abuse [*agandalles*] and chaos [*sacones de onda*]."[33]

A plethora of new Mexico City venues opened in the 1980s, among the most notable of which were Tutti Frutti, Rockotitlán, Rockola, LUCC, and the Tianguis Cultural del Chopo, alongside many other spaces that were soon forced to close due to neighbors' complaints.[34] These venues were established through a combination of organization and opportunism, often by musicians themselves. The Tianguis Cultural del Chopo, created as a "channel of communication" for the exchange of materials connected to rock, was obliged to repeatedly move from place to place due to issues with permits, coming to be established in its current site through a sustained, organized struggle and creative tactics to claim space.[35] Rockola was established when the newly formed band Kerigma convinced a Chinese restaurant in the district of Coyoacán to host a rock concert; after the event proved a resounding commercial success, the venue became dedicated to rock full-time.[36] Tutti Frutti had been a restaurant until the 1985 earthquake prompted its proprietor to flee Mexico City, leaving it to his sister and her Belgian boyfriend; as enthusiasts of the punk scene in Europe, they decided to run the venue as a rock bar. This was a semiclandestine, somewhat informal space that had constant difficulties gaining permits for its activities; in its early years it was promoted with a flyer lacking an address that read simply "*Búscanos*" (Come and find us). As its founder Danny Yerna recounted to me, Tutti Frutti relied on the restaurant below for tip-offs about visits from inspectors and police officers, at which point the sound would be switched off and attendees would be asked to remain silent.[37]

Tutti Frutti is today remembered as a "space of encounter" for different genres, providing an outlet for rock's growing eclecticism in the mid-1980s.[38] Some of these venues may, like Tutti Frutti, be understood as "underground," with no relation to the mainstream. Others played different roles within the scene. Rockotitlán, established in 1985, constituted a significant bridge toward the genre's corporatization, debuting several bands later supported by *Rock en tu idioma*, creating a label that produced live recordings, and organizing a series of popular competitions. LUCC, created in 1987, was a hotbed for professionalization, especially in relation to sound engineering, events management, and artist representation.[39]

Thus, these venues established a social context for increasing specialization of labor within independent production, in which there emerged a wave of new labels and recording projects constituting, as one writer put it, "alternative[s] in our movement's infrastructure."[40] Corporación Sintética, created by the band Syntoma, was created to encourage avant-garde rock production; it consisted of two separate labels and an entity for booking concerts.[41] Other alternative labels included Discos Phallus, Discos Momia (founded by Carlos Alvarado, of the progressive rock band Vía Lactea), Discos Pentagrama, and Comrock.[42] These initiatives were all celebrated in the press. A series of features and editorials in *Conecte* acclaimed rock's increasing reach in the broadcast media, and its appeal for major international labels.[43] The band Syntoma told *Conecte* in 1984 that "in a relatively short time, many things have happened for independent productions. . . . Each day better productions are made, better album covers, better compositions, even better live concerts."[44]

The most discussed of these initiatives was Comrock, created in 1984. Founded by rocker Ricardo Ochoa, Televisa actor Chela Braniff, and her husband, publicist Juan Navarro, Comrock published almost thirty LPs, EPs, and singles between 1985 and 1987.[45] In particular, it sought to promote Spanish-language recordings. In a 1985 interview, Juan Navarro described his vision that Comrock should form "a base for rock, that would be a platform for groups, and that would be a platform for the introduction of rock to the youth" from the outskirts of Mexico City who "didn't have live contact with rock... nor with rock recordings." This dovetailed, he explained, with Ricardo Ochoa's goal to "unify" the rock scene. Navarro emphasized the importance of "constancy" for rock production, saying that "a group is not a success in the first album, a group can't work wonders at their first recording.... The same holds for sound engineers, it's not the same to have recorded two rock albums as the six they now have under their belt."[46] Part of this approach was a strategy, echoing that of major labels, of recording and releasing rock albums at scale.[47] The label also managed bands and organized their own events and tours. They did this, Navarro explained, partly so they could promote their bands' music without giving payola to radio stations.

Comrock faced, however, several pitfalls. The fact that one of its founders worked for Televisa created an immediate challenge of credibility among rock fans, but the most challenging factors were economic.[48] During the time of economic crisis and rampant inflation that would become known as the "Lost Decade," Ochoa and Navarro both insisted on paying rock musicians higher wages and eschewed exclusivity contracts with their artists, a stance borne of opposition to rock bands "selling themselves cheaply."[49] Further, Comrock's promotional tours, however ambitious—one in 1985 went to thirty different plazas across the country—had mixed results. By 1987 Comrock was bought by Warner for its back catalog, and in a *Conecte* postmortem Ricardo Ochoa admitted that the project had suffered from a surplus of ambition.[50]

Overall, then, as *Rock en tu idioma* emerged onto the scene in 1986, it encountered a relatively complex, specialized, and professionalized ecosystem, with a range of venues catering to different audiences and an increasing number of labels. This wave of self-organized or "independent" projects both anticipated and created an organizational context for *Rock en tu idioma*'s market success. Yet, as I will now explore, the shifting conceptual terrain of "independence" created challenges for *Rock en tu idioma* artists seeking to balance corporate backing with their credibility among a rock audience—a problem from which some sought to write their way out.

Punk and Polemic

As noted, the growing tendency toward self-organization accompanied conceptual shifts in the way that "independence" was understood. At the beginning of the 1980s, independence tended to be seen as a stepping-stone toward rock's massification, a tool for the rock movement to advance and reach wider audiences, and a stepping-stone from smaller- to larger-scale business models.⁵¹ Yet by the mid- to late 1980s, it was increasingly common for independence to be perceived as an end in itself, in the manner described by Urteaga.⁵² This tendency toward reification—from independence-as-process to independence-as-thing—cannot be straightforwardly associated with the arrival of punk to Mexico.⁵³ While it coincided in time with the international rise of punk, the emerging emphasis on self-organized production was not an importation of punk's do-it-yourself praxis; the Spanish-language translation of DIY, *hazlo tú mismo*, only came into widespread use in the rock press in the second half of the 1980s.⁵⁴ Within the Mexican rock press, punk transitioned from a target of criticism in the late 1970s to a defended and celebrated genre by the mid-1980s. During this time, the domestic punk scene began to flourish, beginning with the punk band Dangerous Rhythm (formed in 1978) and the New Wave outfit Size (established in 1979).

Punk was a topic of concern in the pages of *Conecte* in the late 1970s, where writers alternated between praising punk as a "refreshing" addition to the rock movement, bemoaning punk as a symptom of societal problems, outright denunciations of punk as a betrayal of rock's values, and the denunciation of *denunciations* of punk in the mainstream press.⁵⁵ In February 1979 Arturo Castelazo praised Mexican punk band Dangerous Rhythm as "a dramatic break with the past . . . Mexican punk music, product of real life, product of the city, of the high level of pollution in the city, of ignorance, of elitism, of snobbery, of the television, of taboos, of ourselves."⁵⁶ Yet an editorial in the following edition of *Conecte* attacked punk for its "poorly studied poses, badly channeled, traumatic rants, horrible musical technique, null expressivity or talent [and] mass non-communication." It warned: "When music abandons its position in the aesthetics of sound and declares itself 'free' to 'do whatever it pleases' (shouting, acting up, breaking drums, strings and microphones), that's when we start to think seriously about what the music of the twentieth century is, or what it should be."⁵⁷

For some writers, punk posed distinctly ideological questions about freedom. In a 1981 version of his ongoing column "The Philosophical Dissertations of Rocky Prex," which consists of a series of fictional political dialogues between children, Carlos Baca criticizes the taxation policy of the United Kingdom's Labour government. He alleges that high taxes caused capital flight, inflation, underinvestment—and the emergence of punk. (Notably, in the context of British political discourse, this account of recent economic history would have been highly contentious, associated with the neoliberal outlook of the recently elected Thatcher government, which was in power from 1979 to 1990.)⁵⁸ As Rocky Prex says, knowingly, to his friend Hermit:

– The reason that [England] has sunk so badly is its Labour government. It spent too much and printed money without any support, which produced high inflation . . . which has affected most those who it was supposed the Labour Party wanted to defend: the proletarian classes. . . . They imposed so many taxes that the capitalists left England and it went bankrupt. When there was no investment there were no new jobs, and the new youth seeking work found there was nowhere to work.
– And they became PUNKS!—exclaimed Hermit.[59]

In this iteration of British history, punks' dependence on the state led to anomie: "Lacking ideals, like the previous hippie generation—which did have ideals of love, peace, freedom, understanding, etc.—the PUNK generation launched itself into the highest madnesses without caring whether they were violent or destructive."[60]

Baca here echoed a recurring criticism of punk: that it took the impulse behind rock and destructured it. Punk was seen as a threat precisely because the energies it was based upon failed to be channeled into ethically ordered individuals and aesthetically ordered sound; criticisms of punk built on longer-standing anxieties about the live rock *reventón* (outburst) as, in the words of a 1977 *Conecte* editorial, "badly channeled energy."[61] José Agustín replayed this logic in his later criticism that punk "lacked a great myth of transformation that would channel creativity and artistic expression toward a higher, greater goal."[62] The dismissal of punk as "mass non-communication" is especially incisive, suggesting a subversion of the purpose of rock: punk achieved collective alienation, rather than communication (see Chapter 1).

In turn, defenses of punk contested received comparisons between punk and rock. Thus, a December 1979 issue of *Conecte* featured an editorial criticizing the ways that "the avid sensationalistic press" had, with "shocking photographs and stories which are mostly exaggerated, systematically categorized the punk movement as a violent and horrible nightmare."[63] This narrative was substantiated in a feature on punk in the same issue, written by Jorge Reyes, which criticized the British press for inventing scandals about punk, as a result of which newer punk groups had taken on "chauvinist expressions." In particular, the British press had ignored punk's "political and social implications" and its contributions to Rock Against Racism; citing the infamous 1977 allegation by the London *Evening News* that the Sex Pistols had ties with the fascist National Front, Reyes bemoaned the way that such misconceptions had caused "public opinion . . . to hate or reject the punk movement."[64] For Reyes, contemporary critics were attacking punk "with the same words they used against Elvis, the Beatles, the Rolling Stones, and rock 'n' roll in general: 'noisy,' 'primitive,' 'in bad taste,' 'brutal,' etc." Reyes thus defended punk by implicating rock and punk in the same ongoing teleology of liberation.

These disagreements over punk thus invoked contrasting conceptions of freedom, but they also had a strong class component, dovetailing with paternalistic critiques of the *hoyos fonqui* and connecting to anxieties about the working-class *chavos banda*, gangs based in the poor outskirts of a rapidly expanding capital that came to embrace punk. Such disagreements eventually led to a rupture within *Conecte* itself. In the mid-1980s, the magazine sought to mediate between anarchist punks and the former generation of rock writers by creating a supplement, entitled *La Banda Rockera*, for those writers most sympathetic to punk. *La Banda Rockera*, however, soon detached from *Conecte* to become an independent publication that, alongside fanzines self-published by myriad groups of *chavos banda*, spread a discourse that was more explicitly antiauthoritarian, liberationist, and anarchist. The *chavos banda* strongly contested the disciplinary governmentality in which rockers were obliged to accept and adapt to government repression as a means of removing disorder. "Government is disorder," one fanzine claimed; since "each individual should be their own truth, their own government," the search for the collective interest would only produce chaos and oppression.[65] "We believe that we're capable of self-governing," another fanzine stated, "without the need for the repression exerted by all current governments."[66] The *chavos banda* also introduced the concept of *autogestión*—self-management—a politicized term within the discourse of punk fanzines whose meaning overlapped with "self-government."

These groups were simultaneously othered from the rock "mainstream" and idealized as groups existing in resistance to government: as one *Conecte* editorial put it in 1987, "The *banda* is *banda* because of oppression."[67] This discourse nonetheless belied more nuanced efforts by government to coerce and influence pathologized working-class youth organizations. The *chavos banda* received continuous support from the government agency CREA (National Council of Resources for the Attention of Youth), a federal institution created from the Institute of Youth (INJUVE) in the late 1970s and which operated throughout the 1980s.[68] CREA sought to co-opt young people by promoting festivals and providing direct funding for punk bands. (Indeed, in 1985 CREA dismissed a group of researchers it had hired to investigate the *chavos banda*, apparently for pointing out that their own project served a "policy of stability, to calm the situation," and for blaming the capitalist system for creating anomie among the *chavos*.)[69] The police also attempted to co-opt *chavos*: in the late 1980s they held a series of meetings for the *chavos banda* in Mexico City in an attempt to "let the *chavos* know that the police are not their enemy," offering rock, food, instruction in running patrols, horse riding, and first aid. These events prompted protests among some *chavos* that participants were being coerced to abandon their principles of freedom in favor of the "control, subordination, and almost always corruption" that typified the police.[70]

The reified account of independence that took hold among the *chavos banda* can therefore be understood as a response not only to marginalization, but also to the proximities to the state effected through organizations such as CREA. It was also, however, increasingly seen as a way to safeguard expressive freedom amid threats from the expanding corporate investment into rock. As I now show, however, an opposition between corporate influence and expressive freedom—and the Catch-22 this created for bands seeking to reach a mass audience—was often reiterated and justified in the 1980s by industry representatives. What may be considered distinctive about *Rock en tu idioma*, in fact, may be precisely the ways that its acts sought to challenge these ideas about the corporate threat to rock's "independence."

Fresificación and Commerce

By the time *Rock en tu idioma* emerged, there had already been a series of distinct concerted efforts to channel increasing demand for Spanish-language rock, some of which attracted significant corporate backing. Notably, several pop acts aimed at young teenagers, such as Flans, Pandora, and Timbiriche, performed in a rock style in the 1980s. These groups were promoted by Televisa, including performances on the primetime show *Siempre en domingo* and the children's show *Juguemos a cantar*; indeed, several had been formed directly by the network.

Those who identified with the "independent" tendency within rock had increasingly come to depict the commercial media promoting these bands as their "other"; they saw them as inherently restricting entities ensuring that rock's subversive edge would disappear.[71] The radio presenter Rodrigo de Oyarzábal, for instance, feared that "they are going to mediatize [rock], they're going to remove its explosive power and its identity."[72] The "very occasional and almost independent" fanzine *La Kaza* bemoaned how rock had been "dressed up" and "had its hair combed"; "they've sent [rock] to school, and now it has an education." The culprit, the fanzine stated, was "commercialism," which had converted "an authentic expression of honesty, rebellion, and communication" into "an exclusive item—only for the beautiful people."⁷³ This was described by some as rock becoming *fresa*—light, unsubstantial, whimsical, of the privileged classes.⁷⁴

The fear that commercialization threatened rock's critical edge was not just based on speculation: occasionally commercial expectations were negotiated openly by industry figures in the press. Thus in a 1984 interview with *Conecte*, Herbe Pompeyo—then working for WEA—blamed rock bands' marginality on their refusal to engage a mainstream aesthetic:

> The fact that they feel marginalized, and are marginalized, has made them take an even more elitist position, to say the least. Some, feeling even more elitist, denote it by wanting to be exclusively progressive, go to the weird stuff of Stockhausen, Tangerine Dream, that kind of thing. I think that what has happened, strongly, is that they have not taken the reality of making pop music with rock elements; it's the ideal way for record companies to get excited about promoting this.⁷⁵

Pompeyo described "pressuring" one of his rock acts, Chac Mool, "so that they grasp the reality that if they want to enter direct competition, there are certain patterns they should respect." In order to make it onto the radio or television, he said, they ought to write music "a little more simply, more digestibly." Further—reproducing a misleading stereotypical association between lower-class status and a lack of aesthetic aspiration—lyrics ought not to be "pretend intellectual" but rather should be accessible, so that "a kid from Nezahualcóyotl will say, I'm identifying myself with this guy."⁷⁶ In Mexico, Pompeyo complained, "rockers believe that writing melodies is *fresa*, and they are absolutely wrong."⁷⁷

Where Pompeyo sought to convince high-minded rockers to compromise their artistic principles to broaden their appeal, other industry actors justified commercial censorship as part of an appeal to the (imagined) middle classes. Alberto Huizar, the director of promotion for BMG-Ariola, claimed that balladeers such as Juan Gabriel and Camilo Sesto had "left behind" the rock scene upon assuming a more popular style built on a "completely white [*blanco*—that is, harmless] rock" that "doesn't attack society and doesn't talk about drugs."⁷⁸ Huizar stated: "The rocker who attacks, uses vulgar words, or who is against society does not interest us. . . . They can criticize society and government, but in this way: without vulgarity, with diplomacy, with quality, and always in a way that the whole family may hear."⁷⁹ Here, commercial censorship is extended across business, government, and society, and Huizar notably justified it as a means to an end: a way to create demand later, as the fans of bands such as Timbiriche came of age.[80] The mainstreaming of rock was, then, overtly intertwined with the politics of respectability in a way that extended government influence over popular culture.

If the concern was that the corporate promotion and mediatization of rock had rendered the genre overly "safe," however, this idea was terribly subverted on September 30, 1987. A free benefit concert was planned in Palacio de los Deportes, featuring the Televisa-promoted bands Flans, Timbiriche, and Fresas con Crema, to raise funds for the Comité Internacional Pro Ciegos (International Committee for the Blind). On the day, the event attracted a far larger audience than anticipated, leading to a crush among the audience and the collapse of a part of the building. The concert left a death toll of four—including girls of eight, eleven, and twelve years old—and roughly fifty attendees injured. Accounts of the collapse varied. One observer faulted the makeshift nature of the supports used inside the building.[81] Official sources, meanwhile, blamed an initial attempt by fans of Timbiriche to enter the event by force, which caused the building's main door to collapse. This led attendees inside to fear that the whole building was falling down due to heavy rains.[82] As a result, there was a panic to exit the building, and an interior support collapsed.

In the wake of the tragedy, it emerged that only twelve police had been present to secure the venue. Yet the general secretary of Protection and Highways in Mexico City denied that the collapse was a failure of policing, blaming the audience instead: "There were enough police officers to provide security to all those attending, but due to the excesses of groups of young people, not even a thousand police officers would have prevented the accident."[83] The press reaction to the tragedy was not mourning or outrage; instead, there was almost complete media silence.[84] Indeed, even in the present, online information about the collapse remains very limited, and the incident has passed almost without mention in scholarship.[85] For some, the reluctance to report the story constituted a potent indication of the power of these acts' corporate backers. Writing in *La Jornada* several weeks later, Víctor Roura took a combative tone: "The incident deserved to be highlighted, at the time, by the tabloid press [*nota roja*]. . . . The press suppresses disastrous results like that day at the Palacio de los Deportes. . . . It would have been another thing if instead of Las Flans or Timbiriche, El Tri or Mamá-Z had performed. Groups that do not have the backing of the television consortium are targets for tabloid information."[86] Of course, the barometer for this conversation was Avándaro, an event that in security terms largely passed without incident but which garnered a hysterical press response and a government backlash nonetheless.

Roura's response to this tragedy indicated stratification between mainstream and "independent" acts. The success of *Rock en tu idioma* depended on its ability to effectively negotiate both a challenging commercial environment and suspicions about commercial censorship. Corporate support for rock, many contemporaneous journalists contended, was inherently censorious, leading musicians toward unacceptable creative compromises. This was often glossed as rock acts shedding their *filo* (edge), something described variously as the loss of a critical stance toward political power, the assuming of the briefer musical form required for radio play, and a stylistic homogenization associated with transnational cultural influence. For one writer in the newspaper *Unomásuno*, for instance, the new corporate influence over rock produced "the image of the ideal rock: all clean, refined, yet not aggressive. It offers a digital look, clearly European," while the industry avoided "burning issues" like the plague. "Rock that motivates people to think and act in solidarity is not of interest" to rock's corporate backers, this writer contended; "the slogan is clear: a rock in our language that could be of any art, without its own sound identity."[87] Although the direct targets of such critiques were often Televisa-backed "light" rock acts such as Timbiriche, *Rock en tu idioma*'s most successful Mexican acts were also targeted in this way as *fresa*, insubstantial, light, self-censoring. For instance, in a *Conecte* interview, the independent filmmaker Sergio García, who had directed several documentaries about Mexican rock, accused Café Tacuba and Maldita Vecindad of being "anti-rock" groups that "make concessions or self-censor so that Televisa allows them onto their programs." "When they appear on Televisa," he claimed, "it's because that group is no longer dangerous. . . . They're complacent, inoffensive, innocuous, inconsequential."[88]

In light of this, it is notable that some media coverage of *Rock en tu idioma*'s most high-profile acts subverted and challenged negative stereotypes about rock bands with the backing of transnational labels. One feature on Maldita Vecindad, published in *Proceso* in 1988, immediately and explicitly addressed the independent/transnational dichotomy: "The Mexican group Maldita Vecindad y los Hijos del Quinto Patio joined the great commercial record industry, under conditions that, according to its members, do not undermine their independence, their musical style or their dissident position."[89] The feature gives several reasons that Maldita Vecindad could still be considered "independent." First, creatively uncompromising Argentine rocker Charly García—who had apparently stumbled on the band performing on a street corner—was entering into talks with their label to produce their music. Second, the band members themselves claim that authenticity was a condition for them to join a label: "They had not joined the record industry because other companies began by questioning them about the length of the group's name, then tried to change their musical concept, and ended up discussing, even in several sessions, their look." By contrast, the band claimed that BMG-Ariola made no attempt to interfere in their music or alter their image. The notion of Maldita Vecindad as commercial-but-independent is also reinforced by descriptions of their music as "a potpourri of genres," helpfully unpacked by "rockologist" Víctor Roura, here drawn upon as an expert voice: "They assimilated styles going from the rudimentary Ska of Toño Quirasco or Desmond Becker, to the impeccable reggaes of Marley or the Irish of UB-40, passing through the mambos of Pérez Prado from 1948 and the melodic ease of Los Van Vans of Cuba and Trabuco." This fluid, dynamic, and highly referential description of Maldita Vecindad's style is echoed in other contemporaneous features on the group, such as a 1987 *La Jornada* article that argues that the band "make the best musical apologia for . . . our allegorical hybridity: we are bastard children of Víctor Jara and Nina Hagen, of the Sex Pistols and the Hernández Sisters, of Jagger and [Mexican Golden Age singer] Angélica María, of [Chilean *bolero* singer] Lucho Gatica and [singer-songwriter] Nina Galindo, of [Mexican Golden Age singer and comedian] Tin Tan and Our Lady of Guadalupe." These associations between Maldita Vecindad and an intimate, mongrel, and eclectic working-class Mexican musical culture subvert contemporary criticisms of *Rock en tu idioma* as homogenizing and constricting.

Indeed, with this in mind, it is interesting that one of Maldita Vecindad's biggest hits, 1991's "Pachuco," performs a certain notion of censorship to establish the band's authenticity and credibility. "Pachuco" opens with a raucous sample of a song performed by Tin Tan, "Mujer Maldita," before the band takes over; the song is built around an up-tempo ska rhythm, backed by an extensive brass section. The song's lyrics dramatize the gaze of the *padre de familia*, who complains about young rockers' dress and lack of decorum: "In my time, it was elegant, no shaggy look, no rock." The protagonist defends their participation in rock by appealing to the moral scandals of the past: "Hey, pa, you were a *pachuco* / They scolded you for it, too / Hey, pa, you danced mambos / You must remember it." "Pachuco" thus reproduces and actualizes a history of societal repression so that the band may show themselves to rebel against it. The paternalistic, censorial gaze that this song invokes in order to resist undoubtedly existed. Yet in casting Maldita Vecindad and their fans as resisting paternalism, and in prominently featuring music intimately associated with Mexican identity, the song also performed independence for a different audience, whose views were more immediately consequential: previous generations of rock writers and audiences who alleged self-censorship among newer acts with corporate backing.[90]

Maldita Vecindad also had avenues besides music through which they could argue for their own authenticity. Their drummer, José Luis Paredes Pacho, was several years older than other members of the band and studied at UNAM in the late 1980s; he quickly developed into an organic intellectual within the rock movement, publishing several books, writing frequent articles in the press, and in the 2000s becoming the director of the Museo Universitario del Chopo. Paredes Pacho's writing tends to maintain a balance: he is consistently critical of globalization and transnational corporate influence in general but produces a somewhat positive account of the impact of neoliberal globalization on Mexican popular culture. This balance is similar to that struck in much later scholarly work on *Rock en tu idioma* emanating from the United States.[91] Paredes Pacho's book *Rock mexicano: Sonidos de la calle* was published in 1992, at a critical political and creative junction: just after Maldita Vecindad's seminal *El Circo* had been released, and as the North American Free Trade Agreement (NAFTA) was being debated. A 1992 article in *Proceso* entitled "Rock y TLC" (Rock and NAFTA) helpfully documents contemporary anxieties about the treaty among rockers: where some expressed optimism about the possibility of accessing US Latino publics, others were apprehensive about having to compete with their contemporaries north of the border and thus called for safeguards for national acts.[92] *El rock mexicano* can be fruitfully read in light of these anxieties and tensions.

Taking what he describes as a sociological approach based on a series of interviews conducted with bands and event organizers across Mexico, Paredes Pacho first explores varied and subtle ways that rock is censored across Mexico. Organizers are obliged to bribe authorities for permits; bands are forced to play pop-rock standards in order to avoid police shutdowns; rock concerts are cancelled due to neighbors' complaints; permits for rock venues are expensive and bureaucratic, and authorities are reticent to grant them due to past disturbances; and elections impede continuity of policies.[93] This nuanced account of censorship is complemented by the specter of a top-down, totalizing, cultural nationalism. "To worry about national identity in the abstract," Paredes Pacho contends, "can justify cultural censorship, especially against rock."[94] Paredes Pacho sidesteps the question of "identity" in favor of rock "community," which he links to the "spontaneous and collective" rock *reventón*, in which one may "express oneself freely and directly with one's own community." The question of a unified, specifically Mexican identity in rock is excluded as epistemologically redundant: "It seems to me unnecessary to standardize, musically or culturally, Mexican rock."[95]

On the basis of this more inclusive sense of rock community, Paredes Pacho dismisses the idea that a United States influence will undermine the "Mexican" in rock, writing:

> Abstract postulates about national identity and the phenomena of cultural hybridity . . . have nothing to offer to those of us who simply want to do our job, from our personal point of view. . . . We are not concerned with our anthropological identity, nor do we believe that more contact with foreign values might lead to a loss of identity. On the contrary. Not even because we play rock, do we feel like *gringos*.[96]

To support this idea, Paredes Pacho describes the Tijuana rock scene, in which rock moved comparatively freely across the border with San Diego, as a bellwether for integration into "international rock circuits." This freedom provided familiarity with up-and-coming US-based bands, leading to greater dynamism and engagement with the international rock vanguard. However, integration was uneven, aligning with wider inequalities: concerts were held in Tijuana but advertised (and priced) for US publics, and Tijuana bands found themselves crowded out from local venues and radio stations by US-based bands, with many opting to migrate to Mexico City.[97]

While observing that such periodic "invasions" have not threatened "national culture" but affirmed Mexican identity in opposition to the United States, Paredes Pacho emphasizes the bitter nature of this oppositionality, rooted in the "anger of not enjoying, even in your own country, the same rights and privileges as a North American with dollars in his pockets."[98] In other ways, NAFTA is celebrated as a potential vehicle for the "internationalization" of Mexican rock and as an aid in a wider process of democratization. A politicized rhetoric of "independence" is here mobilized as a conceptual bridge between antiauthoritarianism and neoliberal economics; Paredes Pacho praises the ways that US rock promotes "independent, free, and democratic thought," while arguing that NAFTA may benefit the rock scene by encouraging "the free circulation of ideas and cultural values."[99] "As rockers," Paredes Pacho argues, "we ought to hope that the Free Trade Agreement facilitates the free circulation of ideas," since this would create "greater access to a wider, more diverse offer of ideals and cultural values."[100] The independent rock venues of Mexico would, as in the following characterization of US college radio, be more fully realized as "independent" through greater exposure to these plural, diverse values: "I have no interest in writing an apology for the United States alternative scene, but what's true is that often in these spaces, plural, creative, and progressive cultural and artistic values are generated. The defense of these already established civil spaces, relatively free, congregates the most diverse of voices and communities, for whom 'their spaces' represent a vital, everyday right."[101] Paredes Pacho thus deftly reverses received connotations of "independence" within the rock scene, transforming the term from a marker of resistance against transnational capitalist homogenization to a signifier of democratic, postauthoritarian politics. In doing so, he effects a familiar, but nonetheless uneasy, intertwining of political democracy and neoliberal economic policy.

It is therefore important to recognize that this author, along with other voices representing *Rock en tu idioma* acts, was responding to a restrictive intellectual context in which commercial success was seen to inherently discredit musical expression. This context has often gone overlooked in scholarship on *Rock en tu idioma*. Corona casts *Rock en tu idioma* artists in opposition to official cultural nationalism, producing vibrant musical work that drew from and celebrated Mexican traditions within a transnational frame, and that defied anxieties about cultural homogenization and commercial censorship within the transnational cultural industries.[102] Similarly, Zolov highlights how mid-1980s rock bands drew on diverse Mexican and Latin American musical traditions and Mexican Spanish linguistic affectations, portraying the former generation of rock artists (in my view incorrectly) as linguistically and stylistically dependent on Anglophone rock.[103] Neither scholar, however, attends to the intellectual context in which this transnationalist/nationalist binary episteme emerged, in the work of writers such as Paredes Pacho, or to the prevalence of ideas about commercial censorship and independence that this episteme was seen to resist. Perhaps most importantly, neither considers the self-interest of the actors who participated in this conversation. Paredes Pacho's contribution should, in other words, be read as a contingently, rather than absolutely, liberatory entanglement between neoliberalism and democracy.

While *Rock en tu idioma* has often been understood as a catalyst for the exponential growth in *rock mexicano* known as the rock "boom," this project in fact emerged in continuity with a series of post-Avándaro projects to advance and construct the rock scene, which came to be described as "independent." I have shown here how an ideological formation emerged at this time that valued small-scale production as the last bastion of musical freedom of expression, under threat from outside commercial censorship. In turn, I have shown how commercial censorship was understood (including by voices advocating for it) as an extension of government power and the gaze of mainstream conservative society. The ability of *Rock en tu idioma* artists to challenge these ideas about commercial censorship was vital for their success. This was reflected in interviews I conducted with several of these artists, all of whom vehemently denied the suggestion that their speech, musical style, or self-presentation was limited by their label. I have no reason to doubt these denials, but it is nonetheless important to recognize that the effectiveness of their denials in the late 1980s was vital to these acts' artistic credibility. *Rock en tu idioma* bands contested received ideas about censorship within their music itself; but as seen above, they also cultivated other kinds of voices through close relationships with the press and through scholarly research. The "boom" of the 1980s was contingent on these kinds of intellectual labor.

CHAPTER 3

The Monopolistic Ogre?

OCESA, Live Rock, and Enclosure

In March 2014, long-standing *rock urbano* outfit Banda Bostik played to a packed crowd at the Vive Latino festival. Partway through, the band performed their 1980s song "Tlatelolco '68," which commemorates the students killed by the PRI regime during the 1968 Tlatelolco massacre: "A time ago, it all happened, people can't forget / In Tlatelolco the blood did flow, of the learned ones who knew the truth." Introducing the song, lead singer El Guadaña celebrated Banda Bostik's enduring defiance of authority: "31 years, *banda*, of throwing shit at the government. We're proud to be a band that's never changed our form of being or living." Guadaña then launched into a speech alleging censorship in the present:

> Talking of guilt and betrayal. *Banda*, the whole world wants you to lift up both hands. Because we're going to lay into that guy who suspended the gig in Texcoco [a zone in Estado de México], on the count of three [shout] fuck his fucking mother [*chingue a su puta madre*]. And the person who doesn't shout with us, fuck their fucking mother [*chingue a su puta madre*]. One, two, three [crowd shouts]. *Viva México*!

The band then launched into the song, while the live online transmission of the concert on the festival's Coca-Cola-sponsored official television channel carried the disclaimer that these opinions "do not necessarily reflect the position of Coca-Cola TV."[1]

Guadaña's speech referenced the recent suspension of an international metal event, Heaven and Hell Fest, by the governor of Estado de México, the PRI politician Eruviel Ávila Villegas.[2] Officials had justified suspending the event—which was to be headlined by Kiss and Guns N' Roses—by alleging that the security arrangements were insufficient. The decision led to accusations of censorship, protest marches, and unsuccessful attempts to move the festival to other states. Taken in isolation, the suspension might seem a comparatively innocuous—albeit heavy-handed and inflexible—administrative decision. Yet Guadaña's speech, occurring before a song about the most infamous moment of the country's single-party dictatorship, depicted the suspension as a repressive act, a naked exertion of state power. Small details in this speech drew continuities between the suspension and the authoritarian legacy in Mexico: for instance, the pride taken by rock musicians in insulting politicians directly responds to the history of the president as an untouchable, uncriticizable *caudillo*; the use of profanities recalls the irreverent, bawdy working-class idiom associated with the *hoyos fonqui*.[3]

Just as important as Banda Bostik's performance itself was its commercial context: Vive Latino is run by the entertainment corporation OCESA (the Operator of Entertainment Centers). After its creation in 1990, OCESA soon rose to dominate the live music market; what was initially a small organization was later incorporated within Grupo CIE (Inter-American Entertainment Corporation), part-owned by billionaire Carlos Slim Helú. (In effect, people often use Grupo CIE and OCESA interchangeably, and often use OCESA to refer to the conglomerate of which it forms a part; I will reflect this simplified usage throughout this chapter.) Although Guadaña was not to know, Hell and Heaven Fest was to be acquired by OCESA from the promotor Live Talent after its suspension. Indeed, some suspect that this turn of events, through which state prohibition caused a small festival to be absorbed by a large, powerful live entertainment company, was no coincidence: OCESA has long been depicted as the beneficiary of collusion between government and corporate power, in a way that complicates any straightforward opposition between monolithic, oppressive state power and popular culture.[4]

In the present, conversations about censorship with rock fans frequently turn to OCESA's anticompetitive practices. As one respondent put it: "If I, a person off the street, want to put on Madonna in Palacio de los Deportes, from the beginning, Palacio de los Deportes is run by OCESA. They oblige you to sell tickets through Ticketmaster, which is owned by OCESA. In the contract, they oblige you to hire the security company provided by OCESA."[5] Independent event organizers who choose non-OCESA services have alleged reprisals on the part of the company; some even fear retaliation if they criticize OCESA publicly.⁶ The company's representatives have not always denied that it constitutes a monopoly; in 2008 its head of Artists and Repertoire claimed that the monopoly was "good for the general public" because "when an artist can auction themselves off, they become more expensive."⁷ OCESA's market dominance has, nonetheless, come under threat from new commercial competition and state regulation. In recent years it has come to be rivaled by Zignia, a live events company backed by the media giant TVAzteca, which has the financial means to compete with OCESA for headline acts. OCESA has also been investigated by the Federal Commission for Economic Competition, which in 2018 concluded that the company had engaged in monopolistic practices; the commission required OCESA to renounce the exclusivity contracts signed with a number of live music venues, and to allow ticketing companies not linked to Grupo CIE to sell tickets to the company's events.⁸

The latter judgment surprised few participants in the *escena independiente*, who frequently talk of OCESA as a "monopoly" and even as a "mafia," and typically define their scene in opposition to the company. Some of my research consultants hinted at an omertà around the organization; as one journalist told me, "There are things [regarding OCESA] I can't say because, you know, it compromises you." One member of a high-profile rock band put it thus: "If you're not there [working for OCESA] there are forms of censorship, labor censorship in some form, ideological censorship, media censorship. Automatically. That's why it's a mafia, because you have to be in OCESA's rules to be able to work."

At the same time, OCESA's rise coincided with a celebrated period, at the beginning of the 1990s, in which Mexico's entertainment infrastructure suddenly opened to international rock acts. Because of this, OCESA is often associated, even by voices otherwise critical of it, with *apertura* (opening or openness) and with an especially vibrant period for Mexican rock.⁹ The company is also linked with the privatization of event security—a process which has drawn criticism, but which also created a vital distance between rock publics and the police and army. OCESA has, in short, come to occupy a paradoxical position, associated simultaneously with an expansion of expressive freedom and commercial opportunity, and with censorship and co-optation of the entertainment press. Reworking a famous phrase coined by Octavio Paz to describe Mexico's single-party regime, OCESA might be described as a "monopolistic ogre": the company's nearly total control of the live entertainment market has been predicated on a set of carrot-and-stick tactics, especially toward journalists.[10] OCESA's influence within the rock scene, however, has been generally overlooked by scholars.[11]

In this chapter, I explore OCESA's ambivalent rise. I am especially interested in the complex relationship that emerged between this company and the entertainment journalists covering its events, and in how the knowledge labor carried out by these journalists shaped histories and understandings of music censorship. I describe this emergent relationship in terms that allow resonances to be heard across OCESA's management of the press, its privatization of security at live events, and authoritarian governmentalities typically associated with previous eras. The vision of rock as an antiauthoritarian practice existing in spite of government was, I contend, convenient for a company seeking to simultaneously commodify and contain rock expression and gain credibility among rock fans. Yet, this vision overlooked how OCESA's rise extended the disciplinary governmentalities of the state. I argue that OCESA's management of the press was vital in normalizing its market dominance and protecting the company from allegations of repression, even in the wake of episodes of violence against fans carried out by its private security operatives. Here, my perspective is informed by Taylor's discussion of what he terms the "commodification apparatus" in music, and Arditi's exploration of the commodification of music as a multiscalar process of enclosure.[12] Live rock's massification in the 1990s was predicated on *apertura*'s opposite: the expansion of practices for the enclosure of bodies, extending rather than breaking with what Zolov calls the "containment of the rock gesture."[13]

Of course, it would be wrong to impute excessive novelty to OCESA's practices for the commodification of live rock—in its earliest years the company competed with organizers of independent venues who had been practicing similar things at a smaller scale. It is nonetheless vital to recognize that the company's commodification practices often involved the exertion of physical violence; that, partly as a result, they were subject to ongoing comment and controversy in the rock press in highly revealing ways; and that OCESA's rise was viewed by many as something very distinct from a harbinger of democracy and "openness." Though some of this controversy reflected OCESA's unprecedented corporate power, I also contend—across this chapter and the next—that the acute attention paid to live rock's commoditization at this time resulted from the intersection of two factors working in tandem: rock's absorption into the cultural enclosures of the mainstream was accompanied by its exclusion from public space. The line of inquiry pursued here is followed by another, in the next chapter, that examines rockers' connections with the Zapatista solidarity movement in the mid-1990s. In addition to examining the specialized rock press and interviews carried out with musicians and organizers, I draw heavily from the culture and entertainment pages of the newspaper *La Jornada* and, to a lesser extent, from the magazine *Proceso*. This is for several interlinked reasons: *La Jornada*'s coverage of live music was influential at this time, features on rock concerts published in *La Jornada* were often reprinted in rock magazines, and *La Jornada* enjoyed credibility among rock publics. Most importantly, the newspaper occasionally published scathing reviews of live events that provide a window into contemporary anxieties about corporate rock, and while most of the press underinformed or misinformed its readers about the 1994 Zapatista uprising, *La Jornada*'s journalists were closer to the Zapatista movement and more willing to report the inside story as well as the official one. The newspaper is therefore an especially useful resource for this period's cultural history.

Monopolizing Live Rock

Much excitement in the early 1990s revolved around the fact that, for the first time, high-profile international rock and pop acts began to perform in Mexico with some frequency. Within three years, from 1992 to 1995, Black Sabbath, Iron Maiden, Aerosmith, Elton John, Jethro Tull, Michael Jackson, the Rolling Stones, Madonna, Paul McCartney, and Pink Floyd all performed in Mexico. At the end of 1992, Elton John held two concerts at the Estadio Azteca; the concerts were organized by a live entertainment company owned by broadcasting group Televisa and effusively promoted on the network's television channels (including by sports commentators). This concert was widely celebrated, taken as conclusive evidence that rock in Mexico could pass without incident and constitute big business.[14] Notably, several of these artists had been subject to, or threatened with, censorship within Mexico. Black Sabbath, for instance, had been denied permission to perform in León, Guanajuato, in 1989 by the conservative PAN (National Action Party) city government. The Rolling Stones concert in Mexico City in 1995 was denied permission until, it is said, former president Carlos Salinas de Gortari directly intervened.

This effervescence also took hold during a time of ideological tumult, in which the legitimacy of the PRI was fading. In 1990, the author Mario Vargas Llosa had caused uproar when, in a televised debate, he had referred to PRI single-party rule as the "perfect dictatorship" (comments which were themselves suppressed by Televisa, which had broadcast the debate, and by the newspaper *El Nacional*).[15] Vargas Llosa's now-familiar conflation of political, expressive, and market freedoms was widely discussed, filtering into the culture pages of newspapers, which were suddenly full of stories about the censorship of music and theater alongside opinion pieces that valorized expressive freedom as an inalienable constitutional and human right.[16] Mexican journalists noted with interest the iconic potency of rock at the end of the Cold War: for instance, Roger Waters' symbolic destruction of the Berlin Wall during a 1990 live concert was widely reported in the rock press.[17] The rapid growth of live rock within Mexico was thus aligned with what was seen as a new, open spirit of freedom of expression.

OCESA was instrumental in the expansion of the entertainment sector in general, into which rock was incorporated. It took over the management of several major state-owned venues, and also created its own. By the end of the 1990s, it began to run an annual festival, Vive Latino, in one of these venues.[18] Another more internationally oriented festival, Corona Capital, followed in 2010. In the process, OCESA took an aggressive stance against its competitors, using its growing market position and power to absorb some and weaken others. Indeed, Elton John's concert may be understood as a watershed in another way: in deciding to perform for Televisa, the artist broke an initial agreement to perform with OCESA. In the buildup to the concert, representatives of the two companies reportedly held "high-level meetings."[19] OCESA and Televisa later forged a lasting alliance; in 2002, Televisa bought a 40 percent stake in OCESA, providing the latter with access to the former's vast distribution network.[20]

Seen from within the independent scene at the time, OCESA's rise was characterized by appropriation, the exploitation of power, and a lot of government help.[21] As a neoliberal model for governance took hold, implying budget cuts and privatization, Mexico City's government began to rent or "franchise" (*concesionar*) its larger venues to private companies. This was justified as a way "to better take advantage of them" while maintaining ownership of these venues, thus allowing the city government to reject the charge that it was privatizing public assets. In 1991 the city government leased Auditorio Nacional, which had a capacity of ten thousand, to OCESA and franchised the Teatro de la Ciudad to the company. The moves were sold as part of "the opening of Mexico to the world stage."[22] In 1996, OCESA was subsequently franchised the Palacio de los Deportes, with a capacity of twenty thousand, and the Teatro Metropólitan, with a capacity of three thousand. Beginning in 1993, the company also erected temporary stages at the Autódromo Hermanos Rodríguez, a racetrack, to host several big-name international artists, and it capitalized on the success of these events to construct the Foro Sol, which could seat sixty-five thousand, on the same site in 1997.

In practice, many of the people hired by OCESA in the early 1990s to run the technical side of live, mass-scale concerts had begun in the independent scene.[23] The poor outcomes of independent groups' efforts to massify live rock are indicative of disparities of wealth and influence, not lack of competence. One example of the impact of these disparities emerged in the small-scale venue LUCC, established in Mexico City in 1987.[24] The founders of this venue, brothers Raúl and Eduardo Barajas, began to organize large-scale concerts at cultural festivals, such as the Festival Internacional Cervantino in Guanajuato. In 1989 and 1990, they had been invited to speak at the New Music Seminar in New York about practices of *autogestión*. Through participation in these events, Eduardo told me, they became aware of the increasing influence of "Latin rock" as a category.[25] Two years later, they sought to import this tendency to Mexico in the form of a large-scale festival, the First Festival of Latin Rock "Rola '92," featuring mostly rock acts from across Latin America. The festival, to be held in the Plaza de Toros, with a capacity of forty thousand, was intended to be large, diverse, and accessible to poorer audiences. However, after the organizers had already booked acts from the United States, Italy, Brazil, Argentina, and Mexico and bought flights for these acts to travel to Mexico City, their license to hold the event in the Plaza de Toros was revoked.[26] The brothers were instructed by a government representative to choose the OCESA-run Palacio de los Deportes. When they did so, OCESA required that they reduce the lineup and pay a substantial amount for a package of in-house security, transportation of equipment, medical services, audio, and lighting, all provided by OCESA subsidiaries. To pay for these services, the pair had to raise ticket prices to at least the equivalent of US$4, roughly four times the minimum price they had initially planned. Moreover, when labels learned of an agreement that Rola '92 be broadcast live on state television channel IMEVISIÓN, they threatened to boycott any bands that participated. The event was a commercial failure and left the brothers with debt equivalent to roughly US$30,000 in today's currency.[27]

Even as it was associated with the expansion of rock, then, the franchising of venues across Mexico City to OCESA had a dark side. Attendees constantly complained about "First-World prices in the Third World" at OCESA events.[28] Artists who had performed regularly in the Auditorio Nacional now found themselves priced out; Tania Libertad, who had played the venue five times between 1986 and 1992, complained that now "you have to pay for a series of unnecessary services, for police, security in the venue ... every light, every microphone." To put the expense in context, she pointed out that in 1991, tickets for Sting's concert in Palacio de los Deportes had cost three times more than for his concert in Madison Square Garden.[29] Libertad's experiences reflected the fact that OCESA was becoming highly vertically integrated, with subsidiaries running almost every aspect of the live music experience: security, production, promotion, ticket sales, venues, and even food and drink. This involved a series of business deals, including with Ticketmaster, the security company Seguridad Lobo, and the promotion company Reed Exhibition Companies. In the mid-1990s OCESA was restructured into a subsidiary of Grupo CIE, which further expanded into other aspects of the music industry, as well as talent agencies and theme parks. During research I often heard stories about corporate-sponsored acts benefiting from payola; yet OCESA's media power, and its ability to influence radio play, went beyond such everyday experiences.[30]

OCESA's market dominance over its rivals was also, however, a consequence of extra financial, organizational, and logistical burdens related to mass-scale events. As one investor in mass-scale rock concerts put it in 1991, live productions of "international magnitude" required collaborations between "two or three businesses," which implied greater costs and a transnational corporate structure, presenting significant barriers to entry for comparatively undercapitalized independent organizers who wanted to participate in the mass-scale live music market.[31] As discussed in the next section, many of these costs were associated with the increased deployment of private security at live events.

Rock, Privatization, and Security

The opening to live rock provided by politicians was not unconditional. "Yes to rock," Mexico City regent Manuel Camacho Solís had said in the early 1990s, "but with order."[32] As already demonstrated, live rock had long been a target of police violence and a source of anxieties over the genre's association with "disorder." Camacho Solís's formulation continued discourse both within and outside the rock scene that perpetuated a censorial downward spiral: past episodes of "disorder" were used as a pretext to deny permits for live concerts, under the premise that they had been provoked by an unruly rock public. It therefore fell to organizers and journalists to "discipline" or "control" the rock public and convince a wider audience that live rock was safe. As late as 1994, Avándaro was still being cited as a pretext for censorship; Arteria, a cultural forum in southern Mexico City, had its license suspended by the *delegación* government after complaints by community groups about its Saturday rock concerts. "We already know about what happens with rock," one community leader said, "there's the example of Avándaro in 1971, which ended in tragedy."[33]

In its public messaging OCESA demonstrated a deep anxiety about maintaining "order," reflected in a somewhat overbearing message often broadcast at its live events: "We remind you that the continuation of these concerts depends on you.... Thank you for your good behavior."[34] Their concern with "good behavior," however, implicated more than just the paternalistic gaze of the state. "There's a lot of talk of the authorities' disquiet" about rock, said the director of OCESA in 1991, "but the greater disquiet comes from the public."[35] The challenge for the new commercial actors, as one industry representative put it, was thus to provide a safe atmosphere for live rock that *padres de familia* would feel comfortable sending their daughters to.[36]

Rock's entry into the massified, commercial mainstream therefore did not constitute a liberation from state control of culture but built on a confluence between commercial interests and those of government. OCESA policed live rock both in order to convince the authorities to award them permits and to form rock into a dependable commodity; after all, "disorderly" acts such as *portazos* threatened both private profit and public morality. In order to constitute a valuable commodity, rock had to be *bounded*—that is, enclosed; and in order for its value to be maintained, it had to be *secured*. Rodolfo Ayala, an investor in live entertainment, stated, "We want there to be guarantees for the public.... We want to provide tranquility." What was often described as the "domestication" of live rock thus gestured toward both government regulation and consumer trust. In turn, ensuring safety at live events was a major theme for cultural journalists in the early 1990s, and security measures were often described in detail in newspapers and magazines. One article in *La Jornada* in 1993 contained information regarding the number of public security forces normally called on to police events in Palacio de los Deportes (200, paid for by the operator, OCESA) and their working hours for these events; it also described the number of private security active inside the events themselves and their cost (150, with a cost of 10 million pesos—roughly equivalent to 100,000 pesos today).[37] Newspapers have continued, until recent years, to publish similar figures regarding security personnel.[38]

OCESA's rapid growth coincided with the dawn of the "punitive turn" in Mexico, characterized by increased securitization, or policing by private security, of public spaces and ambivalently connected to democratization and neoliberalism.³⁹ Part of the arrangement that underpinned the growth of mass-scale rock events in the neoliberal era was the substitution of public forces at venues—including, at times, riot police—with private security companies contracted by the event organizers themselves. This was the case for an event organized by OCESA at Palacio de los Deportes in 1991 whose permit stipulated that no police should enter the venue.⁴⁰ The burden of ensuring security was increasingly transferred to the private sector, partly in order to avoid "the intimidating presence of mounted police, riot police and even plainclothes military" noted in live events in the late 1980s and early 1990s.⁴¹ As one of my respondents later commented, it was largely sensible to reduce the number and visibility of police at concerts; they were a ready target for audience ire, especially given audiences' constant experiences of police abuse.⁴² Nonetheless, this transfer of security responsibilities from public to private hands was often messy and uneven. For instance, in 1998, following a *portazo* at a Rolling Stones concert at Foro Sol that led to violent clashes with riot police, OCESA's director blamed the police for being "soft touch," "negotiating" with those trying to enter without paying and eventually allowing some to do so. Meanwhile, the authorities blamed OCESA for requesting only three hundred police for security at an event attended by sixty thousand fans.⁴³

The private security sector flourished in Mexico in the late 1980s before consolidating around a handful of providers in the 1990s, yet the expansion of private security into live rock has not been without controversy. Private security companies, especially the OCESA subsidiary Seguridad Lobo, have been accused of being heavy-handed and of failing to adequately ensure safety and security. Seguridad Lobo has come to dominate the private security market for mass-scale concerts, partly through its close commercial relationship with OCESA. Seguridad Lobo operatives have, nonetheless, earned a reputation for violent activity since the 1990s, when the company became emblematic of the dark side of rock's commercialization. The practices for which Seguridad Lobo was criticized at this time range from those that, when viewed from the present, seem aberrant to those that now appear entirely unremarkable. In the early 1990s, for example, rock audiences aired constant suspicions about bag checks and body searches. One *La Jornada* journalist wrote, in late 1992, about what he perceived as an excessive front-door check by the company, complaining of "the inspection at the door, the humiliating search carried out by hands eager for masculine skin, [and] the constant mistakes of the doormen who confuse time and again the organization of the queues." Once inside, this journalist was refused permission to leave to make a phone call. The "fear of disorder," he said, had empowered "porters deaf to the voice of reason, determined to carry to its final consequences the expansion of the small aura of power that allows them to build, through arrogant actions, their Darian-Orwellian state of those for whom The Big Lobo Brothers will always be watching you. Bad vibes."[44]

In a neoliberalizing context, "security" also attained meaning beyond ensuring attendees' safety; Seguridad Lobo was entrusted with the securing of intellectual property. As is evident from the following account from a Caifanes concert in 1993, they sometimes did so in disturbing ways:

> Patricia Delgado Robles, a communication student and fan . . . received her first journalism lesson: the accreditation makes the journalist. With her camera, she tries to violate Los Caifanes' copyright. Two security agents on the left wing of the stage ask her for her film, and then they try to take her camera. She flees in terror and they, helplessly, manage only to take away her raincoat, which contains money and documents. She is wearing only a dress. When she tries to negotiate, they demand her camera roll in return. Then, they refuse to identify themselves and assert that they never had the raincoat to begin with.[45]

By mid-1993, in the words of one rock journalist, these practices had become "part of the landscape, and it no longer affects the behavior of the attending youth."[46] Yet it is evident that many opposed the enclosure of rock in live music venues and were suspicious of the intimidatory means through which it could be imposed.

That this enclosure was predicated on the threat of force was demonstrated especially clearly when private security engaged in physical violence against attendees. At a 2005 ska concert at Palacio de los Deportes, dozens of fans decided to jump up to six meters from the stands to the standing area in front of the stage, encouraged by those below who formed human mattresses to catch them. Security personnel, taken by surprise at what one journalist described as "operation monkey," beat and removed those they found engaging in it.[47] *Portazos* were often responded to with physical force.[48] Private security operatives were also associated with far more sinister episodes of violence. At a reggae concert in the same venue held in 2002, Seguridad Lobo operatives launched a vicious attack on a member of the venue's cleaning staff who had just finished work. When he tried to leave, OCESA personnel asked for his badge. Others arrived to request that he remove his shirt and sweater; when he asked why, he was taken into a side corridor, beaten, insulted, and threatened. He was then handed to another group of six OCESA operatives, who beat him for a further ten minutes before ejecting him from the venue.[49] Contemporary participants in the rock scene were often willing to describe violent acts by Seguridad Lobo operatives as "repressive," as in one case at a concert by Los Fabulosos Cadillacs in December 1997, in which five Seguridad Lobo operatives beat up a twenty-two-year-old attendee, leaving him in need of hospital treatment for a collapsed lung. A letter to *La Jornada*, reproduced in the magazine *La mosca en la pared*, complained that the Lobos had been targeting "any youth who'd been dancing euphorically in their place upon hearing Los Cadillacs"; this "excessive security," the signatories stated, created an "atmosphere of repression." "Prepotent, aggressive and always getting off scot-free, the members of the proto-fascist Lobo security force keep getting away with it," concluded *La mosca*'s editor.[50]

Seguridad Lobo was faced with public relations challenges as members of the public began to draw continuities between their activities and past authoritarianism. One 1998 feature from the magazine *Proceso* on Carlos Seoane, the head of Seguridad Lobo—full of puns on the word *lobo* (wolf)—is evidently intended to respond to the company's poor public image.[51] Its headline, "Behind the fear they provoke, there are 500 young people prepared to protect the public," is suggestive of a puff piece. Yet the article directly addresses the apparent concern among "one part of the public . . . that the security Wolves are only sheep on the outside" and that the Lobos had been conducting overly rigorous security checks and forcibly removing attendees over "excesses or drugs." Many, the article stated, considered the Lobos to be "nasty, rude, obstructionist, overbearing, repressive, vile . . . puppets who only obey orders." Responding to this idea, Seoane argued that Seguridad Lobo's work was necessary: "It's not only about violence, but there's also a lot more in play, like the protection of the artists' copyright." Security, for Seoane, was defined as the control of "any insecure act or condition" that could threaten "the physical integrity of participants and venues, or the interests of the client or artist." In defending his company's actions, then, Seoane redefined "security" to include the securing of a musical commodity; it is evident from some of the episodes already discussed above that this logic, simultaneously commercial and governmental in nature, accompanied an expansion of the conditions through which violence could be justified.

Equally, while Seoane accepted that "mistakes have been made," he insisted that Seguridad Lobo operated in a peaceful manner: "We don't use arms, violence begets violence." Moreover, rehearsing a familiar concession to the disciplinary, authoritarian gaze, he claimed that such a nonviolent approach was possible because contemporary rock audiences were "docile and educated." To argue the point, Seoane described how Lobo trained its staff: new recruits were taught first aid, fire safety, and customer service before learning about the penal code, evacuations, and disaster response. Self-defense lessons were an option for staff, but not a priority. The goal, he said, was for employees to learn to "control someone crazy from consuming alcohol or drugs . . . how to dominate that person without striking them, not risking either them or us." "Our job is to serve," Seoane joked, perhaps in bad taste; "if we approached ex-soldiers or ex-police to be Lobos, and if we taught them: first course, taekwondo, second course, how to put people's eyes out, there'd be no mystique to us at all."

OCESA, Journalism, and Public Image

As is apparent, OCESA perceived its public image as an existential issue, especially in the first years of its existence. On the one hand, the company emerged from a period in which episodes of public disorder had been used as a pretext to censor live rock; the comments of politicians such as Camacho Solís, noted above, made it clear that the political tolerance for rock's massification was highly conditional, and could be reversed. Thus, the company depended on the public perception that their events were safe for attendees. On the other hand, the company was also acutely aware of the importance of legitimizing its activities before a rock public as well as the authorities—and, in particular, of narrating their commercial expansion as a break with past authoritarianism.

These competing imperatives informed the ways that OCESA sought to manage the press coverage of its events, as the company cultivated close but conditional relationships with music journalists. Throughout the 1990s, OCESA became increasingly visible in the press; its directors gave frequent interviews, and news and advertisements about concerts frequently foregrounded the OCESA brand. OCESA initially sought to control its public image directly, through the creation of its own rock publications, such as *Rock & Pop*. Some suspected that the company conducted dirty tricks, such as an incident in 1994 in which OCESA allegedly planted rumors in the press that an independently organized festival in the city of Morelia was fraudulent and that it had been canceled, leading this festival to be a commercial failure.[52] As the 1990s progressed, however, OCESA increasingly pursued subtler strategies for managing the press and began to view coverage of its events within mainstream publications as free publicity. The company's directors were opportunistic in pursuing direct press ties; for instance, for several years the director of OCESA's press department sat on the editorial board of the right-wing newspaper *Reforma*.

More important still, however, was the creation of a press division to manage relations with journalists, which at its height counted on ten employees. Members of the organization's press division often assumed the burden of "damage control" in the wake of security failures, seeking to avoid the publication of damaging photos and looking to influence the press coverage of their events.[53] Thus (in a now-commonplace practice) they ensured a strict division between photographers and journalists at their venues; typically, photographers were allowed access to the pit in front of the stage, often only for the first three songs, while journalists were not permitted cameras and were accommodated in a separate room (for instance, in Palacio de los Deportes journalists were allocated the presidential suite). In this way, OCESA's press division was able to limit any damaging photographic evidence of disorder or violence at their events.

OCESA's press division was also able to regulate journalists' activities by distributing a limited number of press passes. On the basis of such controlled access, they built up relationships with journalists that many perceived as coercive. In the words of one rock journalist, the press division had become "a force for pressuring newspaper editors" in order to obtain favorable coverage: "They have the luxury of not inviting [reporters], sending them to the stands, punishing them, if they're not friendly media [*medios amigos*]."[54] One former press division worker I spoke to described having made calls to journalists who published criticism of OCESA: "Hey, why don't you tell us what your problem is, because we see that you're constantly publishing against the company."[55] The worker in question placed this type of call to correct journalistic errors amid an alleged lack of professionalism among rock journalists. Yet on the other end of the phone, these calls might easily be perceived to be intimidatory. Journalists were constantly aware that, given OCESA's domination of the live entertainment market in Mexico City, the revocation of their press pass might make it impossible for them to carry out their work. It is no surprise that journalists have often been critical of OCESA's press division, one writing that they "transformed the work of public relations here in Mexico, by conditioning accreditation for their concerts on favorable news for their activities. Criticism of poor organization [or] about poor facilities for concerts ... would imply the doors closing on journalistic activity."[56]

The open secret of this "closing of doors" has occasionally been reworked into blanket attacks against rock journalism as a profession. For instance, a 2017 post by *provocateur* blogger Peperrock titled "What Journalists Don't Tell You" criticized that year's Vive Latino before giving anonymous (but easily identifiable) "ball-licking" quotes by mainstream journalists praising the festival. The post then provided what this blogger claimed were private quotes from the same journalists criticizing the festival, described as "everything that they can't say in public, faced with the fear of losing future access, and no longer enjoying the grace of the mafia running the Festival."[57] This critique nonetheless overlooks the ways that the conditioning of access to press passes disproportionately affected independent, small-scale publications. Publications with a smaller circulation were at a disadvantage on two counts: their coverage was of less publicity value to OCESA, and fewer people would find out if their journalists were denied passes to live events. Accreditation for members of the press thus significantly favored mainstream newspaper outlets at the expense of the independent, specialized music press, whose journalists often found themselves excluded. For instance, independent journalist Brenda Marín complained in the wake of Billy Joel's March 1992 concert in Palacio de los Deportes that reporters from the underground publications *La Banda Rockera* and *La Afición* had been denied accreditation, and that journalists from the former publication had even been threatened with permanent exclusion. "The specialized press . . . has again been displaced by those who, in the opinion of the 'organizers,' are the journalists who should attend rock events."[58]

Such unequal access is one of the reasons that the specialized rock press began to decline in influence, and that rock journalists increasingly worked for newspapers instead. However, changes were also afoot within newspapers themselves. *Reforma*, a slick operation with close ties to the PAN that entered the Mexico City market in 1993, is credited by some with a cultural shift across entertainment journalism toward more promotional and less critical writing about the creative industries.[59] This cultural shift is also evidenced—albeit in a more complex fashion—in publications claiming comparative independence from corporate influence, such as *La Jornada* and the magazine *Proceso*. *La Jornada* continues in the present to provide space for voices willing to criticize mainstream artists, as well as those promoting them; one of its journalists told me of multiple occasions in which artists and their representatives threatened him with physical violence in retaliation for his writing.[60] Through the 1990s, the newspaper occasionally published stinging reviews of OCESA events that included information about threats to safety and abuses committed by private security.

Yet at the same time, *La Jornada* frequently promoted OCESA concerts within its culture pages, in features on acts contracted to perform for OCESA, as well as in paid advertising. Its coverage often included short news stories highlighting the dates that tickets for OCESA events went on sale; in advance of larger events, *La Jornada* also published extended analyses that served to create hype around the artists due to perform.[61] In the mid- and late 1990s, OCESA and *La Jornada* began to run competitions together, and at the turn of the millennium the paper started to post celebratory end-of-year stories about the annual number of concerts organized by the company.[62] Given OCESA's monopoly on live rock and its corporate power, publishing about the company's events was difficult to avoid; yet it appears that *La Jornada*'s culture section was far more useful to the company than those writing for it might wish to admit.

The high visibility given to OCESA in such coverage allowed the company to take credit for the massification of rock, thus earning legitimacy among a rock audience. Through such coverage, the company's offerings came to be understood as an escape from past repression; as one writer put it, "for lovers of live rock" the creation of OCESA was "like a rain shower in the desert."[63] Indeed, it is noteworthy that writers who depicted the rise of OCESA in this way also began to imagine rock's "long night" of heavy official censorship as extending until the very end of the 1980s, when the company began to operate.[64] In turn, in their interactions with the press, OCESA representatives used subtle rhetorical touches to lend agency to the company within a broader narrative of opening. For instance, during an interview with the magazine *Proceso* in 1991, OCESA's directors stated that it would not be commercially viable for their business to focus only on rock: "If we brought only rock, it would be a mistake."[65] Nonetheless, they emphasized both rock's inherent value and the fact that they and other individuals running the company were fans of the genre. Readers were thus encouraged to see the incorporation of rock into the entertainment mainstream as something approaching an act of corporate largesse—and one that could easily be undone—rather than as a commercial decision to profit from a key youth market. In addition, on the basis of such commercial variety, OCESA's directors portrayed themselves as torchbearers for expressive freedom in rock. For instance, regarding Palacio de los Deportes, they told journalists that they "had managed to get the green light" for "cultural performances" and were at pains to state that "we include rock" within the category of culture. In this way—that is, by prolific and sometimes questionable uses of the active voice—they implicitly took credit for both the cultural opening of state venues and the inclusion of rock within it.[66]

Several events hosted by OCESA throughout the 1990s helped to establish a comparatively new frame: one in which transnational capital had bargained with government in order to create an opening for rock, thus plucking it out of obscurity. In 1998 an event to celebrate the twenty-seventh anniversary of Avándaro was jointly organized by OCESA and Armando Molina, one of the organizers of the Avándaro Festival in 1971. Promoted in *La Jornada* alongside a feature on the festival, the concerts took place in the Teatro Metropólitan and featured several bands who had performed at Avándaro, such as Los Dug Dug's and Peace and Love.[67] While these artists were no longer big names within the rock scene, and were thus of limited commercial value for OCESA, organizing this event served to place the company on the right side of (a conveniently written) history. As was common for the company, OCESA was named prominently in the headline for the *La Jornada* article promoting the events.

The company also found itself on the right side of history during several cases in which performances by high-profile acts came under threat by the authorities. Most notable was the series of Rolling Stones' concerts at the Autódromo Hermanos Rodríguez in January 1995, part of their Voodoo Lounge world tour. When the Mexico City government failed to grant the band a permit, OCESA and the Rolling Stones' manager wrote to the presidency threatening to cancel the band's visit, after which outgoing president Carlos Salinas de Gortari intervened to ensure that the concerts could go ahead.[68] In this situation, OCESA made the case that organizations such as theirs might no longer be able to acquire sufficient credit to organize such mass-scale concerts. Notable publicity coups came in the form of bands who had experienced censorship or were facing calls to be censored. Black Sabbath, for instance, had been denied permission in 1989 to play a concert in the city of León, Guanajuato, by the conservative PAN government in office there; OCESA invited Black Sabbath to play in the Auditorio Nacional in 1992. A concert given toward the end of the 1990s by satanic rock act Marilyn Manson in Palacio de los Deportes was heavily attacked by conservative groups including the Pro-Life Committee, which formally requested of the federal and city governments that Manson be expelled from the country on the basis of allegations of "profanation of religious and patriotic symbols." After the concert went ahead without incident, OCESA put out a statement boasting that Manson's concert had been *blanco*—harmless, "white."[69] These concerts, in different ways, allowed OCESA to assume the position of frontline protagonist, defending rock expression against attack.

Good relations with the rock press were not only useful for the construction of OCESA's public image; they were also vital during moments of criticism and controversy. OCESA's influence over the press was tested during incidents such as a concert featuring the Spanish ska band Ska-P, held in

Palacio de los Deportes in 2005. Before the concert, one journalist convinced the press team to allow him access to the press area with a camera, after promising not to take photos. Once inside the venue, however, this journalist reneged on this promise. During the concert, a thirteen-year-old girl attempted to climb over a security fence, tripped, and fell on her head, later dying of traumatic brain injuries. The photos this journalist subsequently published of disorder at the concert were potentially damaging to OCESA, not just in terms of public image but also in terms of legal liability. In response, the company portrayed the death as the consequence of individualized rule-breaking rather than a failure of security.[70] This journalist has since opted to cover OCESA-run events as a regular attendee rather than requesting a journalist's pass. The subsequent career trajectory of this journalist—who has built up a cult following by publishing independently on social media and in a blog—could be seen to illustrate the liberatory power of digital media; however, for newspaper writers, it is also likely to be read as a chilling example of OCESA's power over their livelihoods.

Conclusion: Privatization, Transition, Ideology

When speaking to me, a former worker at OCESA's press department defended its operations by alluding to a separation of private and public domains: since "we didn't have any legal powers to tell any newspaper what they could or could not publish," the worker asserted, these actions could not constitute censorship.[71] This premise was reiterated by one journalist otherwise critical of OCESA: "the organizer of an event has every right to decide who can enter and who can't." Nonetheless, they said, there was a caveat to this logic: the situation was different "if the key for entry has small print written on it."[72] The ambiguity of this statement indicates a broader struggle to articulate the cumulative, coercive modalities of OCESA's business operations, which have always resisted any positioning within a neat liberal separation of "private" and "public" spheres. OCESA's rise complexly extended the paternalistic, disciplinary state gaze; its commercial expansion was conditioned from the beginning by PRI politicians. A particular, snowballing characteristic of censorship may, here, be discerned: OCESA's actions toward the press, which many have taken to constitute censorship, were themselves provoked by the legacy of rock censorship under authoritarian rule.

This account of the rise of OCESA thus suggests several questions. To what extent could the efforts of a powerful business to safeguard its image by controlling press access to live rock be understood as censorship? In a context in which the boundaries between public policing and private security became blurred, to what extent could acts of violence by the latter be understood as "repression"? The comments of the OCESA worker immediately above would be absurd under single-party rule, in which political power was spread across a range of public and (nominally) private entities; therefore, they highlight how allusions to narratives of democratic transition could be used to contest and shape ideas about censorship. These comments can be seen to prefigure liberal democracy, in the sense of making it present or assuming its presence. From this perspective, whether OCESA is judged to exert censorship over the rock press is radically dependent on a broader judgment about whether Mexico's political system is, in fact, a liberal democracy. In turn, these questions point us toward OCESA's varied efforts to influence the intellectual life of the rock scene, through which the company sought to position itself as an agent of liberation.

Rhetoric around the rise of OCESA often risks a slippage in which commercial "opening" to live rock is connected to a broader sense of political "opening." Yet OCESA's rise speaks instead to the thoroughly ambivalent transition, experienced across Latin America, from authoritarian rule to neoliberal "securitized democracy," characterized by violence, expanding prison populations, blurred boundaries between public and private security, and the privatization of public spaces.[73] Both the failure of independent actors and the success of commercial ones to take advantage of privatization in Mexico City highlighted new conditions for mainstream commercial actors' inclusion of rock. These conditions derived simultaneously from the state and from the demands of commerce, and constituted, as I have argued in this section, a new process for the enclosure of rock. This process, however, was neither straightforward nor self-contained. Rather, as I go on to explore, it relied on crackdowns against rock elsewhere.

CHAPTER 4

On Solidarity and Silence

Music Censorship, Open-Air Performance, and Zapatismo

Rock and journalism come together in the image, broadcast on MTV as part of a 1996 short film entitled *Crónica de un alzamiento anunciado: El zapatismo y el rock en México*, of the lead singer of the band Café Tacuba in rural Chiapas holding a microphone. Before leaving for the autonomous Zapatista community of La Realidad, located in the Lacandon Jungle close to the border with Guatemala, Rubén Albarrán describes the efforts of a collective formed of rock musicians and students, called Serpiente Sobre Ruedas (Serpent on Wheels), to support the Indigenous communities of this region.[1] In the video, he explains that the collective will take "an industrial refrigerator, a sound system to bring music to the party, and a thirty-thousand-watt generator," as well as food, to La Realidad. All of this, he notes, has been collected due to a series of rock concerts organized by this organization in Mexico City. The film then cuts to a number of clips from these concerts, including an extended clip of a speech given by Roco Pachukote, the lead singer of Maldita Vecindad: "Unfortunately, most mainstream media don't give us the truth. Little or nothing is known about what's really happening in the Lacandon Jungle." These concerts fill in that gap; to make the point, the word *informar* (to inform) appears on the screen. The film doesn't tell us, however, about the precarious status of these concerts themselves; at this time, the Mexico City government had prohibited open-air rock.

The stories of censorship discussed in this chapter begin in 1994, with the uprising of the Zapatista Army of National Liberation (EZLN), a revolutionary army led by mestizo Marxist urbanites and populated mostly by Indigenous people speaking Tzotzil, Tzeltal, Chol, Tojolabal, and Zoque languages. When the Zapatistas rose up against the Mexican government in the state of Chiapas on January 1, 1994—the day that the North American Free Trade Agreement was due to come into effect—it was taken by many as a repudiation of neoliberalism in Mexico.[2] While the EZLN's military power was slight, they turned out to be effective communicators; after a ceasefire was declared, the EZLN began to court international civil society and established an enduring solidarity network in Mexico and around the world.[3] In the mid-1990s, Zapatismo—a term often used to denote the ideology and movement that emerged around the autonomous communities of Chiapas—became a symbol of resistance against neoliberal globalization and a source of inspiration for new, utopian thinking. The lasting cultural influence of Zapatismo within Mexico has much to do with the ties created at this time between the EZLN and the emerging rock boom.

The context of Zapatista solidarity solidified a trend that had been occurring since the mid-1980s. In the 1960s and 1970s, rock had tended to keep its distance from popular protest and the student movement. Now, however, within a context of increasingly radical politics, rock began to occupy the same spaces as the protest songs and *nueva canción* that had been sung on the Left since the student movement of the 1960s. From the mid-1980s, rock gained a foothold on the Comité Internacional de la Nueva Canción (International Committee of New Song), represented by the pianist, singer, and composer Guillermo Briseño and members of Café Tacuba and Maldita Vecindad y los Hijos del Quinto Patio.[4] Rock acts engaged in protest in response to several well-documented moments of crisis. The aftermath of the 1985 earthquake that left hundreds dead and thousands homeless in Mexico City is often understood as the moment in which rock musicians began to present themselves as part of "civil society," within a broader artistic response to both the earthquake and the government and media silence immediately following it.[5] Rock musicians also joined protests against the electoral fraud that denied leftist Cuauhtémoc Cárdenas the presidency in 1988.[6] In a less well-documented episode, rock was part of a Mexico City protest against the first Gulf War; the protest featured blues outfit Real de Catorce and goth rock act Santa Sabina.[7]

However, pro-Zapatista solidarity arguably provided something more: a context within which popular music could spearhead politics, rather than complement it. The significance of rock for Zapatismo was recognized in a speech given by Zapatista figurehead Subcomandante Marcos at a roundtable in 1999: "Of music, well, just do-re-mi-fa-sol-la-si and I get lost, but those of us in resistance are hyper-vigilant. The case is that Zapatismo and rock, they're getting up to something together [*algo se traen*]. . . . There was a meeting. There were words that crossed paths, but above all, there were and are feelings that crossed paths."[8] Like Zapatismo, rock began to be encountered as a practice within which radical political alternatives could be imagined; as a seedbed for new worlds. Further, the connections forged at this point were more than only affective and ideological. Rock and its sister genres were central to pro-Zapatista solidarity from an early stage. Mass-scale live rock concerts became the core format for pro-Zapatista demonstrations in Mexico City; and through this activity, direct logistical links were forged between rock and Zapatismo.

The Zapatista movement has also been repressed, especially as the government pivoted toward a model of low-intensity warfare in the late 1990s. Within Chiapas, Zapatistas and their allies have been subject to paramilitary attacks, most notably the Acteal massacre of 1997, which left a death toll of forty-five women, men, and children.[9] Repression against Zapatista-aligned groups also spilled over into other states: the Aguas Blancas massacre saw police murder seventeen farmers who were marching against the disappearance of a peasant activist.[10] It has also continued after democratic transition: both paramilitary and police violence has been implicated in the suppression of peaceful protests by Zapatista-aligned groups in Oaxaca in 2006, leading to an overall death toll of twenty-seven, and in the violent suppression of a popular protest movement sympathetic to the Zapatistas in San Salvador Atenco, Estado de México, in the same year.[11] Repression against the Zapatista movement also affected the cultural sphere, connecting in a complex way to a government prohibition against open-air concerts that singled out rock in particular and that was more explicitly stated than the prohibitions of the 1970s. Yet these histories are less often told than that of post-Avándaro repression; indeed, this episode goes unmentioned in a series of scholarly discussions of Mexican rock covering the 1990s.[12] In this chapter, I ask the question: why? For what reason have episodes of censorship of music relating to the Zapatista movement been discussed so little in histories of the genre? In responding to this question, I emphasize the unusual sense of closure pertaining to these episodes of censorship, due in part to the decisive victory of the PRD in the Mexico City election of 1997, and the incoming city government's decision not only to permit open-air rock but to actively promote it.

As with the previous chapter, I draw here on a variety of media sources, but retain a focus on the output of the newspaper *La Jornada*. This is for a number of reasons. The rock movement developed close ties to Zapatismo, but these ties were not always covered substantively within the specialized rock press. This was also a period of change: the magazine *Conecte* finally ceased publication in 1995. By contrast, *La Jornada* published the work of several journalists who became important chroniclers of the Zapatista movement, such as Hermann Bellinghausen. Finally, *La Jornada* was an increasingly popular site for independent, "civic-oriented" journalism, achieving the second-largest readership of any Mexico City newspaper in the 1990s.[13] For this reason, it was often used as a tool for communication by organizers of pro-Zapatista concerts, who wrote open letters to the publication as free publicity for their events or as a means of denouncing government repression against their activities.

Protest: Rock in (Civil) Society

Rock's massification in the 1990s was not only a question of its entering the cultural enclosures of transnational capital flows. Rock spilled out during this period into public spaces, transforming and claiming them for a revitalized middle-class youth movement. This environment provided Mexican rock bands such as Maldita Vecindad y los Hijos del Quinto Patio, Café Tacuba, Tijuana No!, Santa Sabina, and later Panteón Rococó with a new opportunity to demonstrate their ability to draw a mass audience. By the early 1990s, Mexican bands had already shown that they could sell out large venues—for instance with Caifanes' 1989 concert in the Auditorio Nacional, and Maldita Vecindad's performance in the same venue in 1992. A number of bands were signed to labels created for the Mexican market—especially Culebra Records, a subsidiary of BMG. The growth of Mexican rock was also rapidly accelerated by the peso crisis of 1994, which suddenly made concerts featuring international artists less profitable to stage and led Mexican bands to rise in influence within the live rock scene. In the middle of the decade, the largest venues in Mexico were comparatively inactive; Foro Sol was being constructed by OCESA, and Estadio Azteca featured no large-scale concerts between 1993 (Michael Jackson) and 1997 (Gloria Trevi). By the end of the decade, high-profile Mexican rock acts were routinely recording in the United States, many had recorded live sets for MTV Latino, and many were earning recognition in the newly established Latin Grammys.

Immediately after the Zapatista uprising, rock musicians were instrumental in establishing a movement of solidarity with the Zapatistas outside of

Chiapas. Myriad small-scale benefit concerts were held either to explicitly support the EZLN or to demand a peaceful resolution to conflict and the demilitarization of Chiapas. For example, one was organized in July 1994 by punks in the southeastern margins of Mexico City's metropolitan area at which attendees donated rice and soap for Zapatista communities.[14] These solidarity concerts were highly eclectic, as evidenced by the Festival por la Paz (Festival for Peace) held at the Ángel de la Independencia on February 20, 1995, which featured rockers Botellita de Jerez and Santa Sabina alongside blues singer Betsy Pecanins and folk singer Eugenia León, among others.[15]

This musical solidarity implied new patterns of travel. Many rockers, including members of groups signed to major labels, combined performances at solidarity events in the capital with trips to Chiapas on "caravans" visiting Zapatista autonomous territory.[16] By 1996, caravans were organized specifically for musicians to perform in Zapatista autonomous communities. *La Jornada*'s Hermann Bellinghausen dedicated roughly half of a feature on the Foro Americano contra el Neoliberalismo (American Forum against Neoliberalism), held in Zapatista heartlands in the Lacandon Jungle, to the perspectives and performances of musicians:

> Fully night, without traces of the sun or the moon, and to top it off, clouds of a very black-blue color. And suddenly, to the left of the ear, a stretched out Arabic rumbling and a fine, thin sound of the violin. In the distance, a small light and the silhouettes of a shadow that dance in rhythm. Also clapping, guitars, and a voice. Suddenly a sweet chorus. Around one single, solitary candle, a group of musicians use what they can to sound.[17]

Such accounts indicate the acoustic richness of these encounters; this occasion saw performances by the rock solidarity group Serpiente Sobre Ruedas alongside renditions of "Bella Ciao," the locally popular cumbia "La del moño colorado" (She with the colored ribbon), and traditional marimba music. Rock, the electrified urban genre par excellence, was placed into a rural context outside of the reach of electrical infrastructure, where acoustic music filled up long, dark nights.

Importantly, pro-Zapatista rock musicians recast the imperative to "communicate," in earlier times linked to a postpolitical dream of connection and unity, within an oppositional frame: rock performance itself was taken as a kind of journalism, correcting disinformation about the Chiapas conflict propagated by mainstream media.[18] Rock bands released music in solidarity with the Zapatista cause, such as Tijuana No!'s 1994 album *Transgresores de la ley* (an album ironically named after Carlos Salinas de Gortari's description of the Zapatista rebels in the first days of the uprising), and the acoustic ballad "Prohibido," written by Botellita de Jerez drummer and pro-Zapatista solidarity organizer Paco Barrios "El Mastuerzo" in the few days after the uprising.[19] Pro-Zapatista rockers also took advantage of their increasing media profile to spread awareness about the Zapatista movement. Live concerts sought to "break the media siege" (*romper el cerco mediático*) around the EZLN by interspersing readings of reports from Chiapas, which often contradicted the accounts provided by mainstream newspapers and broadcast media, with musical performances during live events. Reflecting later on rock's imbrication with Zapatismo, Barrios portrayed this conjuncture as a process of "politicization" for many of the newest (and mostly very young) stars of Mexican rock, indicating that pro-Zapatista solidarity events lent rock a renewed sense of purpose: "Art in the capitalist world isn't good for anything. It doesn't have any concrete utility. But we've discovered that thanks to all of those histories behind us, that the concrete utility is to place [art] there, where it's lacking, no?"[20]

One such "lack" was to emerge in Mexico City, just over a year after the Zapatista uprising. In February 1995 a free, open-air concert was organized in the Venustiano Carranza district of Mexico City. It featured the Mexican band Caifanes, by now a stadium rock act at the height of their fame—they had opened for the Rolling Stones in the previous year and had just released their hit single "Afuera." The song's lyrics are both claustrophobic and ambiguous, yet they are especially meaningful for a historical moment in which, as will be seen, open-air rock came under threat from the paternalistic government:

> Y uno cree que puede creer
> Y tener todo el poder
> Y de repente, no tienes nada
> Afuera, afuera tú no existes, solo adentro
> Afuera, afuera no te cuido, solo adentro
>
> And one believes they can believe
> And have all the power
> And suddenly, you have nothing
> Outside, outside you don't exist, only inside
> Outside, outside I don't take care of you, only inside

The Caifanes concert in Venustiano Carranza attracted an audience estimated at between seventy thousand and one hundred thousand, more than twice as large as the audience that the municipal government and the event's sponsor,

Grupo Radio Centro, had planned for. At the last minute, the organizers decided to head off this rush in attendance by starting the concert at eleven o'clock in the morning, an hour earlier than scheduled.[21] Having anticipated a smaller crowd, the municipal government did not provide adequate security and failed to close off nearby streets during the concert. During the performance, the crowd became restless, and some people began to push each other and throw drinks—which in many cases attendees had brought in themselves in glass bottles.[22] Riots then broke out; 200 riot police were then called in, creating a new target for the crowd's ire; small groups began to attack and throw stones at the police, and others attacked the sponsor's truck. The incident left 228 injured, including 21 police officers, and 195 were arrested.[23]

Blame for the riots was ascribed to several different groups: the authorities themselves, the public, the police, and the promoters. Some pointed the finger at the working-class *chavos banda*, or speculated that a rivalry between two gangs had provoked the violence. Others blamed the organizers for poor planning and underestimating the size of the crowd, or complained the police response was disproportionate and provoked greater violence and conflict. Meanwhile, the *delegado* of Venustiano Carranza, the PRD politician Raúl Torres Barrón, denied responsibility and suggested that the riots had been deliberately provoked by young PRI members in the crowd.[24]

In turn, the Mexico City regent, Óscar Espinosa Villareal, responded in draconian fashion.[25] Within a few days he had directed the delegates governing the capital's sixteen districts to cancel existing open-air concerts "and above all rock," and to no longer grant permits to "rock and mass-scale entertainment in the open air." Delegates were ordered to direct these events instead to "closed spaces which count on strong security measures," such as "metal detectors and more thorough body searches."[26] This de facto ban was to remain in force until the election of a new Mexico City government in 1997.[27] "We couldn't organize concerts in the Zócalo," one organizer told me, "nor at the Monumento a la Revolución, nor in any civic plaza in any district [*delegación*], we weren't allowed."[28]

This event and its aftermath rehearsed a pattern similar to that of the Avándaro festival and the government reaction to it in the 1970s: a live rock event associated (however falsely) with disturbances that justified subsequent prohibitions. As with Avándaro, this event was contested from the beginning, with blame shared between the authorities, the organizers, and the rock public itself. For one attendee, reflecting on the incident decades later, the problem was that "we couldn't handle the open space, the open air, period."[29] Many others within the rock scene denounced the incident as a setup, manufactured by the government as a pretext to censor rock: after all, as with Avándaro, it was the government that had permitted the event to go ahead to begin with. "People talk a lot about how, in some way, it was a provocation," Rafael González, a writer and member of Botellita de Jerez, told me that "there were agents provocateurs at the concert. And then there was repression, and it came to blows."[30] Similarly, for Poncho Figueroa, from the band Santa Sabina, the concert was "provoked, in order to cause violence, and then lead to a prohibition."[31] Writing in *La Jornada* just after the ban came into force, the band Maldita Vecindad described it as "Díaz-Ordaz-ist," as "a sad corollary to the symbolic visit of the Rolling Stones" that had taken place in 1994. Channeling the Beastie Boys, they wrote that without a "right to party," there would be no "true democratic opening."[32]

Rock, Zapatismo, Securitization

While the alliance (or "getting up to something," as Subcomandante Marcos had put it) between Zapatismo and rock predated the Caifanes concert in Venustiano Carranza, it grew enormously in response to the ban against rock. Batallón de Corazones Rotos (Battalion of Broken Hearts), made up of a broad base of musicians, artists, and students from the National Autonomous University of Mexico (UNAM), formed from among those who had traveled to Chiapas in solidarity caravans. In 1995, in the wake of the prohibition, this collective began to organize pro-Zapatista solidarity concerts in Mexico City. In 1995 and 1996, concerts were also organized by Serpiente Sobre Ruedas, which was made up almost exclusively of musicians. These concerts generally took place on sites nominally outside of government control, such as the UNAM campus, which has its own independent security force. For instance, events were held in the university's sports arena in late February and late May 1995, in support of "peace and dialogue in Chiapas, and the withdrawal of federal troops from the region."[33] This rapid mobilization in response to the prohibition was described to me by Botellita de Jerez percussionist Rafael González: "The governor of the city, Espinoza Villareal, bans open-air concerts in Mexico City and we responded one week later, organizing the Concert for Peace and Tolerance, to support the Zapatista communities with food and money. It was obviously a challenge to the governor, and it happened in an autonomous zone, UNAM, where the police couldn't operate."[34]

The first of these concerts attracted a crowd of fifteen thousand and raised one hundred million pesos for displaced Indigenous communities in Chiapas.

For the second, organizers also requested that food be donated; subsequent concerts also collected clothes and staple foods for Chiapanecan Indigenous communities. These concerts were economically accessible—organizers either charged a nominal fee or raised funds by *boteo*, the equivalent of passing around a hat.

Pro-Zapatista solidarity actions also provided a pretext for rockers to occupy public spaces officially denied to them. For instance, in March 1995 a cultural event was held in the Mexico City Zócalo as a send-off for a caravan leaving for Chiapas; this came after two weeks in which Zapatista solidarity activists and representatives of Indigenous communities from Chiapas had occupied the Zócalo. While the event featured rock acts such as Tijuana No! and Botellita de Jerez, it was advertised in a letter to *La Jornada* as an "interdisciplinary artistic" event, with no mention made of rock.[35] Open-air rock continued at protests of various kinds, marches organized by the center-left Party of the Democratic Revolution, and generally at any event in which the control of the authorities over public space was temporarily suspended. These attempts to smuggle rock into public spaces are evident in letters by rockers to *La Jornada* that dropped unconfirmed hints that live music would be performed: one signed by Botellita de Jerez, Nina Galindo, Los de Abajo, Maldita Vecindad, and several others before the 1995 May Day parade called for readers to show up "at 10 in the morning on the first of May by the Vips [a chain of restaurants] at the Ángel [de la Independencia], with drums, whistles, and flutes."[36]

Thus, one result of the 1995 prohibition was that the interests of the rock movement and Zapatismo became increasingly entangled. Pro-Zapatista rock events were openly described by organizers as efforts to intertwine solidarity with the EZLN, opposition to the militarization of Chiapas, and material support for Indigenous groups displaced by the conflict with efforts to reclaim public spaces for rockers in Mexico City. Adriana Díaz Enciso, a writer and confidante of Santa Sabina's lead singer Rita Guerrero, wrote in *La Jornada* that the concert held at the end of February had

> two fundamental objectives. One was responding to the recent ban on the Department of the Federal District to perform open-air concerts in Mexico City. . . . Although we have no evidence that the incident was the result of provocation, the ban on concerts we do understand as such: now more than ever, in the context of the pain and uncertainty that unfortunately we Mexicans live, it is necessary to conserve the spaces of civil society. . . . We demonstrated the idiocy of the already out-of-date prejudice that rock concerts are a terrain

for violence. The other objective of the festival, by no means lesser in importance, was to make an urgent call for peace; to inform young people about the conflict in Chiapas, and to collect food for the displaced who are now in the Lacandon Jungle.[37]

As one journalist who had participated in these events later wrote, the Zapatista ideals of self-management, self-financing, and autonomy were vital for the rock movement at this time; since concerts in public spaces received no support from businesses, "following the Zapatista principle of not needing the 'supreme government' or any other authority (label, management, etc.)" became especially important.[38]

As Díaz Enciso's allusion to "civil society" suggests, demonstrating that pro-Zapatista rock events were "civil" was a priority for organizers. One band stated that Doce Serpiente was intended both to inform the public about the conflict in Chiapas and to "demand of the authorities the right of alternative and civil artistic groups to freedom of expression." This choice of language reflects the long-standing premise that the freedom to perform rock was conditional, that the genre could legitimately be repressed if rock audiences were not sufficiently well-behaved. Equally, by engaging with activism understood as part of "civil society," rock was connected to an important episteme within neoliberalizing Mexico. Since President Carlos Salinas de Gortari (1988–1994) chose to accommodate neoliberal ideology with Mexico's nationalistic ideological past in his rhetoric, he did not challenge the notion of "society" and advocate an individualizing process, as had other neoliberal leaders.[39] Rather, the privatizing impulse of the neoliberal project was glossed as giving "autonomy to civil society," which would lend renewed dynamism to Mexican democracy and the nation-building project.[40] Civil society—a term that could index both the public sphere at large and the *sociedades civiles*, some of which were formerly publicly owned venues that had now been privatized—thus came to prominence as an officially sanctioned space for dissent.[41] Civil society became central to Salinas de Gortari's pitch for neoliberal reforms and his understanding of democratization as a cultural phenomenon, rather than as a process of purely institutional change.[42]

Organizers of pro-Zapatista events frequently described them as "civil," "cultural," "artistic," and part of civil society. They also sought to demonstrate "civility" in other ways. First, they spoke to the press in detail about the security measures in place at their events. Security at the UNAM solidarity event in late May, for instance, was managed by a group of four hundred student volunteers, although the organizers also requested support from UNAM's autonomous security forces. They took care to publicize, in the wake of the events, the fact that they had taken place without incident, and they also challenged the ways that security took place at rock concerts elsewhere.[43] For instance, Díaz Enciso highlighted that at the February 28 concert they had taken "preventative" rather than "repressive" security measures, and "shared responsibility for keeping order among organizers and audience"; this showed that "the youth can meet to listen to their music in a peaceful, tolerant atmosphere."[44]

Organizers also managed a certain rhetorical distance from the EZLN. While the funds and goods collected for distribution in Chiapas could arrive at Zapatista communities, and musicians, speakers, and audience members openly supported the EZLN at live events, the material beneficiaries of donations were generally described as "communities," a term often used to denote Indigenous communities in general. Organizers and musicians often framed events with language that hinted at sympathy and support for the EZLN while allowing participants to avoid explicitly endorsing an armed insurrection during a time of government repression. Guillermo Briseño, founder of Serpiente Sobre Ruedas, made this point explicit in an interview given to MTV for *Crónica de un alzamiento anunciado*: "I think that one of the dangers is that they blame us for supporting an armed organization. We're not doing that, we're supporting the communities." Disagreement about open support for the EZLN was at the root of the creation in April 1997 of a splinter group, La Bola, formed of musicians who wished to express more explicit support for the EZLN and Zapatismo.[45]

Distancing pro-Zapatista solidarity concerts from the specter of violent disturbances was not straightforward. The massification of live rock helped to normalize a live music institution directly imported from the *chavos banda* and punk: the "slam" (in some other contexts known as a mosh pit), an ostensibly violent form of dancing in which audience members jump forcefully into one another en masse. The slam, especially associated with ska, was a topic of journalistic intrigue and excitement; it occasionally made it into headlines in unapologetic—and indeed openly celebratory—ways.[46] Writers from different groups wrestled over the slam's origins, and the concomitant right to speak about what it meant and how to perform it. Although it originated in the United States, where people's right to enjoy live rock was far more secure, in Mexico the slam emerged as a challenge to the authority of security personnel at live events. Celebrations of the slam dovetailed with rejections of privatized security, such as at one concert in which Argentine ska act Los Fabulosos Cadillacs reportedly threatened to end the concert if the security presence did not leave: "Here we don't need guards, if one person dies, we all die."[47] This approach subverted the common concern that the slam could be used as a pretext for shutting down rock altogether on grounds of security.

Journalists' open celebrations of the slam thus allowed the practice to be positioned as mere catharsis—a mirage of violence, rather than its actuality. The representatives of pro-Zapatista solidarity concerts collaborated, in their reporting on these events, in this public repositioning of the slam's subversive body politics, on occasion linking the shared bodily autonomy of the slam to a broader right to public space within the capital:

> The concert ended with a *palomazo* [jam], in which the participating musicians interpreted their version of "Give Peace a Chance" by Lennon, sung by thousands of young people still in high spirits, after eight hours of concert and slam, who trust that their desire for peace will not be betrayed, nor their desire for your donation to reach the heart of the Lacandon [Jungle], nor their right to legitimately defend their spaces.[48]

Pro-Zapatista solidarity concerts thus challenged received modalities of providing security for live events; this challenge took place at the intersection of a comparatively novel form of body politics, the right to the city, and a broader struggle for new freedoms of expression across multiple spheres.

Finally, this challenge was not only against the state, but also against a broader disciplinary governmentality practiced in many institutions. Pro-Zapatista activists also struggled against the governance of the UNAM campus where most of their events were held. An early report on Doce Serpiente in May 1995 emphasized ongoing obstacles to free expression that existed on the campus. For instance, the report noted that that the university's facilities were being offered to foreign artists over Mexican ones and that one musician, Jorge Reyes, had made multiple unsuccessful attempts to perform at the university's Sala Nezahualcóyotl.[49] As time went on, pro-Zapatista concerts increasingly came into conflict with the university authorities; on multiple occasions, organizers of Zapatista or Chiapas solidarity concerts were suspended. The highest-profile case is from June 1997, when the student organizer Inti Muñoz was suspended after university authorities alleged—apparently falsely—that he had broken a door to enter a university theater in order to hold a fundraising concert for Indigenous communities in Chiapas. Muñoz's suspension turned into a public controversy that played out in the Letters pages of *La Jornada*: one of the student activist's professors wrote to the newspaper to state that the student had been on the other side of the city just half an hour before the alleged vandalism took place.⁵⁰ The case was taken to a federal court, where a judge ordered the suspension be lifted.⁵¹ Muñoz's case is particularly relevant since, like several others, he went from organizing activist events to creating cultural policy within the Mexico City government. As I explore in the following section, this career trajectory—shared by many activists—is key for understanding why and through what means the prohibition against open-air rock was lifted.

After Prohibition

Taken in the context of the previous chapter, it is difficult not to see OCESA as a beneficiary of the prohibition of open-air rock. The state crackdown had unintended consequences: it encouraged the development of a mass-scale, self-organized domestic rock movement and made evident the limits of government control in Mexico City. Equally, over time it forced rock into the enclosures of the commercial entertainment sector and restricted the scope of "legitimate" organization of live rock. In the present, this history is often taken for granted, as if rockers' defiance of official prohibition was somehow inevitable, but the artists who organized open-air, pro-Zapatista solidarity concerts did so out of conviction and in the face of dissuasion from the industry figures around them. Artists' labels and managers often strongly opposed their participation; some of the bands that chose not to participate, on the other hand, were bemused by the solidarity concerts and sometimes privately ridiculed them. Further, the bands that did participate were not always united in doing so; members of some bands either refused to play or insisted on payment.⁵²

The prohibition against open-air, free rock concerts lasted for more than two years, until the first democratic elections to decide the Mexico City government took place in 1997. As part of its attempt to court the expanding youth vote, the PRD, which eventually won the election, organized a series of rallies on the UNAM campus at which pro-Zapatista rock bands, such as Santa Sabina, also performed.⁵³ After the campaign, the PRD-affiliated cultural figurehead and crime writer Paco Ignacio Taibo II described rock as a linchpin of "cultural revolution" amid predictions that rock would be promoted by "the PRD cultural force."⁵⁴ For their part, rockers such as Roco Pachukote of Maldita Vecindad praised the PRD for the importance they were giving to culture.⁵⁵ PRD promised a festival in December 1997 to mark the inauguration of the PRD administration, "where rock will sound in [public park] La Alameda"—including Santa Sabina, Juguete Rabioso, and Maldita Vecindad—"and rumba at the Palacio de Bellas Artes [Palace of Fine Arts]."[56] Other organizers within the rock scene sought to lay claim to public spaces independently of political support. Paco Barrios "El Mastuerzo" organized a street festival featuring four hundred performers in seven locations across the capital, aiming to "reclaim the Mexican, popular, cultural fiesta [and to] reclaim the street all night, every night," and Serpiente Sobre Ruedas organized an open-air concert in the forest of Milpa Alta, to the southeast of the city.[57] Rockers also took advantage of the meetings held with Taibo to make demands. For instance, Santa Sabina bassist Poncho Figueroa demanded an end to "the law that you can't hold open-air concerts in the city." Maldita Vecindad drummer José Luis Paredes Pacho went further: he demanded an end to closures of "independent forums for theatre, dance, and rock," an easing of the process by which these spaces could gain licenses to operate, an end to cancellations of concerts in public spaces, and a cessation of "harassment, censorship, and repression against non-aligned culture."[58]

Although many cultural figures on the Left were left disappointed at the ideological emptiness of the PRD's cultural policies, the new PRD administration did remove the prohibition on open-air rock.[59] The incoming regime's most direct response to the prohibition came in 1998, when the newly created Institute of Culture established a program titled *La calle es de todos* (The street belongs to everyone) that sponsored concerts in public spaces across Mexico City, including in its Zócalo. While *La calle es de todos* had a wide remit that extended to popular music in general, it brought several high-profile Mexican rock acts to perform in free concerts at the Zócalo, such as stalwarts of pro-Zapatista solidarity concerts Maldita Vecindad, Panteón Rococó, and Santa Sabina. *La calle es de todos* was followed by a similar program entitled DFiesta, and the rock and "world music" concert series Radical Mestizo, both supported by the next PRD government elected in Mexico City.[60] These programs served to bring pro-Zapatista audiences and artists into a relationship with the state.

Live rock also expanded to other spheres in the wake of the PRD's victory. The emergence of a rock festival economy in Mexico, symbolized by the creation of Vive Latino in 1998 by OCESA, has often been attributed to the pro-Zapatista concerts of the mid-1990s. For some, these concerts paved the way for the later commercial festivals at the end of the 1990s by demonstrating that "it was possible to hold festivals of Mexican bands" and that this could be done safely "when security was in the hands of the youth themselves."[61] It is often claimed that Vive Latino adapted the model for large live rock events developed by pro-Zapatista activists through the 1990s.[62] Further, sizable activist events certainly helped, by demonstrating both that a demand for live rock existed and that domestic acts could fulfill it.[63] Equally, a more direct organizational connection between pro-Zapatista solidarity events and Vive Latino is often drawn: the creator of the festival, Jordi Puig, had close ties to the activists that organized pro-Zapatista rock concerts. He was advised by members of La Bola, such as Santa Sabina singer Rita Guerrero, about how to run live festivals, and later credited pro-Zapatista activist events as the inspiration for Vive Latino.[64] It is evident that much of the practical knowledge behind Vive Latino was drawn from the Zapatista solidarity movement—even if in a broader sense OCESA's business model drew from the commercial practices of the wider *rock en español* movement.[65]

The influence of pro-Zapatista solidarity concerts may have had its most lasting influence on the approach to security for open-air concerts. The activists who volunteered to police these concerts demonstrated the possibility of a more consensual and less physically violent model for security at live events, in which audiences as well as artists deserved protection. This consensual policing culture was adopted after 1997 in the new government-sponsored live events. The manager of Maldita Vecindad recalled, for instance, that in the late 1990s the band collaborated with a member of Seguridad Lobo to draw up a new manual for policing, and held extensive meetings with police in advance of an open-air performance in Mexico City's Zócalo: "We had meetings for a whole week with police forces, where we presented to the police of Mexico City a security manual that was well-thought-out, designed by the musicians of Maldita Vecindad so that they could contain the crowd. Yes, we are going to play, but we can't accept the idea that there on the corner [the police] are going to be beating up the kids, right?" Security personnel in the present day, they said, "have a completely different attitude, that their obligation is not only with the artist but with the people."[66]

By the same token, reactions to those security problems that did occur indicated journalism's role in reflecting and helping to form these new attitudes toward security. An especially energetic slam pit and a heatwave at a 2002 Maldita Vecindad concert in the Zócalo, given as part of the Festival del Centro Histórico de la Ciudad de México, left two injured and eighteen with heatstroke.[67] Some attendees also threw projectiles at Los Locos del Barrio, who "had the bad idea to open their set with salsa"; some created bonfires with lecture notes; and some pressured female audience members to expose themselves.[68] Yet the event provoked no political recriminations and little media outrage; indeed, voices from the rock scene responded by challenging the disciplinary logic that had long justified repression. For example, the editor of *La mosca en la pared*, Hugo García Michel, wrote: "It's not rock's fault. ... The *banda*—as some like to call the uncontrolled mass—tends to go crazy when they're together and feel untouchable [*impune*]. It's obvious that not everyone who went to see these groups took part in vandalism. In fact, this is a minority, that minority which always takes advantage of mass meetings to shelter in anonymity and cause problems." As García Michel pointed out, the same behavior took place at protests and football matches; rock itself "doesn't have anything directly to do with it."[69]

Interventions such as this one allow us some insight into a point of curiosity: Why did security at open-air live events become more consensual and less violently repressive during a time when the slam, ostensibly an act of shared violence among a subset of fans, was so widespread? This change can be attributed to a more professionalized security culture, aided by interventions by increasingly powerful artists to protect the rock public, such as that carried out by Maldita Vecindad. Further, as pointed out in the previous chapter, privatization of security was associated with an epistemological sleight of hand in which violent acts on the part of security guards were less likely to be included in narratives about "repression." Yet it is also worth drawing attention to how journalists contested the slam's association with violence, arguing that its body politics was understood as "harmless" catharsis rather than a threat to public safety, and how they increasingly challenged and subverted more general associations between rock and violence. Relief from repression was not only earned by artists and fans: it was also written.

Silencing Censorship

What accounts for the comparative forgetfulness about the two episodes of censorship discussed in this chapter? The prohibition of open-air rock from early 1995 to late 1997 is not entirely forgotten—it is mentioned, for instance, in documentaries about Mexican rock, including *Break It All*. However, it has failed to reach the canonical status of post-Avándaro repression, and it is often remembered hazily by those who lived through it. During my conversations with participants in the 1990s rock scene, there was a consensus that this was an unusually vibrant, exciting period to be a rock musician, and that contemporary coverage in sympathetic newspapers and magazines captured only a small part of this rich experience. However, the details were often murkily recalled. Few seemed to be sure about how long the official prohibition had lasted or when it was lifted. My conclusion that the prohibition of open-air rock lasted until the election of the PRD is drawn from contemporary press coverage.

One answer to this question is about power: the Zapatista solidarity movement has diminished in reach over time.[70] Yet this story of prohibition also shows that stories of censorship fall out of favor when they cease to perform work in the present. There are several interconnected reasons that the prohibitionism of the mid-1990s is remembered so little: rockers worked to make prohibition irrelevant, this story of prohibition reached a conclusion comparatively quickly, and its consequences have often been viewed positively. Many understand the prohibition of open-air rock to have contributed to, rather than curtailed, rock's effervescence in the 1990s, provoking increased, purposeful collective action. Further, this prohibition disappeared through the ballot box, in a way that affirmed the legitimacy of democratic transition. The PRD maintained power in Mexico City until 2015, when it was replaced by another center-left party, Morena. Much as it stands as compelling evidence of PRI repression, commemorations of 1990s-era prohibition do not take place because they do not need to: no contemporary group benefits from commemorating them.

The stories told in this chapter and the previous one fit together: the expansion of an enclosed, corporate-sponsored scene occurred in conjunction with repression against rock in public spaces. This, in turn, can clarify why OCESA's business practices attracted such controversy in the 1990s. After all, the set of practices through which live music was commoditized were not novel; *portazos*, through which the enclosure of live music was undone, were also frequent occurrences in the 1970s and the 1980s. OCESA's privatization of live rock was criticized partly because it was supported so transparently by the single-party regime. But it was also criticized because a utopian counterpoint had newly emerged in the form of performances at protests and occupations of stadiums, where engagement with the Zapatista movement inspired participants to imagine radical alternatives to the historically closed, mainstream account of democratic transition and other ways of organizing live rock.

CHAPTER 5

Listening Down the Rabbit Hole

Independent Music Venues, Democratic Governance, and the Performance of Transition

In 2009, independent hip-hop artist Akil Ammar was hired by the newspaper *El Universal* to make a series of videos based on brief topical raps; the videos were then uploaded onto the newspaper's website under the title "Reversos." These videos were highly political; many launched direct attacks on mainstream figures in Mexican public life, alleging systemic collusion between politics and organized crime, and denouncing government repression and the influence of the Catholic Church over politics. They also aired deep cynicism about the country's political system, to the point of implying disengagement with electoral democracy: for instance, one described Mexico's political system as "Only smokescreens / Honest? Nobody / That's why at the ballot box, my vote is null."

Akil Ammar made frequent reference to one topic, specific to the music scene in Mexico City. On June 20, 2008, the capital police, under the orders of the government of the Federal District, had launched a raid against New's Divine, a small nightclub in the city's northernmost district, Gustavo A. Madero, that tended to attract a young clientele. Carried out under the pretext of stopping underage drinking and drug use, the raid ended in disaster. It left 13 dead and 16 injured, after the police blocked the venue's only exit, trapping a large group of attendees in the venue's narrow entrance, causing many to be crushed and asphyxiated.[1] Many of those who died were minors. In the aftermath of the atrocity, evidence accumulated of police

[113]

brutality and sexual violence against attendees. The situation was worsened by a situation of impunity in which the intellectual authors of the massacre had been allowed free, while the only person prosecuted was the venue's owner, for the crime of "corruption of minors." "Almost one year from 'Divine,' and where are the homicide charges?" sang Akil Ammar in one "Reversos" video.

One year after the tragedy, Akil Ammar's decision to base a "Reversos" video on the New's Divine atrocity led to the whole series being scrapped. A track entitled "20 Junio 2008," which had already appeared on *Requiem*, his album of the same year, discussed the atrocity in detail, based on witness testimony given by survivors. This track went beyond a general condemnation of the events: it pointed the finger at Marcelo Ebrard, then the head of the city government (and now a candidate in the race to represent Morena in the 2024 elections). In May 2008 Ebrard had created by decree the police and judicial forces that perpetrated the attack. The fact that the song accused Ebrard directly was, the rapper felt, one step too far for *El Universal*: "I sent it, like any other week, to the newspaper. And I was waiting to see it published the following day. And they didn't publish it, obviously. They didn't publish it, and they told me that there ended my participation in the newspaper, too. So I obviously didn't want to know anything more from them. It's the only time that I've been censored for something I've said."[2]

The rapper subsequently uploaded the video onto his personal YouTube page, where it has accumulated almost ninety thousand views to date.[3] The most viewed version of the video, however, was uploaded the following day under a separate YouTube account, with the title "'Reverso' censored by El Universal 17/06/09."[4]

Akil Ammar understood the suppression of this video as a missed opportunity to communicate beyond a regular hip-hop audience. In fact, the New's Divine tragedy continues to be common knowledge within the Mexico City independent music scene in which Akil Ammar frequently performs, and comparatively uncommon knowledge outside it—including within the academic world, where it has barely been discussed at all. Raising awareness of the atrocity was only half of the challenge. After the New's Divine deaths, the capital government and most of the press engaged in a shared act of brazen victim-blaming, spreading false allegations that the victims had been heavily intoxicated and had provoked a stampede. The account of police repression that subsequently emerged came from testimonies of survivors of the attack; it is still common to hear people blame the tragedy on those attending rather than on the police who caused it. Perhaps it is no surprise, therefore, that not all viewers of the video agreed that its suppression did, indeed, constitute censorship. For one YouTube commenter, accusing Ebrard directly "would not be wrong if Akil Ammar could support his accusations. . . . Akil Ammar is followed by many young people, most of them even minors and easily manipulated. This is a great responsibility, this man should be better informed to be able to communicate it, since he is not a journalist."[5]

The raid was, nevertheless, disastrous for the relationships between music venues and the city government controlled by the PRD, which had long depicted itself as the party of freedom of expression, and of youth culture. Yet for many venues in the independent rock scene in Mexico City, the New's Divine raid constituted a particularly violent instance of less remarkable forms of repression that they experienced on a daily basis. The New's Divine tragedy simply peeled back the facade of PRD tolerance, showing that questions continued under electoral democracy relating to the repression of youth subcultures; the expressive freedom promised by transition remained elusive. Akil Ammar's struggle to draw wider attention to the experiences of the victims was also indicative of the dangers of being voiceless. It pointed toward wider musical and journalistic practices of generating voice that have served to protect venues against police abuse and venue closures. And it raised questions about the trajectory of censorship under democratic rule in the city. Could democratization in Mexico City be contained within a narrative of straightforwardly expanding expressive freedoms? Or was this process messier than depicted in official rhetoric? If the latter, how could repression within transition be understood?

In this chapter, I explore the experiences of the venues often termed *foros culturales*—small and midsize venues dedicated to original music, generally with a capacity not over four hundred. These venues typically guard an identity fiercely opposed to the mainstream cultural industries and tend to organize around a set of principles known as *autogestión* (self-management).[6] The chapter is based on ethnographic research carried out between 2018 and 2022 in nine such venues, most of which are (or were) located in and around the center of Mexico City. Moments of violent, state-initiated censorship such as the New's Divine tragedy, I emphasize, are not the norm; *foros culturales* experience ongoing, everyday, grinding repression that condition the cultural labor undertaken in these spaces. The banality of these experiences of repression means that narrating it as censorship is an ongoing affective and aesthetic challenge. I finally seek, therefore, to show the ways that links between these two trajectories of censorship—the spectacular and apparent versus the everyday and insidious—are performed within these venues. Distinct kinds of performance, I argue, serve as a layer of protection against local repression and censorship.

Organizing Scene

Perhaps the most prestigious independent venue in Mexico City's rock scene in recent years is called Multiforo Cultural Alicia. A self-managed space (*espacio autogestivo*) operating since 1995, "El Alicia" has been closed down by the authorities on at least twenty-four occasions, often ostensibly on public health grounds; the authorities also targeted it in more violent ways.[7] Multiforo Cultural Alicia has, in turn, been featured repeatedly in the press, especially during or after closures, partly due to its status as a hub for music journalism; it has also been celebrated in multiple books and featured in documentaries.[8] When, in 2023, the venue finally decided to close the doors on the small venue in Mexico City's Roma district it had always called home, it was a major cultural event that made national and international news.[9] The venue's reopening in March 2024, in a larger premises in the Santa María La Ribera district of the capital, was also widely reported in the national press.[10]

Censorship serves as a key motif for those visiting El Alicia. As with many centers for activism in Mexico, this is a ramshackle, vibrant space, every inch painted in vivid colors. The venue gained particular fame for the distinctive posters that adorn its walls. These posters bear the venue's logo, which depicts the grinning Cheshire cat from Lewis Carroll's *Alice in Wonderland*, indicative of the epistemological challenge effected as one enters this space: we are provoked to reimagine the world we have left behind as oppressive and tyrannical, and consider this new terrain as a refuge for expressive freedom.[11] Multiforo Cultural Alicia's ramshackle decor is presented as a gateway to the Other. In block capitals and bold primary colors, its posters continuously depict the space as under threat. This threat often emanates from the state: "No more closures, respect independent cultural spaces," reads one poster; another, "No to VAT on culture," and another, "We're not criminals, we are cultural spaces." Equally, oppositionality is here broadly drawn. Many posters contain the phrase "culture against power," in small letters in the corner, and they are just as likely to denounce misogynistic violence ("Inoculate yourself against violence against women and girls," "Abortion is a woman's choice only") as they are to condemn OCESA's market dominance ("No to monopolies"). Multiforo Cultural Alicia was created as an explicitly anarchist project, and some posters cite the Italian revolutionary anarchist Errico Malatesta and the Mexican journalist Ricardo Flores Magón, a figurehead for anarchism in Mexico. One Malatesta quote featured on a poster, for instance, read: "I embrace you, to not lose myself in the rancor of a broken country."

The latter phrase, in particular, can be taken as a synecdoche for the *escena*

FIGURE 1. Graffiti in Multiforo Cultural Alicia's original venue (now closed), located in the Roma Norte district of Mexico City. Photograph taken by the author in May 2019.

independiente more widely; as in many subcultures, identification is here predicated on resistance and the suspension of exterior injustice. The posters present Multiforo Cultural Alicia as a "lettered" venue: the written word, presented in austere, minimalist, block font, dominates over the image.[12] Visitors are almost as likely to encounter a book presentation, poetry reading, or seminar in Multiforo Cultural Alicia as a concert. The diversity of cultural offerings of a space such as this one—the multi- in *multiforo*—is, it might be said, contained and channeled by an ever-present narrative of externalized repression. The unavoidable allusions to threats of censorship one witnesses when entering Multiforo Cultural Alicia perform multiple roles—including holding together a sense of scene.

At the same time, I experienced a more mundane side to Multiforo Cultural Alicia upon my first visit to the venue in 2018: it was old. A part of the ceiling was missing, covered over with an often-dripping tarpaulin. Repairs to the building were constantly put off due to lack of funds. It was run by a tight-knit group who believed in the project, but they all received low pay. Even its founder and owner, Ignacio Pineda, was poorly remunerated and worked long, grueling hours; among other forms of labor, he cultivated a large following on Facebook, where he continuously promoted the venue's events.

Playing Multiforo Cultural Alicia has always attracted a great deal of prestige for artists. The venue is valued as a stepping stone toward success, an important line on an act's CV. It has also been praised as "the quintessence of the independent and self-managed scene."[13] Multiforo Cultural Alicia has long been held up as a model to follow among those running other *foros culturales*, especially because of the tenacity and perseverance of those running it, and to the organizational model of self-management (*autogestión*) it was seen to follow. In presenting independence as austere self-sufficiency, Multiforo Cultural Alicia is accompanied by the majority of *foros culturales* in Mexico City, which live an economically precarious existence. Often unprofitable, such small and midsize venues are nonetheless vital: as in many other live music scenes, they provide a vital first step for growing artists.[14] Economic precarity breeds legal precarity: *foros* are often threatened with closure by representatives of local governments, but they also struggle to make enough money for the repairs and equipment needed to comply with regulations.[15] Especially when based in its now-defunct Roma venue, Multiforo Cultural Alicia was occasionally attacked for precisely this reason: some critics derided its radical self-positioning as a cynical ploy to evade compliance with health and safety legislation.[16]

Yet the organizational practices and attendant ideological trappings of venues like El Alicia did not emerge in a vacuum, as the result of abstract, nongrounded choice. Rather, their organizational practices and aesthetic posture respond to a context marked by corruption, extortion, and violence. Most *foros culturales* have been closed down by local governments or INVEA (Institute of Administrative Verification) on multiple occasions, often too numerous to count. Inspectors often make threats of closure as a means of extorting bribes. Extortion is a systemic occurrence; in 2015 allegations surfaced of an organized network of corruption in the municipality of Cuauhtémoc, through which PRD functionaries were receiving bribes totaling 7 million pesos (around US$285,000) each month in exchange for permits, including 2 million per month (around US$82,000) from restaurants, hotels, bars, and shops.[17] Owners of *foros culturales* often felt that such corruption was facilitated by inflexible licensing laws that constantly presented inspectors with pretexts to close venues. One respondent described this extortion to me as follows:

> I mean, if the people coming to check you are really trying to help you, they'll say, "Hey friend, you're missing this license, you have until December to present one." You say to yourself, ah well, that guy came, but he told me. And there are others who can arrive and tell you, "You know what, friend, if you don't give me [the license] by tomorrow, you're getting closed." You know they won't give you [the license] from one day to the next. What does he want you to understand from that? That you have to "arrange" it directly with them.[18]

The best response, this respondent told me, was to prepare administratively as best as possible, "fight your corner" when inspectors arrived, and accept at face value threats of closure.

Venue closures were also associated with local elections: incoming administrations would trigger waves of closures as new personnel either found paperwork anomalies or sought to impose their authority. Elections were therefore often experienced as destabilizing events that created possibilities for corruption. *Foros culturales* were also affected by a generalized context of insecurity that manifested in several different ways: organized crime ran extortion rackets, and business owners perceived to be rich often felt threatened by kidnapping or burglary. *Foros culturales* tend to balk at promoting reggaetón, for example, but one venue, located in an insecure and poor part of Mexico City, made an agreement with local young people to hold a reggaetón event once per month, explicitly to avoid trouble from criminal elements within the community.

At the confluence of these factors exist the organizational practices of these spaces themselves. Often, these practices are as horizontal as permitted within the law, especially in assigning property ownership. The founder of one space told me that "we are all owners. . . . [The venue] belongs to whoever makes it theirs. You turn up, and you want to paint a mural here, and you want to put music on, the space is yours, that's what it's for." *Foros culturales* present as spaces for shared creative ownership, rather than spaces ordered by hierarchical curation. Equally, many *foros* eschew hierarchical organization in which decisions are taken by a small number of leaders (such as managers or owners). As far as is practically possible, decision-making is decentralized into cooperatives usually comprising the venue's workers. One venue told me they had no defined manager (*encargado*, literally "person in charge"), but that "we all manage as equals. And when there's something [to decide] we have a general meeting and ask for the opinion of everyone. Why? Because that's important to us."

Often, but not always, these organizational practices are understood as expressions of *autogestión*—a term often linked to the politics of autonomy, anarchist praxis, and the Zapatista movement. The founder of one *foro*, based in one of the capital's richest districts, described *autogestión* as "our ethics, our philosophy.... We have a punk ethics, do-it-yourself, take control of your life and not wait for the future, or for revolution, to be happy. It's our revolution, our happiness, our liberated world has to be built right now." In practice, this meant rejecting interest from "entrepreneurs who aren't part of the scene" seeking to invest in the venue.

Although many such spaces are internally managed in a communitarian or horizontal way, horizontalism presents challenges. First, staff working for *foros* may be temporary, transitory, and underpaid. There is no reasonable requirement or expectation that they be committed to the "cause" or cultural "mission" of the venues they work in. Second, translating this horizontalism into legal terms—by, for instance, registering as a cooperative—is challenging. It is also difficult to convince government to recognize collective ownership. David Graeber recounts the difficulty caused when the New York Direct Action Network, an autonomous collective, was donated a car.[19] The car either had to be registered as the property of one member of the group—who then was obliged to take on a series of administrative responsibilities relating to it—or the group had to create a formally recognized organization with a hierarchical structure. Choosing the former option led, over time, to the car being treated as its named owner's personal property rather than that of the collective to which it was donated. The overall effect, Graeber claims, is that "government regulations essentially enforce a certain model of society, in which individual actors or hierarchically organized companies seek profits, and anyone who wishes to organize themselves differently—around any sort of conception of common good—needs to either be part of the state apparatus, or to register with it as a nonprofit corporation."[20] Although it is difficult to make comparisons across legal contexts, the situation Graeber describes is very pertinent for *foros culturales* in Mexico City.

The most administratively convenient form of formal organization for *foros* is to name one or two individual owners, but that approach has some disadvantages. In Mexico City there are disincentives, mainly related to insecurity and corruption, for the individuals presented as "owners" of these venues. For instance, the owner of one venue did not want their identity to be publicly known, as they felt that this would increase the risk that they or a member of their family might be kidnapped or extorted. Horizontal decision-making also presents venues with a layer of protection from extortion by the police and inspectors because it is unclear who precisely would be targeted. Would-be extorters may therefore be passed between members of staff, and generally placed in an atmosphere of confusion, until they leave.

For these reasons, many of the *foros* in which I conducted research have adopted what may be best understood as a hybrid model of organization, in which they are legally codified as private property with a small number of owners, but organized and presented as nonhierarchical and horizontalist. The notion that egalitarian social practices can serve as a tool for evading state control is common within anarchist thought, as in the case of Scott's exploration of Southeast Asian history.[21] Within the *foros culturales*, horizontal and fluid organizational practices can be seen both as a product of a shared anarchist politics and as a bulwark against multiple threats to these spaces' existence and day-to-day operation. In this sense, criticism of these venues' alleged hypocrisy misses the point: there are well-founded practical reasons that these venues operate in the way that they do, rooted in taken-for-granted operations of exploitation within rentier capitalism.[22]

In turn, a particular kind of economy has tended to predominate in *foros culturales*, connected to these venues' self-identification as spaces for the promotion of "culture." What distinguishes a *foro* from a bar is its emphasis on "culture"; indeed, within these venues culture often implicitly takes the place of monetary value. As the manager of one *foro*, Multiforo 246, told me, "As a business it's not so profitable. . . . At this kind of venue it's often about love for art."[23] The waitstaff in this venue, they said, tended to receive less than they would for such work elsewhere; many chose to work there because they had their own bands and musical projects and valued the venue's musical offerings. Some *foros*, furthermore, prided themselves on signing generous contracts with live performers. Since it began operating in the mid-1990s, Multiforo Cultural Alicia maintained generous financial arrangements in which the venue retained less than half of concert receipts, with the remainder being distributed to bands. Its owner contrasted this approach with the business model most prevalent at this time, in which "venues had you perform as a favor, and they got you to sell tickets so that the headline act could charge."[24] Multiforo Cultural Alicia also sought to provide bands with the ability to hold their own events, produce their own promotional materials, and record their own music. Indeed, this venue has long been more economically dependent on sales of beer than on concert tickets.

It is important to recognize that *foros* pursue a variety of business models.[25] Many venues, lacking the exposure and iconic status of Multiforo Cultural Alicia, operate under a greater set of constraints that do not allow such

FIGURE 2. El Mundano, a small venue (now closed) in the historic center of Mexico City. It carries the slogan "Revolutionizing ideas, sharing alternate realities." Photograph taken
by the author in July 2018.

generous agreements with artists. Nonetheless, it is clear that practices of self-management in these venues, these venues' mission to promote "culture," and their business models are often mutually intertwined.

Liberation and Curation

As discussed, *foros* depict themselves as spaces in which freedom of expression is valued. In stylistic terms, they are "heterodox" venues.[26] In other ways, *foros*' claims to provide a space for liberation—freedom from the expressive constraints of the world outside—encounter internal contradictions, which I explore in this section.

Foros culturales' apparent freedom of expression presents as a posture of noncuration, diversity, and inclusivity: *foros* provide space to be appropriated by a creative community. For instance, Foro El Mictlán describes itself online as an "alternative space open to all artistic expressions"; Bajo Circuito as an "open space for culture"; El Mundano, which shut down during the pandemic, as "a collage: here we don't know of genres or boundaries." Finally, the venue Multiforo 246, partly owned by members of the ska band Panteón Rococó, self-defined as a "free territory."

Such curatorial freedom implies a permissive, aesthetically open stance concerning the bands allowed to perform. This posture is nonetheless complex since it implies a contrast with the apparently controlled commercial mainstream. Where opposition to the mainstream has long been common to rock and other subcultures, in Mexico such oppositionality is complicated by the country's authoritarian history.[27] Narratives of censorship were vital in establishing the musical diversity of *foros*, as this quotation from the founder of Multiforo Cultural Alicia, Ignacio Pineda, indicates:

> This [venue] started in 1995, we saw and thought that there was a lack of a space where loads of bands could play that weren't on the radio and didn't belong to any commercial institution. . . . We saw that there was a subterranean universe of music not broadcast on the radio or in concerts. . . . There were bands playing ska, soul, hip-hop, punk, garage, rockabilly, metal that didn't get played on the radio. . . . There was a whole musical culture that because of censorship and anti-democracy, didn't belong to the official scene.[28]

In practice, *foros* establish boundaries that resemble those of rock itself: they tend to feature ska, blues, surf, indie or pop-rock, and hip-hop, and to exclude nationally popular genres such as *banda* and reggaetón.[29] These boundaries are justified by discourses that either critique the mainstream as morally ambiguous (for instance, by making claims that reggaetón lyrics are misogynistic) or present the corporate mainstream as lacking in freedom of expression. In the words of one venue worker: "The only thing that doesn't go with our style is *banda*, reggaetón, and *norteña*. The space doesn't lend itself to that kind of music. . . . As [this venue] is more anarchist, we might say, [reggaetón] doesn't fit with the ideas of [the venue]. We have a clear idea of what the venue is. So those vibes don't fit with us [laughs] more than anything." These exclusions are also justified through an inversion of market logic: performers of *banda* and reggaetón have no economic need to play in *foros culturales*. One event organizer suggested, by way of example, that if someone went to a *foro cultural* to propose an event featuring *música norteña*, you might be told, "Well, there are other places this music might fit better."

In turn, this othering of the perceived mainstream allows rock—a highly diverse genre—to be conceptually unified according to an oppositional logic.

Often, as the above quotation from Ignacio Pineda indicates, such oppositionality rhetorically entangles the perceived cultural and political "establishments." For instance, Paredes Pacho contrasts the "citizen resistance" of independent cultural spaces with the "monocultural authoritarianism" both of the state and of free-market "standardization."[30]

Some managers of *foros* have instead chosen a more formal, "professionalized" route, rooted in more direct curatorial control over live music, in turn reducing performance opportunities for rock. Those running the midsize venue Bajo Circuito (named as such because it is located under a motorway bridge) found a noncuratorial approach to be economically unviable. One worker described the venue's previous attitude toward performers as "come and play, and it doesn't matter if it doesn't sell." As they put it, bands would arrive claiming, "'No, my band will definitely fill this space'—and we had events with only fifty people, terrible, the venue had to pay our staff with that."[31] In response, they created a curatorial team in which each member was assigned a genre of music and tasked with finding artists with large social media followings, especially those based outside the capital. The venue dedicated Fridays and Saturdays to more well-known artists, leaving Wednesday and Thursday evenings to the "independent scene" and "cultural" acts. They also lengthened and formalized the contracts they signed with bands, and created new contractual options for performers so that the venue could avoid losing money on slower days.[32] These options included one in which performers were paid a small amount for each customer after forty had entered, and one in which performers were paid a percentage of bar sales. Finally, Bajo Circuito even began to require advance payments for bands with large followings: a cultural shock for many, but a business necessity for the venue.[33]

These spaces' association with "freedom" is also complicated by factors other than this formalization of curatorship. The economic and legal precarity of *foros culturales* means that they can be especially strict on illegal behavior that might present a pretext for closure, especially the sale and consumption of illegal substances.[34] *Foros* may in other cases take a lenient approach toward security, which creates different kinds of problems. An organizer of the metal venue Real Under complained that "we should have a very strict, very punctual way" to deal with people who had too much to drink. While bars and clubs have private security, Real Under would "try to deal with things in perhaps a more humane manner. We try to be nice, we try to understand what's going on with those people . . . and how to solve it before it harms us or harms them."[35] As this worker indicated, a lack of specialized security personnel may constitute a marker of antiauthoritarianism, but in practice it also has the potential to cause harm. One blogger described an incident at Multiforo Cultural Alicia in which, after a group of drunken anarcho-punks became violent and pushed a young woman down the stairs, the venue threw out the woman and her friends rather than those that had attacked her, leaving her to wait for an ambulance on the sidewalk outside. "A multicultural space without people trained to respond to events like this?" the blogger asked. "You still want to carry on worshipping that *hoyo fonqui* disguised as a multicultural center?"[36] Incidents such as this one serve as a reminder that the antiauthoritarian self-presentation of *foros culturales* could exist at a remove from the messy realities of fomenting inclusion. Freedoms collide in these spaces: the freedom to become intoxicated versus the freedom to enjoy one's evening in safety, or the freedom for performers to express themselves onstage without constraint versus the freedom to self-identify without encountering misogyny or hate speech.

Finally, although it is common to contrast the creative freedom present in *foros culturales* with the corruption and *amiguismo* (cronyism) apparently prevalent at OCESA-run events, in practice this distinction is not quite so clear-cut. As we have seen, the rock "mainstream" in Mexico is perceived as a closed shop, with entries guarded by a few gatekeepers; artists are either inside or outside. Yet as Paredes Pacho puts it, "community" is a constitutive feature of self-managed or independent venues.[37] Multiforo Cultural Alicia, for instance, is a center for sociality, run by and often featuring musicians, organizers, and journalists with long-standing friendships. One account of the curation of artists to record in this venue, given by its owner, indicates the ways that sociality and selection tended to overlap. "We [the organizational team] work with those who want to start," comments Ignacio Pineda. "We request a recording, listen to it, and see if it fits the profile of El Alicia. We work on it, give them a certain confidence, then when there's an opportunity, we record them."[38] Curation here builds on an undefined sense of the venue's identity developed by those working in it. In this form, curation can overlap with gatekeeping, fomenting suspicions about unstated forms of exclusion, such as those based on gender.

By the same token, there are varying levels of "professionalization" of management and artist promotion in the independent scene in Mexico City, such that some acts get to perform by approaching venues directly, and others benefit from hiring professionalized promoters as intermediaries. One venue manager described three routes to getting to play at a *foro*: contacting a given venue directly via social media, contacting venue workers face-to-face through sustained visits to the same space, and finding an effective event organizer to work with—itself difficult without a preexisting network of contacts.[39] Networks and personal contacts are of perennial importance in the creative industries.[40] In this context, the need to build such networks invoked anxieties about so-called *coyotes*, corrupt intermediaries that steal resources from genuinely productive (creative) workers.

This latter situation, in particular, belies the self-presentation of *foros culturales* as open, accessible venues that mirror the closed corporate spaces run by OCESA. While it is difficult to deny that most *foros* are more accessible to a range of artists than large-scale venues or events, we cannot apply a straightforward binary distinction in which the former is delineated as a space for "free" expression and the latter is dismissed as an entirely closed, controlled space. More broadly, *foros culturales* do not suspend the power relations found outside them; instead, external power relations are often replicated within these *foros* in complex, intersecting ways that contain and channel musical expression—within some genre boundaries, through certain social groups, and within certain principles for ordering society and economic exchange. A complex governmentality is at play within these venues that makes it difficult to untangle the "free" from its opposite.

Support and Assimilation

There is, however, another side to this coin: those running *foros culturales* complain simultaneously of a lack of government support and official efforts at co-optation. As Ignacio Pineda told *La Jornada*: "At times, political power gives you a squeeze. They say, either you work with us or we shut you down. Either you contribute to our campaign, or we shut you down."[41] In turn, what is understood as co-optation is often very subtle. The Mexico City government has created several programs to support and found small-scale cultural venues, providing city dwellers with an eclectic cultural offering often resembling that of *foros*. This situation suggests a paradox: given the scarcity of resources for *foros* on the one hand, and constant low-level repression on the other, it is surprising that these venues choose to maintain their distance from the state. *Foros* have refused to participate in these programs for reasons that relate to "post-transition" forms of censorship and silencing.

Since the turn of the millennium, the capital government has created a series of vibrant new cultural centers: since 2000 as part of the Faros program, and since 2018 as part of the Pilares program.[42] The Faros program was founded by a PRD city government seeking to democratize access to cultural activities, reacting against the elitist cultural institutions created by the PRI.[43] The writer Eduardo Vázquez Martín, who had directed the Mexico City Institute of Culture (the PRD-created precursor to the city's Secretariat of Culture), declared in a 1999 speech that "promoting culture is promoting freedom," while criticizing cultural investment constituting "decoration for parties thrown by those in power." For Vázquez Martín, the capital's "source of wealth" was its "cultural, ethnic and social plurality."[44] An essay he published the following year advocated a series of actions to realize this vision, including the following recommendation: "It is necessary to recuperate or create cultural infrastructure for the local governments. Almost all have cinemas in ruins, run-down theaters or auditoriums that are unequipped or with obsolete or inadequate equipment."[45] If municipal governments refused to invest in these venues, Vasquez Martín wrote, then it was the Institute of Culture's responsibility to take them over.[46]

This was the ideological context in which the Faros program emerged: a rhetorical admixture of "freedom" for culture understood as a positive project for the state, achieved through the appropriation of disused venues. Faros venues began to proliferate across the city's peripheries; many of the buildings in which venues were established had been created by the single-party regime and subsequently abandoned during the PRI's turn toward neoliberalism. At the same time, some had also been appropriated and managed as independent, self-managed cultural spaces by autonomist or community-led collectives.[47] Although there is a mismatch in resources between such self-managed venues and cultural spaces administrated by the Mexico City Secretariat of Culture, the cultural offer of these two kinds of venues overlaps considerably: both tend to provide an eclectic mixture of concerts, film screenings, visual art, sculpture, performance art, theater and storytelling, and workshops from across various artistic disciplines. Even in government-run spaces, one is just as likely to encounter workshops in hip-hop as sessions on more "elite" forms of art. The most high-profile venue, Faro de Oriente in Iztapalapa, regularly features concerts with the biggest names in Mexican rock, but it also provides access to diverse kinds of cultural workshops. This overlap in cultural offer is indicative of the fact that such cultural venues have often alternated between state governance and *autogestión*.

For their part, the Faros venues have successfully developed a sense of autonomy from politics while being funded by government. Although they helped the PRD to distinguish itself from the PRI, and mostly served this party's young support base, the Faros sites have escaped the widespread perception that they serve as a tool for the PRD's legitimation. Something similar appears to hold for the Pilares program created by the Morena administration that has governed Mexico City since 2015, though this is by no means total: while many of the musicians I worked with distinguished between the (nonpartisan) Secretariat of Culture and the (partisan) sources of funding for culture specific to political parties, other more skeptical voices assumed that state funding of culture was inevitably clientelistic.

Partly due to the legacy of clientelism in culture, spaces that the state was starting to run after years of *autogestión*, or that received government cultural funding or support from political parties, were especially likely to attract distrust in the local community. One small independent venue I visited in July 2019, Foro Cultural Zirahuen, was subject to local suspicion because its owner—a retired electrician called Baltazar who had bought a multistory house with severance pay after the firm he worked for shut down—rented the top floor of the building as office space to the leftist Worker's Party (PT). It is not difficult to see how some in the local community concluded that the space was now run by the PT; the first thing one saw when approaching the venue was a small canvas sign bearing the party's logo and advertising workshops and events. Indeed, during our interview—ironically, precisely at the moment that Baltazar was expressing his frustration at the situation, and his worry at the damage it might do to the space's reputation—he was approached by a member of the community mistakenly asking him to sign a PT document. Especially troubling for Baltazar was the fact that the PT organized diverse cultural events that resembled the offerings of Foro Cultural Zirahuen.[48] This venue, then, faced challenges indicative of transition: the financial power of political parties, combined with a postauthoritarian suspicion of public spending.

There are also downsides to accepting state help; these relate principally to a transition between informal and formal organization. Here, I explore the case of one cultural space, Centro Cultural La Pirámide (CCLP), located in the northwest district of Benito Juárez, building on press reports and an interview with a director of the venue.[49] CCLP had been founded in the 1990s and served as the center for the Association of Writers in Mexico, a civil association that had taken over a pyramid-shaped building belonging to, but abandoned by, the local government.[50] Initially used as an administrative center, it became a cultural space as the writers running this civil association started to invite friends from the community to give workshops in music and dance. As a result of this community-led approach, the venue developed diverse cultural offerings; in particular, it hosted cultural activities not often found elsewhere due to elitism and racism, such as African dance, circus arts, and capoeira.

The administration of the space developed as members of the community demanded to use it, requiring individuals to organize schedules, pay for utilities, open and close the premises, and maintain the building. Eventually, the group running the venue consolidated into a small group of coordinators who worked on the basis of principles of autonomy, horizontality, and consensus decision-making: "We practiced anarchism as an ideology, but it was working."[51] As one of these coordinators later reflected, the snowballing nature of these tasks, and the increasing diversity of the space's activities, resulted from the fact that the space was self-managed: "That's what *autogestión* entails—you get confronted with things you hadn't considered."[52] While many of these directors had first begun to engage in the project as artistic instructors, they took up administrative roles as their commitment to self-management and community engagement transcended their own direct enjoyment of artistic participation.[53] As this director told me, this period also presented challenges: the building was extremely dilapidated, with an "archaic electrical system that didn't work" and "a lot of wear and tear." The precarity of the project meant that "we couldn't just repair things that broke"; as they reflected on their experience, they told me that "it's a feature of *autogestión* that there's often no budget. So the problems build up."[54]

The early 2000s were remembered as an especially vibrant period for this venue: CCLP attracted several high-profile rock acts to play there, and birthed a successful circus troupe called Cirko de Mente that outgrew the venue. As it grew, CCLP began to attract the attention of the local authorities who, beginning in about 2006, started to threaten "to close the space . . . to come and forcibly remove people." Amid rumors that the local *delegación* government was deliberately allowing the building—which legally belonged to them—to degrade so that they could remove the cooperative assembly running CCLP and then demolish the building to create blocks of flats, the co-operative launched what they termed "cultural resistance."[55] Footage from a small-scale protest (numbering some twenty people) outside the local *delegación* government building in 2012 shows a vibrant demonstration of the breadth of cultural practices that CCLP offered, including polyrhythmic drumming with West African instruments, circus skills, and poetry readings. One sign held at the protest read "Democracy is rooted in the people, and in the cultural center."[56]

This process of resistance intertwined support for cultural diversity with democratic ideals and antiauthoritarian politics. Reporting on the controversy, the news website *Desinformémonos* praised CCLP for maintaining "a cultural offering independent from political parties and governments," and described it as "a reference point for self-managed artistic activities" without any "subsidy or governmental budget for its operation." In response to "harassment on the part of the government," they reported, CCLP had set up a "permanent assembly in defense of the project," effectively ensuring a constant presence in the building.[57] Over time, however, it became increasingly difficult to resist local government, and CCLP was obliged to negotiate with the authorities in about 2015. An initial compromise was reached in which the management of the building was passed to the capital's Secretariat of Culture and the cooperative was allowed to continue running the same cultural events. Then, after elections in 2018, the new city administration arrived with the intention to take over the space entirely, but they were convinced to allow the cooperative to be absorbed into the city's Secretariat of Culture, leaving the space's cultural offer intact.

These changes were made with the idea that they would bring access to greater resources. This promise was fulfilled to some extent—for instance, the venue was now given police personnel as security, and the venue also began to enjoy greater access to broadcast media. In 2018, the city government television news program *21 Noticias* ran a feature on CCLP's cultural and educational offer (implied, through the choice of Concerto No. 2 in E minor from Vivaldi's *La Stravaganza* as the soundtrack, to have been more rarefied than was in fact the case). The feature made no mention of the space's past as a locus of self-management and cultural activism, nor of its contentious recent past.[58] Nonetheless, the Secretariat of Culture had also made promises regarding maintenance that were slow to be fulfilled:

> It had its good side, and also its inconvenient side. Because when the Secretariat of Culture came to offer its help it was like "I'm coming to help you, I'm going to offer you everything you need," really nice. When they took possession of the building, those promises, it wasn't like that, they couldn't come through on them. . . . For instance, maintenance of the building, if you see all the lights, only three work. All the rest don't work because there's no budget.[59]

The final statement, that there was "no budget," is less hyperbolic than it sounds: in the first few months of the new administration, cutbacks and budget holdups led to many teachers and instructors on the Secretariat of Culture payroll going without pay.[60]

Yet another catch related to formalization. The directorial team of the

FIGURE 3. Centro Cultural La Pirámide, a community cultural center located in the Benito Juarez district of Mexico City. This cultural center has long fought with the local state for its independence. Photograph taken by the author in June 2019.

venue was now obliged to create a cooperative and register with Hacienda (that is, Mexico's finance ministry), and they had greater obligations to the Secretariat of Culture. Accepting state help created a significant new administrative burden and activities that may be meaningfully described as "bullshit": ultimately pointless administrative exercises that concretize and deepen a lack of in-work autonomy.[61] In both the Faros and the Pilares programs, teachers who give workshops complained about the amount of paperwork they had to submit. While I was attending a hip-hop course at a government cultural center in Mexico City, we would routinely take the final thirty minutes of each session to register. Anyone who lived outside of Mexico City wasn't allowed to register, and since this space was on the edge of Mexico City, participants often gave fake addresses. Something similar occurred in the case of CCLP. The representative of the venue I spoke to in 2019 had just had a report to the Secretariat of Culture rejected because it "was missing a heading. They told me, no, you have to do everything again. I go in with a pile of papers, and it's missing a pointless frippery [porquería]." This individual taught classes and administered the venue, but much of their time now was devoted to apparently pointless tasks, like writing reports "detailing all of my activities, I mean, everything I do every day." The apparent pointlessness of these reports was heightened by the fact that their contents were never verified: "What I include in it, how do you know it's true? There's a bureaucracy that from my point of view, you say, well, it's pretty useless."

Here, the meaning of *autogestión* had passed from providing freedom from needlessly onerous bureaucracy to the freedom to allow the management team to become martyrs to bureaucracy so as to protect instructors in the venue from excessive paperwork:

> Despite passing... from being completely self-managed to now being dependent on the Secretary of Culture, we still maintain a self-managed [*autogestivo*] process of organization. We do what the Secretariat of Culture requires, but we also work so that if for example... you need to put something on in one of our rooms, if you go to the Secretariat of Culture, well [they'll say] "send me an application, I have to sign an agenda and it has to be written, and in a certain format... and I'll have to send a Secretariat of Culture representative to observe what you're doing, and afterward you have to create a report, and with a photographic report as well, and hand it in on a compact disc as well as printed out"—a complete absurdity.... But if you come to us directly to say "I need a room," look, at 4pm I've got one free.[62]

What the coordinators perceived as a hard-fought victory, then, was the ability to afford their instructors and artists both the freedom to decide on their own activities and the time to dedicate to them. Power and autonomy inhered not in resisting onerous bureaucracy per se, but in the ability to direct or control bureaucratic flows.

The story of CCLP is important for understanding why, even in highly adverse circumstances, independent venues have often refused state collaboration. One factor is trust: constant changes lead to uncertainty about the future behavior of governments, which means that accepting state help can be a losing bet for cultural spaces. Another is bureaucracy: government procedures impose pointless, unnecessary, and unproductive tasks that obstruct meaningful cultural labor. Independence and self-management, then, vicariously underscore the status of a system in transition, in which democratic actors' struggle for credibility itself constitutes an ongoing legacy of authoritarianism.

Responses: Journalism and Performance

This chapter opened with an act of violent repression against an independent music venue and has gone on to describe a complex situation of ongoing, low-level repression against small- and medium-sized *foros culturales*. This repression is overdetermined: it emanates from many different spheres, including the operation of electoral democracy itself. It is, furthermore, not straightforwardly resisted by *foros culturales*, but instead is often replicated in these venues' modes of operation. Characteristic of these patterns of low-level repression are continuities: first, between present and past experience and, second, between the organizational practices of these spaces and their corporate and governmental "others." The coincidence of strict licensing laws and local corruption has antecedents going back to the 1970s and 1980s. So does the inflexible licensing situation itself, under which no appropriate license exists for the *foros culturales*' situation. Furthermore, the association between waves of venue closures and changes of administration, ostensibly a repressive by-product of democratic elections, is also inherited from single-party rule. Just as with repression under the PRI, these venues' understanding of their marginalization combines deprivations of liberty (such as venue closures) with acts of apparent support (the co-optation of venues into government).

Derrida claims that for "finite" entities "there is never any lifting of censorship, only a strategic calculation: censorship against censorship."[63] This poststructuralist position finds strong resonances in the forms of governmentality that have made their way into the independent scene itself. It is a topic of practical importance, since this more nuanced account of the marginalization of this scene is more difficult to articulate and mobilize around than the oppositional rhetoric with which *foros culturales* tend to describe their marginalization, in which their struggle against authoritarianism in government simultaneously traverses political times and complicates the distinction between them. The notion of "censorship against censorship" is also reflected in language that reiterates the most common pretexts for music censorship in Mexico. Ignacio Pineda, for instance, told me that Multiforo Cultural Alicia was subject to closures "because they [the government] don't like what we do. . . . They don't want young people to meet, to have their own space." Yet, he said, "this is a really calm space, you've seen it. There aren't people rioting, at all. People behave really well."[64] Pineda here reproduced the governmentalist logic underpinning censorship across dictatorship and democracy—in which the existence of youth culture was predicated on "good behavior"—as well as invoking and criticizing the repressive history of government prohibitions on youth gatherings.

Many instances have demonstrated, in turn, that the prevalence of these discourses within media narratives is vital for *foros culturales*' ability to operate. In the summer of 2015, Multiforo Cultural Alicia was shut down for several months and handed a fine of 167,000 pesos (roughly US$7500). Nonetheless, voices within the independent scene were able to set the agenda during the closure, portraying it as an act of dictatorial overreach and implicitly linking it to the paternalistic politics of single-party rule. The closure was covered in *La Jornada*, as well as a plethora of independent online media, such as *Regeneración* and *Sopitas*, which called the venue "a vital lung for musical expression" in Mexico City.[65] A number of high-profile musicians also condemned the closure, and an online petition was created calling for an end to the authorities' "harassment" of the venue. Pineda was quoted in *La Jornada* as saying that the closure had been "a little political. I don't think they like young people or culture. They don't want to accept it."[66] The day after this interview was published, the *delegación* government was forced to deny that the closures were politically motivated or that they constituted "an attack on culture."[67] In the end, the fine was rescinded, and Multiforo Cultural Alicia was allowed to reopen five days after it had been closed.[68]

This episode also demonstrated how responses to censorship often spill over into affective acts of performance and interpretation. Following the closure of this venue, a number of Twitter users shared the hashtag #noalcierredelalicia (No to the closure of Alicia), with one sharing in the same tweet the Dirty War–era Three Souls in My Mind song "Abuso de autoridad"—a song containing the famous lines "Living in Mexico is the worst / The government is really bad . . . / And the rock concerts / They want to take them away."[69] Indeed, in their creative practice within *foros culturales*, musical actors perform vital interpretive labor, carrying out the cultural work of linking everyday experiences of repression with sporadic, spectacular censorial acts, invoking musical and extramusical histories in the process, and drawing affective continuities between authoritarian and contemporary rule. In what remains, I explore three examples of this interpretive labor.

In August 2019 I went to Multiforo Cultural Alicia to attend an event held to promote a book of poetry; the event also featured live rock. Rafael Catana, who headlined the event, was a singer-songwriter who began performing in the 1980s *rock rupestre* scene and whose music combined a range of influences: rock, blues, jazz, and salsa.[70] On this occasion, he performed with a five-piece band. Catana opened with a performance of his 2001 song "Dices,"

FIGURE 4. The stage prior to an event in Multiforo Cultural Alicia's original venue (now closed), located in the Roma Norte district of Mexico City. Photograph taken by the author in June 2019.

a melancholy, restless ballad whose verses narrate endless travel through the city, each concluding with distinct narratives of postponed closure: "You say you're going to kill me / And you don't kill me"; "You say you're going to love me / And you don't love me"; "You say you're going to leave me / And you don't leave me." "Dices" weaves key figures in the history of Mexican rock into the song's hazy, palimpsestic, multireferential poetry: "I think of the kind of Walkman that follows you / You have the glasses of [León Chávez] Teixeiro, and the hair of Pájaro Alberto."[71]

As is common in performances at Alicia, the venue itself was frequently invoked. Catana reminded us that his most recent album was recorded at Multiforo Cultural Alicia and released on the venue's label, Grabaxiones Alicia; he dedicated his song "Rock sobre ruedas" to Ignacio Pineda, sitting in the front row. "Rock sobre ruedas" (Rock on wheels) reminds us of the precarious existence of rock in the early 1970s by commemorating the collective of the same name that put on continuous live concerts out of the back of a truck. This collective's thirst for electricity is, from the outset, playfully depicted as an addiction: "Come on, come on, I just want a bit of electricity / Baby baby, I just want a bit of electricity." The song is based on an ostinato guitar riff that recalls the rock of the late 1960s and early 1970s. Its lyrics are unsettled, with lines constantly shifting between variants; the song's recurring trope that 1970s rockers "bit the dust" indexes the genre's history of repression.[72]

> Venga venga, solo quiero un poco de electricidad
> Nena nena, solo quiero un poco de electricidad
> Ellos mordieron el polvo, cruzando la ciudad
> Con una bolsa de naranjas, menuda tempestad
> Ellos mordieron el polvo en un pedregal de flores
> En un camión carguero lleno de amplificadores
> Rock sobre ruedas
> Ellos mordieron el polvo en esta mi ciudad
> Conectando un poste de luz a un amplificador
> Ellos mordieron el polvo en esta mi ciudad
> En un camión carguero lleno de electricidad
> Rock sobre ruedas
>
> Come on, come on, I just want a bit of electricity
> Baby baby, I just want a bit of electricity
> They bit the dust, traveling across the city
> With a bag of oranges, such a commotion
> They bit the dust, on the stony florid ground
> In a cargo truck full of amps
> Rock on wheels
> They bit the dust in this, my city
> Connecting a light pole to an amplifier
> They bit the dust in this, my city
> In a cargo truck full of electricity
> Rock on wheels

Censorship is not confined to the pretransition past in this artist's music. On Catana's 2016 album *Terregal*, "Rock sobre ruedas" is followed by the Santana-esque "Punta Cometa," a track commemorating the victims of the September 2014 mass kidnapping of forty-three students in the state of Guerrero, a horrific act carried out with the complicity and support of the military and police.

Catana is a well-known and respected name on the scene, but his music has never enjoyed commercial success. He tends to perform at small-scale venues such as government-run cultural centers, *foros culturales*, museums, and book fairs. Catana has a charismatic persona, at once learned and serious, playful and provocative. Yet Catana does more than perform: he presents a radio show on Radio Educación; he has collaborated with poets on spoken word performances; he appears on panels, such as that presenting the poetry collection at the event at El Alicia. What does Catana offer a venue such as Multiforo Cultural Alicia? His performances stage certain versions of musical-political history and locate the venue within them; they constantly present rock expression as precarious, rough, tenacious, fleeting, transitory; as dirty, material, produced from the city's physical infrastructure; and as underground, under threat. In this way, he contributes a value that is at once aesthetic and narrative: his performances both invoke the apparently aberrant music censorship of the past and make it do affective work in the present. As both a performer and intellectual, Catana has the gravitas to pull off this conjuring trick that places us simultaneously in and outside of transition.

I went to the same venue two months earlier, in June 2019, to celebrate the fifth anniversary of the Front for Freedom of Expression and Social Protest (FLEPS). The first band that performed was Los Nakos, a long-standing act performing parody songs that formed in 1968 as part of the student movement. Playing with a three-piece ensemble of bass guitar, acoustic guitar, and *cajón*, they opened with a song dedicated to the Zapatistas. Like Rafael Catana, Los Nakos were able to bridge the single-party rule of the past with the present. This bridge was here effected in a more direct way, through testimonial: they engaged their own experiences of struggle under single-party rule with present-day struggles under multiparty democracy.

Through the performance, Los Nakos intertwined their own history of engagement with social struggle with introductions to their songs, many parodies of popular songs that introduce political themes. This history began with the student movement of 1968, continued through the Zapatista uprising of 1994, and crossed paths with many other leftist social movements up until the present day. The group also recounted this history in such a way as to subtly weave together the musical cultures of the student movement with rock culture. Thus, they told the audience that they began to perform during student rallies at the UNAM campus in 1968. "At the University Flagship Campus," they said, "there performed, for the first time, Los Nakos. Then, everything was cooler" (*todo era más chido*), a statement that recalled Botellita de Jerez's Guacarrock and its strapline "what's corny is cool" (*lo naco es chido*).[73] Los Nakos went on to perform their song "¿Soy naco y qué?," which unpicks the history of the term *naco*, a slur with a racial origin (the Indigenous Totonaco people, from the eastern coast of Mexico) that became prevalent in Mexico City as Indigenous people migrated to cities through the twentieth century.

They also performed the parody song "La balada del granadero" (The ballad of the riot police), which they introduced as an anthem of the student movement.[74]

Like Rafael Catana, Los Nakos are not a big commercial draw (although they claim to be the anonymous composers of several highly popular songs for children). During this event, indeed, the crowd took a while to start paying attention, although the band eventually left the stage to a big cheer. Yet their presence here was significant for several reasons. Los Nakos draw continuities between the period before and after the transition. They targeted for mockery Luis Echeverría Álvarez, the "*loco* responsible for the Tlatelolco massacre . . . who is now 94 years old, they're going to hire him for a movie called Walking Dead." But they also made fun of outgoing president Enrique Peña Nieto and the *panista* Vicente Fox, "Peña Nieto's hippie dad." There are nonetheless exceptions within this critique of party politics: the band's mockery tends to target conservative, establishment parties rather than the Morena government. The line between political repression and resistance against it is drawn subtly, in performance, and with humor.[75]

Los Nakos form bridges across different times through personal testimony; they provided descriptions of their performances in the 1968 student movement and spoke of their recent experiences playing at protests and union events: "It was a year singing in different places," Ismael tells us. "Through so many years, we've made many connections with . . . the movements for freedom, with all of the movements that make it possible that today's event can be a party." The implication was that democratization is a consequence of grassroots struggle rather than political leadership, and that electoral democracy constitutes bread and circuses, a veil obscuring real change. This implication was made explicit at other events held at this venue, such as a concert in December 2018, titled *Cuarta Transformación Fest*, which ironically celebrated AMLO's declaration that his election would usher in the country's "Fourth Transformation."[76] Its organizer was a member of a recently formed band named Little Mechanic, a singer-songwriter named Aldo, who spoke to me before the event started. His personal background had shaped his expectations of Mexico's political system; several family members were public intellectuals who repeatedly changed their party affiliations after elections. When asked whether Mexico could be considered a democracy, Aldo responded in the negative: "I don't think so. . . . I don't believe in the Mexican democratic system specifically, more generally the Latin American one." Aldo held up Multiforo Cultural Alicia as a counterpoint to corruption in the musical mainstream; it promised "liberation" and "freedom" from both Mexico's political system and its commercial musical elite.

These musical accounts of democratization in Mexico are of existential significance for *foros culturales*, whose survival in situations of precarity has repeatedly depended on their ability to pivot from official discourse about health and safety into conversations about freedom of expression. More broadly, these venues' survival depends in part on the ability to connect everyday experiences of marginalization with repression in its most dramatic form, in a way that resonates with publics attending these spaces. As the above explorations of performances by Los Nakos and Rafael Catana show, these kinds of connections are made affectively and creatively, and they are made in such a way as to place at the forefront of democratization the organizational labor of the venues in which these performances take place.

Let's return, to conclude, to the self-definition of many of these *foros culturales* as *libertarios* (liberationists) rooted in creative freedom—something that I have sought to complicate in this chapter. The account of freedom that results from observation of how these venues are actually organized, I have suggested, is messy, ambivalent, and open-ended. In resisting the dominant celebratory, teleological, universalistic narrative of democratization, the discourse of these spaces often simply inverts this narrative—for instance, in the way that a purportedly democratic government is exposed as "really" tyrannical, and the democratic transition is revealed as insubstantial or illusory. Most important, when the rough edges of these discourses come into tension or encounter movement, they sound, becoming audible in the performances of the musicians playing in these venues.

Although the looking glass of the *foros culturales* can be understood in reference to the books of Lewis Carroll, in closing this chapter I want to propose another literary avenue through which to disentangle the resonant frictions encountered in these venues. In his novella *The Crying of Lot 49*, Thomas Pynchon introduces the concept of "anarchist miracles" through an encounter with Jesús Arrabal, a fictional Mexican anarchist.[77] On the one hand, Arrabal uses this concept to allude to the miraculous nature of autonomously generated solidarity based on "the soul's talent for consensus," and, on the other hand, he uses it to point out that things never "really happen that perfectly."[78] The concept also indicates the miraculous nature of antagonists who are "too exactly and without flaw the thing we fight"—a description that could be applied to authoritarian governments in Mexico, and corporate monopolies within live entertainment, as they appear in the discourse of the independent scene.[79] There is indeed something miraculous about many of the *foros culturales*, as spaces that are able to exist amid constant repression, precarity, and poverty of resources. They persist despite often falling afoul of health and safety regulations. They mediate between groups with distinct political allegiances and differing accounts of repression and democratization. They simultaneously occupy different accounts of political time, between the teleological and agonistic. And they present themselves as, to borrow another of Pynchon's phrases, "another world's intrusion into this one."[80] Yet, as I have argued, it is through a combination of music and journalism that these discrepancies and rough edges are smoothed over. As in the novella, whose protagonist experiences an "anarchist miracle" as she is swept through a dance with bewildering, undecipherable steps that nonetheless guide its participants away from each other, the stuff of this "miracle" are the affordances of musical performance itself.

CHAPTER 6

Foros culturales, History, and the Right to Culture

The problem is that word that is repeated: "CULTURE." It contains room for so many things that, even if we accept the limits that the words "Underground" and "Resistance" look to place on it, they give us space not for a roundtable, however square, but for a great intercontinental meeting that would last light-years, not including the time it takes to fix the microphone, to say hi to everyone [*saludar a la raza*], or to fall asleep because someone has decided that culture can also be boring and has insisted on showing it.

—SUBCOMANDANTE MARCOS, during a speech given for the roundtable "De la cultura subterránea a la cultura de la resistencia," Multiforo Cultural Alicia, October 26, 1999

"Culture is not a luxury" reads a slogan on several images produced by Multiforo Cultural Alicia, "it is a right." This phrase appears on a poster, often put up in the entrance to the venue, which also declares in black and white: "We are not delinquents; we are cultural spaces." It also shows up on a painting in vibrant colors emulating the aesthetic of the Zapatista movement. The artwork depicts a house inhabited by a rocker wearing the anarchist symbol, a young woman reading a book, and an Indigenous couple, sitting underneath the phrase "Abandoned buildings for the cultural community and community art!" Both images are shared online by representatives of the venue itself, and by the Coordinator of Independent Cultural Spaces (CECI), a group organized to lobby for the interests of a series of small venues based in central Mexico City whose offering is dominated by rock. The slogan "culture is not a luxury, it is a right" has also been circulated in the press, especially among groups with a close relationship to CECI, such as *La Jornada*,[1] and it has also made its way into political debates, especially on the Left.[2]

This slogan has become especially relevant to recent political developments in Mexico City. In 2016, twenty years after its first elections, Mexico City underwent a series of administrative changes to give the capital full recognition as a state of Mexico. It was renamed—the Federal District (DF) became the City of Mexico (CDMX)—and its districts were denominated as elected *alcaldías* (mayorships) rather than *delegaciones* (delegations).[3] As part of this administrative change, the capital created its own constitution, which entered into law in February 2017. Passed by a city government dominated by the leftist Movement for National Regeneration (Morena), which won the election in the capital in 2015 (Morena would go on to win the national elections in 2018), the constitution sought to establish a "right to culture" for the capital's citizens.

This constitutional right to culture was far-reaching and ambitious. It both identified and challenged censorship in the cultural field, and established a role for government promotion of culture. As the new constitution combined negative and positive conceptions of freedom, it presented both conceptual and practical dilemmas: How could one satisfactorily distinguish "cultural" from "noncultural" activities? What kinds of state interventions could guarantee the universal right of access to a diversity of cultures, and could such interventions create losers as well as winners? How could one marry a definition of "culture" in the broad anthropological sense with a project to claim a special status for cultural venues?

Discrete initiatives to establish a right to culture in law have emerged in cities across Latin America in recent years.[4] For instance, in 2006 the Bogotá city government passed Acuerdo 257, consisting of an administrative reform to the governance structure of the capital, which created a right for its citizens to access and participate in culture and sports, and established a duty for relevant government bodies to serve as guarantors of these rights. In the same year, the government of Buenos Aires passed Ley 2176, a cultural rights law, followed by a more recent Law of Independent Cultural Spaces in 2018; both laws directly inspired the right to culture initiative in Mexico City.[5] These initiatives build on diverse antecedents, including declarations of the pluriethnic character of Latin American nation-states, recognition of the rights of Indigenous peoples, and the establishment of intellectual property rights. Importantly, the right to culture has tended to imply antagonists: for instance, a document issued by the Bogotá city government to explain the history of cultural rights in the city notes "the progressive expansion of modernity to all corners of the planet."[6] The nature of the perceived threat to rights tends to condition the actions taken to support them; thus, in the Bogotá law, the state serves as the guarantor of rights in the face of threats against them seen to be external to the nation-state itself.

Critiques of human rights have been made from many different perspectives, as human rights have transitioned from a "revolutionary and vulnerable ideology of contestation [to] a rather established mode of governance."[7] Feminist, queer, disabled, and Indigenous writers have argued that human rights are often framed in ways that benefit those doing the framing.[8] Human rights have been critiqued as vague and ill-defined, and for frequently coming into conflict with one another.[9] Human rights have also been critiqued for universalism, imposing an individualist conception of the human being and normalizing liberal "structures and values of governance."[10] These critiques are relevant to the "right to culture" drive in Mexico City, which both invoked the universalizing logic of rights and was dependent in practice on the need to engage specific communities of cultural actors. Following a framework proposed by Gross and Wilson, the "right to culture" may refer to two things: the right to participate in the shared cultural life of one's choosing (what has recently been called "cultural democracy") and the public right of access to rarefied, elite culture (the so-called deficit model).[11] Though in reality these distinct iterations of cultural rights often intertwine, the fact that they have very distinct implications for policy means that the "right to culture" has, in Mexico City, become contested among actors within the cultural field.

In this chapter, I draw connections between the right to culture in Mexico City, the emergence of collective action to support it among representatives of *foros culturales*, and received histories of rock censorship in the capital. Where previous chapters have explored the ways in which histories of censorship have taken shape, in this chapter I focus on the affordances of these histories, following the increasing emphasis in the humanities on "productive" forms of censorship, and the ways that censorship may catalyze new forms of social organization.[12] The right to culture, I highlight, was contested in ways that reflect fissures within the Mexican Left; *foros culturales* have, as such, had to mobilize to demand recognition within it. Histories of rock censorship, I argue, became important to the ability of *foros culturales* to mobilize, represent their interests, and claim recognition before the state. I describe the emergence of several groups established to lobby on behalf of *foros culturales* and explore how stories of marginalization, repression, dictatorship, and transition informed this process. Such shared histories have helped to draw together and motivate lobbying activities related to the right to culture. This chapter thus engages with music censorship not only as a "lack" of musical expression but also as a generative social fact with complexly intertwined aesthetic and extraaesthetic affordances.

Cultural Rights and the Independent Scene

The PRD politicians that came to power in Mexico City in 1997 were accustomed, under PRI single-party rule, to the use of cultural spending to maintain political power. PRI clientelism extended to using cultural programs, especially through Sociocultur and Fonca (National Endowment for Culture and Arts), as a means to gain influence and legitimacy within Mexican intellectual and cultural life. Indeed, the latter program was established precisely during a crisis of legitimacy after the 1988 electoral fraud.[13] Political influence within cultural spending was notorious and has continued long after Mexico's transition to multiparty democracy. One cultural administrator told me, for instance, of portraits of PAN politicians hanging on the walls of *delegación* Secretariats of Culture in Mexico City well into the mid-2000s.

By contrast, the PRD sought to establish horizontalism in its cultural policy. For PRD functionary Eduardo Vázquez Martín, the party's responsibility was "to guarantee the greatest space of freedom possible for culture" while avoiding clientelism, corruption, and elitism.[14] Just before the 1997 elections, all parties in the city government reached an agreement to dissolve Sociocultur and replace it with the city's Institute of Culture (to become the city's Secretariat of Culture in 2002), whose mission was to "circulate, promote and preserve the culture of the Federal District."[15] Change came both through the figureheads of "official" culture themselves and from engagement with the popular, mass-scale mobilizations described in Chapter 4. PRD politicians included writers and essayists who had received government funding under single-party rule, such as Alejandro Aura, and individuals connected to activism, such as Inti Muñoz. That the PRD was a coalition was reflected in its cultural policy, which both continued to sponsor "elite" culture and painted cultural capabilities as innate expressions of shared, multicultural freedoms.

The notion of a "right to culture" had been discussed in the Mexican political sphere since at least the early 1990s, when it was understood either as a move to further entrench Indigenous rights or a universalistic and far-reaching move to widen access to cultural resources from libraries to live entertainment.[16] In the late 1990s, at a time when the San Andrés Accords were being negotiated between the EZLN and the Mexican government, the former account of the right to culture became especially prominent.[17] This resonated with developments on a global scale, where the concept of a right to culture was principally related to ethnic minorities whose language and cultural practices were under threat. In 2000 Carlos Payán Velver, a PRD senator in the National Assembly, attempted to establish the right to culture in the Mexican Constitution, with the intention of defending Mexican folklore and traditions from "the globalization that allows large transnationals to take control over the cultural products of the peoples [*los productos culturales de los pueblos*]." It would not be possible, Payán Velver said, "to construct the nation on the basis of homogenization of all groups," excluding "pluriethnic and cultural diversity."[18]

There are echoes, here, of the definition of "national" territory as an inalienable resource that needed to be defended against implicitly foreign entities, a tendency that goes back to the earliest years of independence.[19] Payán Velvér's invocation of globalization as a threat against which "national" culture needed to be defended presented a productive "operative logic"—but one that could be subverted.[20] Excluded from Payán Velvér's definition of the culturally "inalienable," rock could be seen as the kind of external cultural threat against which this right could be defined; musical imports such as rock had long been perceived as agents of transnational homogenization.[21] By the same token, since this account of the right to culture apportions rights in particularistic fashion to those cultural traditions seen to be under threat, the target of "right to culture" protections could shift, depending on the ways that histories of repression were established, performed, and textured.

Participants in the rock scene had long defended their genre against repression by arguing for its "cultural" status. Starting in the 1970s, rock writers wrote of the genre both as intrinsically cultural and as part of broader culture; the latter logic is evident in the title of the television program *Rock en la cultura* (Rock in culture), established in the early 1970s. Indeed, a similar phrase, *El disco es cultura* (The record is culture), was carried on vinyl records distributed throughout Mexico in the 1970s, as the recording industry sought increased social acceptance. Occasionally, rock journalists developed this logic in a more explicit way, such as in a 1978 *Conecte* article by Roberto Vázquez entitled "Reading and Culture," which argued that rock audiences should enhance their appreciation of the genre by engaging in wider reading and education.[22] Equally, the idea of rock as intrinsically cultural is stated in the full title of the iconic market for rock recordings and magazines, Tianguis Cultural del Chopo (Chopo Cultural Market), established in 1980, and the slogan "Rock Is Culture," which was frequently published on the front page of the magazine *La Banda Rockera* in the late 1980s. Appeals to "rock as culture" have often followed episodes of repression against rock, as a defensive measure: for instance, rockers highlighted rock's "cultural" and "civil" nature in response to the 1995 prohibitions against live rock and after a wave of venue closures in Mexico City in 2001.

This inclusive stance toward rock as culture found support in the work of the PRD cultural functionary and director of the Institute of Culture from 1997 to 1999, Eduardo Vázquez Martín. A writer with anthropological training, Vázquez Martín made frequent reference to the right to culture, which he framed in a universalistic fashion. In a 2001 talk titled "Culture: Space of Freedom," Vázquez Martín attacked the idea that "the nature of culture should be circumscribed exclusively to the fine arts, or to the ceremonies that adorn the parties thrown by Power, and gain audiences and legitimacy for political discourses that would otherwise be discarded." While critiquing cultural clientelism, he also defended proactive government action "to guarantee the largest possible space for culture" and to encourage "the encounter of artists with publics"—something achieved by appropriating neglected or abandoned buildings in order to create new cultural spaces, especially under the Faros program (see Chapter 4).[23] In a later essay reflecting on his experience in the city government, Vázquez Martín wrote that they had "awakened a new citizen's demand: the right to culture, understood as a core part of the right to the city."[24]

The policy of creating cultural venues in abandoned spaces triangulated across distinct factions within the PRD: the intellectual and artistic elite on the one hand, long supported by government grants, and the mass-scale popular movement that had coalesced around rock on the other. It enacted proactive interventions to support a universalistic "culture"—with the attendant associations with clientelism and politically motivated censorship—while distancing the party from the task of choosing cultural "winners" on the basis of hierarchies of taste. The emphasis on space was directly linked to the rock movement; Vázquez Martín wrote in one essay that "the growing fear that was felt in 1997 of a wave of violence [upon a PRD victory] was halted; the idea that large concentrations of youth in rock concerts necessarily implied violence, was discarded."[25] Thus, rock's inclusion within the right to culture was directly connected to its recent history of prohibition. As I will now show, the ability to claim this right for rock was central to rock venues' ability to mobilize in support of their interests.

Toward CECI: Solidarity, Lobbying, and Knowledge

One specific history of community mobilization in favor of rock in Mexico City can be traced back to the turn of the millennium.[26] As has often occurred after elections, there was a wave of closures of small and midsize music venues in 2001, which affected Multiforo Cultural Alicia, Circo Volador, Café de Nadie, and Octavo Día.[27] Furthermore, in 2002, Tecnogeist, an open-air, free-to-attend festival of electronic music in the Cuauhtémoc district of the capital, was denied a permit amid complaints from neighbors and concerns about safety and drug consumption.[28] In response to these closures, several venues created the Forum of Alternative Spaces (FEAS) and established a set of demands and principles that would dominate the politics of alternative rock until the present.[29] FEAS demanded not only the reopening of venues, but also a special license differing from restaurants and bars that would permit them to "sell alcohol and also protect cultural activities."[30] FEAS also lobbied for greater government support for these venues, and for the creation of an independent commission to prescribe cultural policy.

After these venues were allowed to reopen, FEAS was dissolved, but another organization emerged in 2004 to represent a slightly larger group of independent venues. This organization, called the Network of Independent and Alternative Spaces (RECIA), had a core of seven venues but sought to represent the interests of some twenty-five more.[31] Its members mobilized in favor of an amendment to the Law for the Functioning of Mercantile Establishments, which had been passed in 1996 and updated in 2002.[32] They also called for a status of "Independent Alternative Cultural Space" to be included in the 2003 Law for Cultural Fomentation in the Federal District.[33] RECIA gained a significant voice in the print media that allowed it to publicize and denounce closures of venues represented by the network; for example, in 2005 an article written about the network noted two closures of member venues, and further threats of closure against five others.[34]

After entering a period of inactivity, RECIA was replaced, in the summer of 2013, by the Coordinator of Independent Cultural Spaces (CECI), which has operated until the time of writing.[35] CECI's demands continue those of RECIA and FEAS: they demand an end to closures, the provision of financial support for cultural venues, and greater legal rights for venues whose offering is deemed "cultural." CECI is led by Multiforo Cultural Alicia, but has represented newer spaces such as Gato Calavera, El Mundano, and Multiforo 246; all of these venues are located close to the historic center or the conjoining

Roma district.[36] Although this is a small network, it punches above its weight, partly due to press interest in venues such as Multiforo Cultural Alicia.

CECI's first activity was an open forum, held at Multiforo Cultural Alicia in August 2013, arguing for the creation of "the right to culture, the recuperation of abandoned spaces, and dialogue between the city government and independent cultural spaces." This "right" was fleshed out in a brief manifesto, printed on a poster, demanding that "abandoned public spaces" be recuperated by the "cultural community" for "forums for artistic and cultural expression," and requesting government recognition of CECI as "interlocutor" for the cultural community. As with CECI's predecessors, the most concrete demand in this manifesto was the creation of a category of "independent and alternative cultural spaces" (*espacios culturales independientes y alternativos*) within the preexisting citywide Law of Mercantile Establishments. This would imply the creation of an independent council composed of members of government and "civil and artistic society," and the creation of "operative, administrative and fiscal support to facilitate the adequate functioning of the spaces in question." CECI subsequently lobbied, over several years, for legal recognition for what came to be formally known as ECIs (independent cultural spaces).

These organizations have been especially visible in the press. In 2005, RECIA challenged the PRD government to a debate "about the cultural project of the Left in the city," an offer that was not accepted.[37] CECI continued in this vein in 2016, when in an open letter to *La Jornada* its members condemned the recent closures of two venues and called for the capital's government to address problems with their legal status.[38] These lobbying groups have used their press visibility to influence public debate, consistently framing rock as under threat, arguing that the entertainment industry depends on them as a pipeline for talent, and seeking to hold successive city governments to their promises of support. Most importantly, representatives of *foros culturales* repeatedly connect the right to culture to histories of repression against youth movements and against rock; they also constantly articulate continuities between present-day democratic governance and past authoritarianism. Speaking to *La Jornada* about the denial of a permit for Tecnogeist in 2002, José Luis Paredes Pacho argued that cultural projects that were "independent, alternative or with youth roots" would "never be allowed to exercise their right to culture": "It's sad that we still have to suffer the inheritance of '68 and '71 with these democratically elected authorities in this city, which are supposedly of the Left; it's lamentable that they maintain a similar attitude toward youth expressions as with the Uruchurtu regime [regent of Mexico

City from 1952 to 1966], which repressed nightlife in the city and stigmatized rock, and with the case of Avándaro."[39] Notably—but typically—Paredes Pacho draws continuities between "democratic" and "nondemocratic" repression against rock.

Those speaking on behalf of RECIA and CECI have also depicted rock as a form of cultural expression that is in need of protection and that poses no threat to public safety. "These alternative spaces are not places for *reventón*," said the founder of Multiforo Cultural Alicia in 2001, recalling past ideas of rock rebellion; "they are natural schools for art and culture."[40] The headline of a 2005 article in *La Jornada* introducing the activities of RECIA warned of "Cultural Forums under Threat"; the article went on to describe how these venues suffered under inadequate licensing regimes in Mexico City.[41] In a feature on Multiforo Cultural Alicia from 2012, the venue's founder connected cultural rights with the right to the city, depicted the independent scene as resisting the entertainment industry, and demanded that the city's leftist government "act to guarantee the right to culture [since] if we leave it to the laws of the market, a large part of the population will lack access."[42] In lobbying for rock's protection as "culture," these discourses implicitly circumscribe the genre's political impact—for instance, through discarding *reventón* as a legitimate form of cultural expression. The discourse concerning rock as culture is thus embedded in a wider logic in which freedoms are extended conditionally, through concessions to the imagined disciplinary state gaze: we, the rock public, have earned the right to exist because we have reformed our behavior.

In addition to lobbying government, these organizations have had several other important roles: resisting or postponing state appropriation of community-led cultural activities, aiding everyday operations, and responding to other threats to spaces' operations. CECI has shown itself valuable as an expertise-sharing hub and as a representative of member venues in the public arena, especially in response to threats to their activities. The previous chapter recounted how new independent cultural spaces created in Mexico City aim to follow a model of self-management (*autogestión*). This involves learning on the part of venue organizers, who have to communicate with the authorities, comply with a complex and changing set of regulations, and turn enough of profit to pay staff, performers, and the cost of goods. In this sense, Multiforo Cultural Alicia serves as a blueprint for new independent cultural spaces, and as a focal point for organizational knowledge. That other spaces are modeled on Multiforo Cultural Alicia is evidenced in nomenclature, as with the case of Multiforo 246. but it is also reflected in the fact that spaces are often run as horizontally structured cooperatives and in the diversity of artistic genres they host. One of my respondents, who had managed multiple independent venues that formed part of CECI, told me that Alicia would "always be the model to follow. Because it's one of the first *foros* I know, the first that is in resistance, the first that passed through a time of being constantly closed and got through it." This respondent compared cultural spaces to children: "Every *foro* is like a person, as it grows it starts to understand what it is, and we all have to understand that [a new] *foro* is like that; it's like an entirely new person."⁴³

A solidarity organization such as CECI is, furthermore, an important bulwark against extortion and robbery. Most of the venues that form part of CECI are located close to each other and are thus able to share information about thieves operating in the area and government inspectors seeking bribes.⁴⁴ In turn, these tactics are most effective if an organized group such as CECI, well-connected with a network of journalists and a high social media profile, is able to exert pressure on local government in response to closures. This has occurred repeatedly since its creation, especially during multiple closures of Multiforo Cultural Alicia itself, starting in early 2001 when the venue was shut down for a month and a half.⁴⁵ As already seen, press coverage from sympathetic media outlets has been vital in framing debate about venue closures. While press attention has long been focused disproportionately on Multiforo Cultural Alicia, belonging to these networks means access to some of this venue's voice and exposure. This was the case after the 2007 closure of RECIA member Dada X, which came about after an anonymous complaint; it was supposedly oriented around technical infringements that invalidated the venue's security permit. The closure was reported in *La Jornada* the following day.⁴⁶ The day after that, RECIA published a statement denouncing what they described as an irregular closure about which the venue had not been forewarned; the *La Jornada* journalist covering it added a sympathetic note demanding "that the Cuauhtémoc *delegación* government cease the harassment against venues which foment youth culture."⁴⁷

CECI has also organized collective visits to municipal government buildings in response to extortion, criminal activity, or venue closures. On one occasion, a venue was approached by two men claiming to be from a criminal organization that was looking to establish an extortion racket. Asking for the owner, they were told that the space had no owners, upon which one reportedly replied, "If you don't start to cooperate [that is, financially], in monthly payments or however you want, we're coming here to kill people." After this chilling moment, CECI helped to unite spaces to file a collective report to the municipal government:

We were really active with CECI, this happens, and then we start to get messages "hey, you know what happened [at that venue]" ... because we were really active with CECI, someone from the municipal government arrives and says to us "you know what? It's the time to talk to someone from the municipality," who at that time is Ricardo Monreal, the delegate for Cuauhtémoc. We all go, there were like ten of us, to the municipal building, and Ricardo Monreal arrives ... then they close doors, switch off cameras ... get rid of reporters and ask: "right, what really happened?"[48]

This respondent described initial defensiveness on the part of the senator, who was under the initial false impression that their complaint had to do with a corrupt government employee. Once the senator realized the incident was caused by a nearby criminal group, journalists were invited into the room and the senator preached the "nauseating [anti-crime] discourse of all the politicians." The group was then referred directly to the municipal police attorney (*procurador de la policia*); however, faced with bureaucratic slowness, several left without filing a formal complaint.

While the members of FEAS, RECIA, and CECI have continuously reworked and retextured histories of censorship to justify and contextualize their lobbying activities, focusing on the right to culture has allowed these groups to shift the terrain in their negotiations with the city government: rather than requesting permission to carry out their activities, they demand legal recognition and support. To identify rock with "culture" may suggest a limited account of the genre's political potency, which is contained within a deliberative, representational frame; rock is here valued for its ability to articulate political visions, demands, and claims, rather than its capacity to move bodies and forge resistant subjectivities. Asserting rock's status as "culture" therefore functions simultaneously as a practical means of resisting authoritarian actions against rock and a concession to imagined authoritarianism in government. Yet it is on this basis that CECI has cultivated constructive relationships with politicians, pushing for changes in local licensing policy and for the inclusion of their work within the right to culture in the capital's constitution.

Morena and the "Right to Culture"

The cultural policy pursued by Morena politicians since 2015 has followed the precedents established by the PRD: Morena has articulated a similarly bottom-up, democratic vision of cultural policy in Mexico City that both responded to histories of censorship and connected to grassroots, independent cultural organizations. Morena has also appealed to "culture" as a postpolitical remedy for conflict and violence, reflecting both López Obrador's "hugs, not bullets" 2018 campaign slogan and discourses long prevalent within *foros culturales*.[49] The notion of cultural spending as a linchpin of conflict transformation has also, more recently, taken hold in the national political conversation. For instance, the federal government's 2019 Development Plan contained a subsection entitled "Culture for peace, for wellbeing, and for all," which declared that "humans live in cultural systems that go from language to celebrations and commemorations. . . . Nobody should be excluded from the activities and circuits of culture, which represent in current circumstances factors of peace [and] social cohesion."[50] In March 2019 the new head of the federal Secretariat of Culture, Alejandra Frausto, stated that the government would continue past emphases on hosting cultural events in public spaces, "principally in zones of conflict."[51] Frausto placed arts funding at the heart of conflict transformation and repeatedly described culture as a right.[52] As with the PRD, her rhetoric triangulated between popular and elite constituencies of Mexico's cultural community; Frausto declared, for instance, that the government would promote "a dialogue between deep Mexico and universal culture."[53]

Cultural rights have been affirmed most strongly within Mexico City's government, championed by successive individual politicians from Morena. Thus, after the party's victory in the capital in the 2015 midterm elections, a Morena city senator (*diputado*) named Alfonso Suárez del Real included CECI within a series of discussions to establish a right to culture in law.[54] After 2018, the task of coordinating this drive fell to a younger, incoming *diputada* called Gabriela Osorio, and in 2021 it was taken on by another *diputada*, the director and cabaret performer Ana Francis Mor. The right to culture was contested; it is noteworthy, for instance, that in the wake of Morena's 2015 election victory a group of anthropologists with ties to the National Institute of Anthropology and History (INAH), based in Mexico City, put forward a declaration, based on an anthropological account of culture centered on "national identity and cultural identity" threatened by "globalization," that was endorsed by almost four hundred academics and handed directly to the Culture Commission of the city government.[55] This declaration, accompanied by several position statements by anthropologists, reflected a frame through which Mexican cultural traditions, especially those connected to Indigenous identity, were undermined by state and market "homogenization."[56] Popular, industrialized, and transnational cultural expressions with comparatively recent provenance in Mexico, such as rock, were implicitly excluded from this account of cultural rights.

Yet the right to culture that was finally given constitutional recognition in 2017 reiterated prominent discourses from the independent music scene, and eschewed language attacking cultural "homogenization" and "globalization." The new constitution established the "unrestricted right of access to culture" for "all people, groups, and communities," and explicitly prohibited "all forms of censorship." It stated a right to "cultural identity, in the diversity of its modes of expression"; guaranteed access to "cultural heritage" and the right to "access and participate in cultural life"; and established a right to "exercise one's own cultural practices." Most notably for independent venues, the new constitution established the rights to "constitute spaces which are collective, self-managed [*autogestivos*], independent, and community-led" and "to participate, through democratic means, in community cultural development." The authorities were called on to "favor the promotion and stimulation of the development of culture and the arts. Cultural rights will be able to widen in accordance with the law in the matter also established by the mechanisms and modalities for their enforcement [*exigibilidad*]."

Clearly, the constitution's definition of rights married the deficit model with cultural democracy, alluding to both the right for cultural practices not to be censored and the rights of "culture and the arts"—however these were to be defined—to receive government support. As with the PRD's post-1997 approach to cultural policy, such conceptual inclusivity reflected the diverse set of interest groups making up Morena's base of support in the capital.

The constitutional right to culture was followed by a series of legal initiatives and reforms; Suárez del Real pushed for the creation of a Law of Culture and Cultural Rights to catalog a series of defined "cultural rights" and establish that a minimum of 2 percent of the city budget should be spent on cultural activities.[57] A fiscally stripped-back version of this law was passed in December 2017, tasking the city's Secretariat of Culture with administering a system of coupons for cultural events.[58] In turn, a number of institutions were created to advocate for the new cultural rights. The Law of Culture and Cultural Rights created an Institute of Cultural Rights, which soon became the Institute for the Defense of Cultural Rights; the Culture Commission was rebranded in 2018 as the Commission for Cultural Rights, led by Gabriela Osorio. As with Suárez del Real, Osorio and her team rooted their approach in dialogue with the city's community of cultural organizers and artists. Osorio's team organized a series of meetings to consult on how the right to culture should be implemented. The meetings were held in diverse venues across the city, culminating in a final consultation at the government-run Museo de la Ciudad de México in August 2019, which I was invited to attend as a participant observer. This consultation was intended to hear feedback on a draft summary of a bill to support cultural venues, provisionally entitled the Law of Independent Cultural Spaces (Ley de Espacios Culturales Independientes, or Ley ECIs). Here, I do not provide an exhaustive legal analysis, but rather build on participant observation and interviews with participants in this process to explore how the consultation both responded to venues' needs in the present and invoked received histories of censorship.

From the beginning of the consultation, organizers framed the Ley ECIs as a way to extend democracy and defy the capital's repressive histories.[59] Osorio gave a brief speech asserting that the purpose of the law was to provide ECIs with "legal certainty" and praising ECIs for their resilience in the face of lack of recognition and constant closures. Meanwhile, Inti Muñoz— now working for Morena—affirmed that corruption and extortion had been a common feature of these venues' interactions with the state and recognized that the "legacies of the old authoritarian regime" persisted, especially in licensing regimes for these venues.

A member of Osorio's team then summarized the proposed law and provided a timeline for its implementation. The Ley ECIs created legal bases for considering ECIs as a separate juridical category, and it aimed, by establishing a series of norms around the organization of cultural venues, to both "guarantee the absolute respect of freedoms of expression and association" and "foment the knowledge, dissemination, promotion, encouragement, and development of culture and the arts." It also created a legal definition of a "cultural space," built on an understanding of culture as "a set of distinctive spiritual, material, intellectual, and emotional features which characterize human groups and which comprise, beyond art and literature, ways of life, human rights, systems of values, traditions, and beliefs." Culture identified "our country through its richness, diversity, and originality," and constituted "processes generative of identity, individual, and collective symbolism." ECIs themselves were "organized in a self-managed [*autogestiva*], community, and independent manner" with the goal of "promoting and fomenting social interaction" through the creation, dissemination, exchange, and commercialization of "artistic-cultural goods, products and/or services." *Autogestión* was, in other words, defined in such a way as to include government-supported spaces as well as for-profit venues.

ECIs would be supported in the following ways: First, they would be recognized by the Secretariat of Culture as "organisms of public utility for common well-being," for which a letter of support from local residents would be required. Second, a publicly accessible database of ECIs would be created. Third, administrative processes would be simplified and made more transparent. Fourth, an official ECI certificate would be created, to be renewed every two years free of charge. Fifth, it was proposed that ECIs would be exempt from taxes on public spectacles, though this proposal later encountered problems. ECIs would in turn assume certain responsibilities to the state. The draft bill mandated ECI organizational teams participate in training workshops on neighborhood mediation, civil protection, and first aid. In order to gain recognition as ECIs, venues would have to provide names of *responsables* (responsible persons) and taxpayer numbers for members of the collectives running them, information about venue capacity and documents showing ownership or rental agreements, and a program for assuring the security of the venue. They were required to allow regular monitoring visits from Secretariat of Culture personnel, and to install a plaque created by the Secretariat of Culture "in a visible place on their exterior" containing contact information for the Institute for Cultural Rights—a proposal intended to mediate between ECIs and residential groups in cases of conflict.

Finally, those attending the consultation were divided into different tables and asked to provide feedback on aspects of the proposal. It is notable that much of this feedback strongly reflected specific everyday experiences that were not necessarily replicated across the board. For instance, one venue organizer requested that ECIs receive protections against frivolous complaints, alleging that neighborhood groups asked for bribes in exchange for not filing complaints. Others requested clarification on the rules around alcohol sales; while most music venues described as ECIs made a majority of their income from alcohol, the draft law contained a clause excluding venues selling alcohol from ECI status. The experiences of repression that emerged through the consultation varied widely: some implied government action and others implied government inaction, and many such experiences raised questions about conflicting rights. How could politicians mediate, for instance, between the constitutional rights of culture and assembly and residents' right to political participation (expressed through lodging complaints about ECIs)? How could one disentangle policies that supported public safety—for instance, by reducing noise pollution or insisting on safety standards for cultural venues—from those that extended Mexico's authoritarian legacy?

These questions remained open within this consultation, after which the Ley ECIs passed a vote in the city's senate in June 2020, and another in October 2020. It has since technically passed into law. At the time of writing, it is difficult to understand this law's effects in full. Equally, the process of passing this legislation has raised several policymaking challenges, which I will now describe.

Challenges: Trust, Governmentality

The Ley ECIs promised material benefits that were welcomed by many; participants also praised the consultative nature of the process.[60] At the same time, this law created practical problems of jurisdiction and implementation. While the law sought to ensure rights for cultural venues, the task of administering these venues fell to local *alcaldía* (formerly *delegación*) governments. These *alcaldías* were "the first government of contact," the sites for most disputes around licensing and compliance with the law, the entities that "can shut venues down, grants licenses for the sale of alcohol and food, which carry out safety checks."[61] They constantly had to mediate between constituencies with opposing perspectives and interests, including "nimbyist" neighborhood groups and ECIs. As such, while they did not write the law, *alcaldías* were the first to be accused of censorship after venue closures. Indeed, while the Secretariat of Culture had the task of implementing the Ley ECIs, the Law of Mercantile Spaces was implemented by the *alcaldías*. Establishing the right to culture in law, then, required coordination across various government entities with varying levels of commitment to the project.

This commitment was contingent on the culture of governance itself and the specific ties between various government entities and the cultural sphere: interlinked issues I discuss here in turn. For those within the *escena independiente*, the Ley ECIs could be understood as a tool of appropriation. ECIs would be effectively "branded" with the logo of the Secretariat of Culture, be obliged to comply with some Secretariat of Culture organizational guidelines, and be listed on a government-administered website. Some community cultural organizers who defined their role in terms of cultural resistance found the level of personal information requested difficult to accept. In an interview, one of Osorio's functionaries admitted that they had to face an "inherited distrust" of the authorities among ECIs, which made implementation difficult. Partly, they said, this distrust dovetailed with a "logic of opposition" in the Morena party now governing, and in the Mexican Left more generally. Equally, in the independent scene there was

> a lot of distrust, inherited from the seventy, eighty years [of single-party rule] in which, today we're still seeing news of diversion of millions in funds, of censorship, the previous government in Mexico City had enormous police operations against protests, it's not easy to create trust when in reality in the whole history of the country there weren't participatory processes. We think it's normal for the citizenry to have those reservations.[62]

This distrust reflected unwittingly onerous forms of statecraft; *foros culturales* knew from experience that administering a complex new regime of rights might create new administrative responsibilities. In turn, in order to combat distrust, functionaries sought to bypass bureaucracy by highlighting their personal approachability and proximity to the cultural community: "We've been either researching it or working in it, or we're arts managers or lawyers close [to the cultural scene]. . . . We're from the same cultural orbit and that creates a certain trust."[63] Within this vision of effective public administration during democratic transition, a good public administrator was characterized as an active social agent whose effectiveness was rooted not in the "production of indifference" but in a partisan affiliation to the cultural community, with which discrete personal connections would be nurtured.[64]

The problem of trust was a complex one, however, for two key reasons. First, distrust of government was vital for the ways that the right to culture was given value by the lobbying groups and policymakers pushing for it. An understanding of cultural rights as under threat was fundamental to the policy initiatives of Gabriela Osorio and her team and was inscribed in the names of institutions such as the Institute for the Defense of Cultural Rights. In turn, the argument that the right to culture applied to rock and the various related genres performed in *foros culturales* built on narratives depicting these genres as subject to historical and ongoing state repression. Second, where the personal relations of trust that politicians and functionaries sought to develop with stakeholders within these *foros* depended on continuity, such political workers often moved between government posts. Cultural organizers often complained that cultural policy was undervalued by politicians, cynically used as a career springboard (or, as one cultural organizer put it, a "political catapult") within the political profession.[65] Political transition also posed an obstacle to passing coherent laws: the election cycle caused significant breaks in politicians' ability to legislate and led to some politicians losing their jobs. Gabriela Osorio left her position in the city government to run for mayor of the *alcaldía* of Tlalpan in the 2021 midterm elections (which she lost to a candidate from the PAN), and many Morena policy initiatives were undermined when the party lost seats in these elections. The Ley ECIs responded both to specific experiences of repression and marginalization in the present and to a shared intuitive, affective, generally unspoken knowledge about Mexico's repressive history. It is perhaps no surprise that venue organizers often found that new functionaries had little understanding about the purposes and context of the Ley ECIs. This problem was compounded by patterns of media attention: as one functionary complained, cultural policy in Mexico City attracted scarce press coverage.[66] As a result of these factors, growing dissatisfaction with the Ley ECIs within independent venues combined with confusion about it: "We don't know what it is," one venue organizer told me in late 2021.[67]

To add to its challenges, the Ley ECIs coexisted with several other legal initiatives or reforms made by the Morena government that were relevant to the right to culture: the Law of Cultural Heritage, the Law of Films and Cinema, the Law of Cultural Promotion, the Law of Public Spectacles, and the Law of Mercantile Spaces. Most relevant to the topic of this chapter were proposed reforms to the Law of Mercantile Establishments, which regulated the licensing of commercial venues in the capital. A reform to this law was put forward in August 2020 to create exemptions to licensing requirements for ECIs. However, through this process, skepticism emerged among city lawmakers about potential misuses of the law—for instance, through bars which occasionally featured live music benefiting by declaring themselves "cultural spaces." Problems such as this one, as well as a legislative slowdown relating to the pandemic and the 2020 city elections, meant that this particular reform was not heard in the city congress.

These setbacks were indicative of broader challenges regarding the disciplinary governmentality still embedded in the capital's political culture. One functionary complained that politicians still tended to treat nightlife with suspicion, as something the state ought to limit or control: "The predisposition is always negative, that is, how can we control, verify. They never start from a promotion or creative or cultural industries perspective."[68] The process of implementing the Ley ECIs, in 2021 and 2022, was repeatedly frustrated by policymakers who tended to understand policymaking in disciplinary, prohibitional terms. Indeed, the Ley ECIs should be understood as part of a broader set of policy initiatives through which a group of Morena politicians and functionaries sought to challenge disciplinary governmentalities coded into law as a legacy of past authoritarianism. Such tensions were on show in one exchange during a panel on cultural rights organized by the Secretariat of Culture in August 2022 as part of the process of renovating the Law of Public Spectacles.[69] Juan Carlos Bonet from the city government's System for Supporting the Creation of Cultural Projects opened the panel by denouncing "lamentable spectacles" in public spaces in the capital, and advocating a curatorial role for the Secretariat of Culture in adjudicating what kinds of cultural expressions were "worthy, correct, [and] relevant." He explained that "public spectacles in a city to strengthen your identity, they have to be curated in some way" by a government agency empowered to censor art for being "noisy, raucous, rude, unworthy." Another panelist, David Mendoza, lead singer of the *sonidero* group Sonido Retro, responded by strongly challenging the premise of this governmental logic:

> Our city is still very young in terms of democracy. . . . We know that many of the laws, norms, regulations that have not been discussed or updated have a conservative bias in terms of society. Practically at the time they were drawn up, the character of our laws or our regulations was based on restriction or prohibition. In other words, the vision of the legislator and the executive . . . was to prohibit and restrict as far as possible.

What was required, Mendoza claimed, was a posture in which cultural expressions were regulated and facilitated by the authorities, but which refused "any vision that intends to prohibit or restrict . . . a cultural or artistic manifestation."

The disciplinary governmentality Mendoza here critiqued was reflected in the reception of the Ley ECIs among the city's political classes, who held up the law's implementation over concerns about "black sites" (*giros negros*)—venues or bars that were fronts for illicit sales of alcohol or drugs from which *foros culturales* frequently distanced themselves. It was also manifested in a clause excluding venues that sold alcohol from ECI status; the clause was introduced in order to prevent potential abuse of the Ley ECIs by unscrupulous bar owners, which caused dissatisfaction among venues within the independent music scene whose business depended largely on beer sales. Disillusionment was also driven by the messiness and length of the political process (drawn out in part by extensive consultation with the cultural community to begin with), leading to what one functionary described as "fatigue and exhaustion" in civil society.[70] By the end of my research, many of the venues that formed part of CECI had therefore ceased to engage with the drive to establish the right to culture. This was an ironic turn: marginalized spaces, which had been instrumental in the push for the Ley ECIs to begin with, saw their marginality reinforced as they engaged with it.

Final Reflections: Historical Affordances

As of 2024, the Ley ECIs has just begun to be implemented. Indeed, the city government has achieved somewhat of a public relations coup through its implementation: when Multiforo Cultural Alicia reopened in a new, larger venue in March 2024, it did so as the capital's first officially recognized ECI. Although the news was received with jubilation by most fans, some voices have criticized the venue's decision to accept official support.[71] It therefore remains to be seen how the venue will manage the tension between "cultural resistance" and official recognition, and the extent to which ECI status will protect the venue from closure by the authorities.

In this chapter I have argued that the drive to codify the "right to culture" in Mexico City law has taken an idiosyncratic path. I seek to show here how this idiosyncrasy reflects the specific nature of the coalition that has pushed for it—and in turn, the histories and experiences of censorship which this coalition has formed to resist. In practice, the concept of the "right to culture" is extremely vague, and exists in continuity with a broader postpolitical turn in Mexican cultural policy. Those tasked with making the (political) decisions about which cultural expressions deserve the protections ensuing from it have continuously invoked histories of censorship as a way to make sense of the task. In this sense, the coherence of "right to culture" policy depends on an affective politics of threat that is unstable and multidirectional, such that the state was here simultaneously engaged as guarantor of the right to culture and rejected as an assimilating force, originator of bureaucracy, and threat to venues' operational freedoms.[72] These downsides reflected a still-pervasive disciplinary governmentality, in which cultural life in Mexico City was seen as a source of danger in need of disciplinary control.

The "right to culture" drive uncovers affordances of histories of censorship. Lomnitz explores Mexican modernity as a struggle to establish terrain that is "inalienable" and subsequently used to define "relationships of differentiation."[73] It is thus instructive to note how the newly defined (inalienable) "right to culture" is built on differentiations between powerful corporate and governmental entities and small-scale independent spaces. Yet—following Lomnitz's analysis through to its conclusion—politicians encountered a challenge of putting into practice inalienable cultural rights without appealing to "the tutelage of the state," which had increasing relevance as the city's government grew more sympathetic to CECI's requests.[74] External threats are often constitutive of "rights," and many of those seeking to legislate the right to culture were motivated by and conversant in histories of cultural censorship, which were now taken as read, indexed rather than described. In turn, as within *foros culturales* themselves, histories of censorship tended to be reproduced in affective ways, producing a generalized affect of threat that motivated and conditioned collective action. The right to culture drive also catalyzed organization among *foros culturales*, and it helped to turn requests of the state into demands on it. Such collective action also had practical importance for the everyday activities of cultural venues in Mexico City, especially in a context of insecurity.

Rock could occupy an ambivalent position in relation to the right to culture: while its proponents reach back to the history of repression against the genre to position it as terrain in need of protection, rock could also be taken as the archetypical foreign, "invasive" cultural force. Its right to state protection was not a given; it was instead earned by solidarity groups such as FEAS, RECIA, and CECI, and the journalists who worked to amplify their voices, marshaling histories of censorship to this end. Nonetheless, this historical labor was ongoing and incomplete. As one functionary observed, it built on affective responses to past repression that varied depending on positionality and that were often difficult to articulate:

> Perhaps parents, grandparents, or [earlier] generations of the Left are very clear that there was a very clear repression and censorship, from movies to music, and that at least from our perspective it was part of the motivation behind the law, this lack of recognition in the different laws is no coincidence, there's a reason that there were no meeting places for youth, for political dissidence . . . but this link is not always made between repression, censorship, freedom, and human rights.[75]

This historical work, the same functionary reflected at a later date, could take different forms across different facets of the capital's shared cultural life; for instance, they stated that rock had a "very clear" history of censorship when compared to other artistic disciplines such as theater and film.[76] Although I have sought, in these pages, to complicate such historical "clarity," the right to culture drive reveals the potency of the same for present-day political contention.

While those promoting the right to culture faced challenges concerning institutional procedure, their work fundamentally depended on ideas, language, and history. They faced the challenge of convincing people within the cultural community to integrate rights discourse into their everyday language, such that episodes of censorship could be reinscribed as attacks against cultural rights. Vital, too, was the retelling of disparate histories of censorship against culture in such a way as to establish their relevance for the present and articulate a shared narrative of democratization of cultural rights across artistic disciplines. In this sense, the innovative policy initiative that accumulated around the "right to culture" was contingent on the affective and epistemological complexities of stories about censorship.

CHAPTER 7

Write for Your Right to Party

Rock Knowledge and the Opening of History

It's December 2019; I'm at a book presentation held at Multiforo Cultural Alicia. Rafael González, otherwise known as Señor González, a percussionist who has performed with the pathbreaking *rock en español* group Botellita de Jerez since the 1990s, has just published the last of a three-part book series on Mexican rock, *60 años del rock mexicano*. The room is, for this midsized independent venue, fairly full: about eighty turn up. While the event is free, many attendees buy bottles of beer to keep the venue running, and there's a long queue for the book signing at the end.

Much of González's introduction to the book emphasizes the difficulty in getting this book published in a changing environment. The series' initial publishing house, Ediciones B, approached him about writing an encyclopedia of Mexican rock bands after the same proposal was rejected by Chava Rock, a well-known rock journalist and blogger. As González began to write, the project ballooned into a series of three parts. Ediciones B was then taken over by Penguin Random House, who promptly cut its support for the series; the final volume was published independently under the name "Sr. González Producciones." The Herculean nature of the project is further highlighted by struggles with ill health: the writing process was delayed by González's battle with cancer.

Rafael González is accompanied in a roundtable discussion by long-standing rock journalist David Cortés, who opens by emphasizing the paucity of books written about rock (although, in truth, at a local level it is one of very few genres that receives this kind of literary attention). Cortés highlights the importance of the collective "labor of documentation" of rock in Mexico and praises González's contribution: where projects such as this often focus on the writer's friends, he says, *60 años del rock mexicano* is genuinely invested in presenting a more complete, less partisan account of the genre. This comment is revealing of an enterprise that is simultaneously predicated on "objectivity" and rooted in a decidedly "interested" attitude to rock as a genre. Rock journalism is, fundamentally, a shared meaning-making pursuit oriented around a rich social life. I'm reminded of other fieldwork encounters with the journalist, such as one occasion when I bumped into Cortés buying CDs and vinyl at the Tianguis Cultural del Chopo and we got talking about rock's history of censorship. He began to criticize a younger journalist who denied that rock was prohibited in the 1970s and roped in a series of nearby friends who had lived through this era to weigh in as well: "[El] *rock estuvo prohibido, ¿sí o no?*" [was rock prohibited, yes or no?]. Soon, there were several of us participating in engaged, friendly, personal discussion.

Through interactions such as this one, interviews, and conversations with González, Cortés, and many others, I've come to negotiate this terrain myself somewhere between interestedness and detachment. The most common praise I hear for my own work is that it is "objective," in the sense of being distanced from particularistic interests within this scene, yet this is also a backhanded compliment: it still paints me as an interloper, making a virtue out of my perennial status as outsider. Of course, the idea of the researcher as cool, detached, disinterested observer is neither feasible nor desirable, and I have not encouraged this idea in the process of doing research. However, it speaks loudly to a situation in which knowledge work is profoundly interested in the production of cultural life. The questions about research, commitment, and inclusion suggested by this praise relate to how knowledge work structures Mexican rock history and the social function it plays within the local scene, for which González's book constitutes an interesting case study. He takes an encyclopedic approach to Mexican rock history, profiling 137 acts seen as representative of the genre. While the first two volumes studied the periods 1959–1979 and 1980–1989 respectively, the third begins in 1990 and runs until 2016. Each volume contains periodic historical overviews, which are generally brief and journalistic in tone, yet most of this work consists of descriptions of individual artists' musical contributions and biographies. This is, principally, an exercise in documentation for the purposes of historical memory; it seeks to "rescue" and reevaluate long-forgotten predecessors to the stars that emerged from the 1980s and 1990s rock scene. A similar purpose is indicated more overtly by the subtitle of one of the precursors to González's series, David Cortés's *100 discos esenciales del rock mexicano: antes de que nos olviden* (100 essential albums from Mexican rock: Before they forget us).[1]

The fact that González's project is not intended as an exercise in boundary or canon creation is underscored by the inclusion of five pages, toward the end of the book, listing the hundreds of artists who were "on the table, but never made it to these pages."[2] The topic of inclusion and exclusion is also a subject of roundtable discussion, implicit in audience questions about whether Mexican rock has a distinctive sound and about González's definition of rock. In turn, the author is keen to downplay the "definitive" status of his book; some albums, he highlights, were featured simply because of an abundance of information about them. Something more nuanced, playful, and alive is taking place here, therefore, than the creation of an "imaginary museum of musical works."[3] As it happens, the pair are asked whether a dedicated museum for Mexican rock ought to be created, to which David Cortés gives an impassioned affirmative response. A museum, especially one containing the rock magazines that "kept us united with the world" during the 1970s and 1980s when rock struggled to achieve radio play, would aid the memory of the scene and combat the perception that Mexican rock "begins with [bands from the 1980s boom] Caifanes and Los Amantes de Lola."

González's book has a vibrant social life: it's a focus of enjoyment and conviviality, to a far greater degree than most academic books.[4] Neither the author nor Cortés hesitate to share their musical tastes; both are engaging, charismatic, and sympathetic speakers. The distribution networks for González's book are revealing in themselves: initially, fewer than a thousand copies were printed and the book was promoted locally, at a handful of small-scale events such as this one. After this point, the book took on a reasonable momentum within Mexico; in a few months it was being sold in Gandhi, one of the biggest bookstore chains in the country. When I saw González once again upon my return to Mexico in late 2021, he was looking to gain the rights to the first two volumes of the book in order to republish them; by Autumn 2022, he was selling a Kindle version of the book on Amazon, where it's been purchased in the United States and Europe, as well as (mostly) in Mexico.

Such international reach points toward questions about what happens when Spanish-language books on Mexican rock travel to the Anglophone world. Those based north of the US-Mexico border can purchase many such titles online with comparative ease, although this is not always the case. I was only able to purchase Teresa Estrada's *Sirenas al ataque* directly from the author, with whom I met over a coffee, because the book was out of print. For scholars writing in English, such books provide source material for the production of historical narrative and the performance of historical expertise. In some cases—for instance, where books are out of print and no e-book exists—the facts of distribution enhance their prestige. Ethical questions thus arise about how people such as myself, participating in these books' international circulation, may perpetuate or challenge extractivist tendencies in transnational flows of knowledge, as well as about the relationship between our research and the local scenes we write about. As I have tried to point out, at no point in engaging with the histories of this independent music scene can we escape the question: What does knowledge do? I have attempted to reckon with this question, tracing complex entanglements between knowledge production—in documentaries, recorded music, and performances, as much as in books, magazines, and newspapers—and the production of a scene.

This conclusion becomes more intuitive when considering the many figures mentioned here who have combined careers in rock journalism with careers as performers and organizers, such as Walter Schmidt, Chava Rock, Federico Arana, Rafael González, Rafael Catana, and Patricia Peñaloza. In these figures' writing, which I have sought to foreground, the connection between the stories told about the rock scene in Mexico and action within it is intuitively understood, yet they are less celebrated than the canonical intellectuals cited most often by academics writing about Mexican rock, such as Carlos Monsiváis, José Agustín, and Parménides García Saldaña. The work of the former set of writers tends to have fewer literary aspirations, it speaks to a local audience rather than an international one, and it is harder to access. It addresses local necessities, looking to speak, intervene, and act as participants in a creative community. Rarely does it produce conclusions that, in Spanish parlance, "transcend"—in other words, that impact wider debate, especially conversations held outside of Mexico. Rather, this is work with existential stakes for venues in Mexico City's independent rock scene. Journalistic labor, for instance, influences whether, and for how long, these venues are closed by government. Such knowledge acts powerfully within this scene.

This knowledge-action invokes contentious histories. On the one hand, Lomnitz has critiqued the ways that scholars based in Mexico have been able to create what amount to personal fiefdoms predicated on their ties to the nation-state and on their ability to act as interlocutors for intellectual traditions from outside of Mexico.[5] On the other hand, we may understand the unusually close, enduring link between creative practice and distinct forms of journalism as part of a broader cultural and affective legacy of Mexican authoritarianism. Rock musicians in Mexico have long had to negotiate their existence before government and society. The intuitive sense among many rockers who have entered journalism that they have to "write for their right to party" has a long inheritance.

In this final chapter, I am to account and advocate for the documentary aim of books such as those discussed above, and for rock journalism as a documentary practice in general. I am inspired by the (now very long) legacy of work critiquing notions of historical "closure" or "settling" and work that sees in historical "openness" a path toward counterhegemonic politics.[6] I explore how knowledge actors such as journalists, who are significantly engaged with what has been explored here as the *escena independiente*, work to open the history of their genre and undo its inherited historical closures. And I argue that such labors of historical "unpicking" may contrast sharply with the metanarratives often foregrounded in international scholarship on the same topic.

At the same time, this chapter also explores how rock journalists have experienced Mexico's neoliberal historical "closure." I assume the "ecosystems" approach to journalism: that is, a perspective that highlights journalists' interventions in broader flows of knowledge, mediated through assemblages composed only in part by journalistic labor. I am interested in different ways that rock journalism may be positioned: as adversarial, as socially valuable within a given cultural community, as a project for imparting ideas about citizenship.[7] This chapter draws on ethnography conducted in two areas. First, I discuss workshops given by rock journalists in Mexico City. These workshops not only teach students about histories of rock censorship but also function to preserve a model of journalistic citizenship in a conflictive context. By destructuring prevailing accounts of the censorship of rock in Mexico, they draw attention to other, less recognized patterns of music censorship. Second, and to conclude, I present an ethnographically informed reflection on ColectivaMente, a project created by a group of rockers, journalists, and academics that engages several different kinds of activities (and many meetings) to the task of documenting rock. I open, however, by exploring how rock journalists in the present have understood recent transformations in their profession and, in turn, how this changing setting has affected their opportunities to produce and fashion knowledge.

Writing, Professionalizing

Starting in the 1990s, rock journalism has undergone transformations linked, ambivalently, to neoliberal globalization. Reflecting the "fragmentation" of rock into many "small universes,"[8] there emerged a number of increasingly diverse commercial rock publications catering to different audiences. The magazine *La Banda Rockera*, for instance, began life as a supplement within *Conecte* before it became independent from its parent publication in the late 1980s; *La mosca en la pared* emerged in the mid-1990s as glossier competition for *Conecte*, which eventually became commercially unviable. For many, the field has become more competitive as a result. A diversity of rock publications certainly helps to avoid the problems of the 1970s and 1980s, in which the "overwhelming" power of *Conecte*—a magazine in which "everyone wanted to appear"—allied with informed suspicions that labels gifted the magazine LPs in exchange for favorable coverage.[9] From the mid-1980s, the style and presentation of rock magazines also began to change significantly. Magazines began to use the now-standard gloss-coated paper, and they began to use fewer colloquialisms, opting for a writing style that could reach beyond an audience of rock insiders. The editorials that characterized 1970s rock journalism—addressed to the "rock movement" as a whole, and often articulating shared values and dreams, or denouncing catastrophic events—were now *outré*.

Especially notable was the appearance of a Mexican version of the international magazine *Rolling Stone* in 2002. Though rock journalists had been reporting from outside Mexico as "correspondents" since the 1960s, *Rolling Stone*'s global reach presented it with an enormous advantage: the same interviews with high-profile acts could be carried across multiple iterations of the magazine. Transnational integration could place magazines at the mercy of international events: after the global financial crisis of 2008, the Mexican edition of *Rolling Stone* was discontinued for six months. In addition, the magazine's global reach has complicated its relationship with the national music industries. Its editor has argued that because it is able to syndicate content from its US affiliate, it is less economically dependent on national labels and more able to be "objective," but this has disadvantaged Mexican acts: in 2009 the magazine implemented a policy of not placing Mexican or Latin American artists on its front cover, since this correlated to significant declines in sales.[10]

Rock journalists have also been affected by the sector-wide crisis brought about by the Internet. *La mosca en la pared* was forced to close in 2010 as readers moved online, sales declined, and bankrupt labels ceased to advertise in the magazine.[11] Members of Mexican rock journalism's old guard are often critical of bloggers for lacking professionalism and critical reflection; perpetuating stereotypes, myths, and misinformation; using obscene language; and conflating critique with criticism.[12] As the comparatively stable journalistic work of the past is also threatened by the shift to online news media,[13] these older writers have found opportunities to be paid for their writing increasingly limited.

These experiences of change draw attention to the ways that rock journalism is valued by those practicing it. The rock magazines of the 1970s and 1980s played a practical role in the growth of the rock scene; as such, the editorial policy of a magazine like *Conecte* was "to tell the truth, being positive."[14] Such an attitude continues today among some journalists: for instance, for the writer Patricia Peñaloza, to be able to "communicate" through journalism one must first "delimit what is your community" and quite literally embed yourself within it: "go to get covered in mud at Corona Capital, go to the slam, where you get covered in piss."[15] In the present, however, it is less clear what precisely constitutes that community; rock journalists tend to find magazines unreceptive to any insistence that they should specialize in a single genre, especially at a time when "there isn't even a consensus about what rock is."[16] "Those writing today," some have written, "aren't committed to the idea of being a professional journalist, or to rock."[17] The occupation has, then, diversified out of necessity. In many cases, rock journalists have found livelihoods in new terrain, such as the "pool profession" of pedagogy.[18] The rock journalists who turn to teaching in some form tend to use, and play upon, the prestige formed through published but often unprofitable writing.

Rock journalism has also become a more "professional" pursuit. While the term "professional" leaves plenty to be defined, the professionalization of rock journalism comprises several tendencies.[19] The first pertains to language: where well-known journalists of the past employed a freewheeling, richly subjective, and often scathing style, contemporary rock journalism tends to be more formally written; it contains fewer spelling errors; it is less inventive with its use of language and punctuation, especially eschewing older generations' frequent capitalizations of words and use of ellipses; and it is more "objective" in the narrow sense of focusing on the object at hand (generally, artists and their music). It produces credibility by removing the writer from the picture rather than by intensely foregrounding the writer's sensory experience. Some trace this shift to the 1990s, when *Conecte* was put out of business by *La mosca en la pared*, whose editor insisted that the magazine's writers use more formal language.[20] As former *Conecte* editor José Luis Pluma later reflected, "We addressed people on the street, who preferred a simpler read"; unable to compete with the "quality and journalistic perspective" of its new rival, *Conecte* soon folded.[21]

Second, it is suggested that present-day rock writers have a more deep-rooted sense of professional ethics. Some cite the case of a 1971 *Piedra Rodante* interview with *la encuerada de Avándaro*—a young girl who was photographed topless at the festival; it was common knowledge that this interview had been fabricated by the magazine's editor, with little concern for the real-life experience of the person involved.[22] Rock magazines in the present also take intellectual property more seriously. Past rock magazines reused images and articles "from American magazines with singular glee and without scruples."[23] For former *Conecte* editor José Luis Pluma, stealing content from these magazines "was valid. They stole our territory years before, it was time to steal something back, fuck it [*chingue su madre*]."[24] This approach is no longer an option: the risks that plagiarism will be discovered are greater, and the penalties are higher.[25] Evidently, both developments reflect the abundance of information in a digital age and the entrenchment of a neoliberal model of intellectual property. One consequence of this trend is that internationally syndicated magazines such as *Rolling Stone*, which can freely adapt and translate content across multiple versions worldwide, have an advantage over independent, local publications.

This conjuncture of digitization and neoliberalization has also affected the way that knowledge about rock is produced. In general, there is a lack of publicly accessible archival material on rock. Editors of magazines and newspapers have a legal duty to submit two copies of each issue they publish to the Hemeroteca Nacional de México, a public archive. In practice, however, editors have often failed to fulfill this obligation; in the 1980s it was estimated that 60 percent of editors did not do so, a situation worsened by the rampant inflation of the 1980s and 1990s, when magazines' operating costs rose significantly.[26] As a result, the archival record of rock publications is patchy; the only public record of several significant rock magazines from this period are mentions in other magazines. In response, some rock writers have organized new archiving initiatives. The Museo Universitario del Chopo has established a so-called *fanzinoteca*, which holds fanzines from Mexico City's self-managed rock scene since the 1980s.[27] At the Fonoteca Nacional de México, an archive generally dedicated to Mexican folkloric music, journalist Ricardo Bravo has created a catalog to document Mexican rock history and "rescue and join together the pieces of Mexican rock."[28] Nonetheless, these efforts still leave this field piecemeal and disjointed—a practical impediment to producing any grand narrative about the genre's history, and an obstacle to documenting it.

As a result, even at a time of informational abundance, the work and prestige of rock journalists often depends on private collections. There is a significant market for rock magazines at sites such as Tianguis Cultural del Chopo, the informal rock market that appears each Saturday close to Metro

Buenavista, in the north of Mexico City. At this market, several stalls sell old vinyl records of *rock mexicano* and rock magazines. While the former are far more visible than the latter, vendors often keep a more extensive collection than they place on display, bringing them out when passers-by show an interest. Some competition exists between established stalls and itinerant vendors. The price of a single issue of a magazine can range from twenty to a hundred pesos, depending on its contents and condition; many magazines sold at the Tianguis are reprints. Magazines featuring especially popular bands, such as Caifanes, on the front cover fetch a premium, as do older editions and untouched copies. The offering here is equally patchy, and stalls often sell the same issues of *Conecte* and *La Banda Rockera* repeatedly.

Rock journalism may, therefore, be a costly undertaking, built on competition for limited resources. Prestige may rehearse preexisting patterns of economic privilege, converting economic capital into social and cultural capital. Journalists often suspect, in turn, that some of their contemporaries may have stolen archival material from the holdings of the Hemeroteca. Some advocate the creation of a new, accessible library of rock magazines, although this would require goodwill, work, and a shared recognition of enlightened self-interest.

This piecemeal access to information about Mexican rock also extends to recordings. "In the past," one journalist wrote, "we had to buy thousands of books and albums; now, perhaps, it's all online."[29] This form of connoisseurship was described by Carlos Monsiváis as *estar al día* (being up-to-date): "being submerged in the music for hours and days on end, acquiring discs and cassettes with an expert eye, exchanging information, memorizing lyrics, obsessively reading magazines and fanzines, following with a little skepticism the energy of the cultural industries' trends."[30] In recent years, many more recordings of Mexican rock have been made available on streaming services such as Spotify. Yet many rock recordings from the 1960s and 1970s are still hard to find online and dependent on individual uploads. For instance, *Viaje fantástico* by Pájaro Alberto y Conjunto Sacrosaurio, released in 1974, is still not available on Spotify, although a version has been uploaded to YouTube. This compounds another problem: many otherwise accomplished Mexican rock bands from this era never recorded their music to begin with.

The comparatively recent transition to neoliberalism, then, has had complicated effects on rock journalists' ability to give an account of the scene in which they are situated.[31] Even in the Internet age, David Cortés and Rafael González's concern that many rock bands might drop out of history is entirely feasible. These actors' structuring of rock knowledge—in the form of anthologies and chronicles that both provide biographical information on artists and closely describe musical style—constitute a pragmatic response to a frequently articulated local necessity, implying a certain purpose for rock journalism: one of conservation and restoration. Genre-specific rock journalism, indeed, has proven to be a remarkably enduring pursuit, even as, in contemporary times, rock is a diminishing part of the wider entertainment industry. Much of this, it is recognized, is down to the genre's specific histories. On the fiftieth anniversary of Avándaro, José Xavier Návar criticized rock journalists' and collectors' obsession with the festival: "Avándaro, where on the day itself groups were included who didn't ask for money; today these same bands are, as they are part of official history, thoroughly envied by collectors, in their discographies; by orators and academics, professional organizers of homages, conjurists and blusterers, for whom Avándaro legitimates them."[32]

Yet in fact rock journalists articulate varied motivations for their activities: at times they are connected to the specific cultural project of the rock scene, at times they are understood as engaged in a disinterested informational project, and at times they are linked to democratization and the development of a skeptical citizenry.[33] The next section explores how varying ways of doing and valuing rock journalism intertwine within free-to-attend workshops about Mexican rock history.

Rock Journalism and Education

Education has, in recent years, constituted an increasingly important aspect of rock journalists' livelihoods. Rock has found, to some extent, a foothold in the academy. David Cortés has a doctorate in education from the National Pedagogical University (UPN) and has given classes on rock at universities, as well as free-to-attend seminars at Multiforo Cultural Alicia. Patricia Peñaloza, a rock journalist and musician active since the late 1990s, gave a rock journalism workshop in Centro Cultural José Martí, a cultural space administered by the city government in Mexico City's historic center, for several years until 2018. A seminar on heavy metal has been established at UNAM since 2018, and rock-related education is increasingly a fixture at state-run cultural centers. Most notably, a dedicated rock school, Escuela de Rock y la Palabra (School of Rock and the Word), has been established by the rock pianist and composer Guillermo Briseño with the support of the Secretariat of Culture of the Mexico City government. Rock journalists, increasingly obliged to diversify their livelihoods, take on such jobs out of economic necessity. The status of rock journalism as a discipline worth pursuing as part of formal education in its own right plays on the importance of literature to the counterculture in Mexico and the respect accorded to some of its high-profile exponents.

From May to July 2019, I attended a weekly workshop held at the Faro de Oriente, a large government-run space in Iztapalapa. Faro de Oriente is a visually arresting site, awkwardly situated between two metro stations. To arrive, one must pass by open-air stalls selling rock-related paraphernalia and food on a road that borders one of the largest informal markets in Mexico City, where one encounters piles of stolen clothes, electronic equipment, and other goods. The venue's campus—which is bordered by a high fence and has a small entrance guarded by police ever since an episode of unrest during a Panteón Rococó concert—presents an island of comparative security in the midst of threatening surroundings. It was created by the PRD city government in 2001 with a large open area that can host mass-scale rock concerts and a large building that is the site for many workshops serving the surrounding community.

Titled "Mexican Rock and Journalism," this workshop has been hosted at the Faro de Oriente for several years and is free of charge. Students at the workshop are mostly, although not exclusively, from surrounding neighborhoods on the eastern fringes of Mexico City. Students participated in the workshop for various reasons: while many were attracted by the chance to record radio programs, some saw it as a chance to improve their writing, some were enthusiastic about learning journalism as a craft, and some were drawn to the workshop as enthusiasts of rock. The workshop has accumulated an online community of present and past students, oriented around the *Rock con filo* (Rock with an edge) Facebook group, which proved especially useful during the Covid-19 pandemic, when the course was delivered online. It is convened by Javier "Chelico" Hernández, a long-standing Mexico City rock journalist who started to write at *Conecte* in the 1980s, and now writes a column for *La Jornada*. As a participant (and later as contributor), I became interested in how the course made history speak to the present, how the act of producing Mexican rock history was deployed as a proving ground for a form of journalistic subjectivity grounded in empiricism and skepticism of received wisdom, and how Chelico frequently intervened to ensure that the history told in the workshop was open rather than closed.

The format was the same for most sessions: during the first hour Chelico delivered a talk, after which we moved to the Faro de Oriente radio studio to record a one-hour show on the weekly theme, to be published on the radio station's MixCloud account. Weekly themes progressed in linear fashion from the 1950s to the present, although they paid most attention to the 1960s and 1970s. Shows were supposed to be planned the week prior, but in practice were often organized ad hoc on the spot; on a couple of occasions Chelico approached me just before the show started recording to ask if I could prepare a four-minute section. After recording the radio show, we returned to the classroom to plan for the following week.

The radio program was not the only practical activity in the workshop: a key assessment was the collaborative production of a fanzine, which students had to organize and write under Chelico's guidance.[34] This assessment mediated between the administrative expectations of government and an engagement with professional practice, which tends to be emphasized in the Faros. Equally, key to the workshop were certain iterations of journalistic values, which interacted in complex ways with the ways that rock histories were retold. In the workshop, Chelico modeled a certain journalistic subjectivity—rooted in rigor, humility, neutrality, and skepticism—and dedicated time to explicitly defining a specific social role for journalism. In doing so, he began to unpack received histories of rock in Mexico, looking to "[tell] a better story in relation to the current conjuncture."[35]

A journalistic matter-of-factness played out in everyday language used in the course: *ahí va la información* (there's your information) was the mantra repeated after each segment on our radio show, and Chelico consistently emphasized the importance of correct information during classes. This emphasis on "information" reflected a commitment to rigor and skepticism of received narratives. As one student put it to me, the workshop taught them to think independently, rather than being a *fiel seguidor*—a faithful follower.[36] At one point—just after Chelico had asked me to prepare a snap five-minute segment about the Summer of Love for the workshop radio show—the journalist discussed with me unwitting inaccuracies made by other students during the live broadcast, before entering the classroom to set the story straight. An especially prominent bone of contention were the *hoyos fonqui*, which in fact predated Avándaro but were often mistakenly understood as a product of post-Avándaro repression. Not only did Chelico intervene immediately to correct students implying that *hoyos fonqui* were created in the 1970s, but students even began to correct one another on this point in the instructor's absence.

While Chelico valued accuracy, he told me that it was most important that students not contradict what the group was learning in the workshop. Misinformation only became intolerable when it began to undermine pedagogical authority, suggesting broader questions about the ways that journalists and connoisseurs act to shore up their own prestige, especially in a digital age. Chelico repeatedly linked misinformation with online media, both in private comments and to the class: "There's a lot of garbage on social media," he told me. In turn, although the instructor's authority was never challenged, he acted proactively to protect it. Authority was asserted in the studio: in addition to effectively acting as producer, Chelico sat by a microphone during most segments, ready to intervene to correct speakers or add to their contributions. In classes the instructor drip-fed us information from his personal collection, especially photocopies of newspaper and magazine clippings, and occasionally books now out of print. For example, on one occasion he brought a copy of the safety policy shared with attendees of Avándaro, showing that festival organizers supported the police and military presence at the festival, that they had organized medical tents and information points, and that effective security was seen as vital to the success of the festival ("We're going to show the world that we can do this!" it opens). This demonstrated the planning that went into organizing the festival and indicated a communal spirit among attendees. But at a time when journalistic authority was challenged by a new generation of bloggers, it also underlined the importance of "analog" knowledge not available online.

In turn, Chelico connected effective journalistic practice to "observing ... and being humble." This "humility" was linked, he told us, to ways of acting and being in everyday life; good journalistic practice was good living. It is notable that the distinct ways that Avándaro had been remembered became central to this journalistic combination of attention to detail and personal humility: the credibility of contemporary journalists and musicians had become so dependent on their attendance at the festival that many who were not in fact present had made up false stories about it.[37] Other moments during class permitted the instructor to perform comfort with his own fallibility: after he asked how many acts performed at Avándaro, one student looked the answer up on Wikipedia, finding a list of twelve bands. Chelico didn't agree, providing a figure of ten, before going through the list and finding only one act that had not, in fact, performed at the festival. Undermining his own status as "authority" on Mexican rock and authority figure in the context of this classroom, he concluded jovially: "The problem is, I don't know how to count." This self-deprecating comment made particular sense when contrasted with what the instructor described as "mythomaniacs" in the rock scene who had invented stories to boost their own reputations or to create a narrative of "victimization." Here the insecure, fragile rocker was contrasted unfavorably with the calm, detached, self-confident journalist, modeled throughout the workshop by Chelico's reserved, serene, softly spoken persona.

This mixture of journalistic values clearly resonated with many students. One participant described the values taught in the workshop as "humility, simplicity, trust, knowledge, generosity, lightness of touch, playful adventurousness."[38] Students valued the workshop's systematic emphasis on verification of information and informed skepticism, and appreciated the ability to deepen their familiarity with comparatively unknown Mexican rock in order to recuperate and "rescue" this music. For some, rock had declined in influence and reach; others complained that Mexican audiences tended to listen to and value rock from overseas, leading to ignorance about the rich history the genre enjoyed within Mexico.[39]

Rock history was transformed in these workshops into a litmus test for such journalistic empiricism and skepticism. Chelico tended to challenge received ideas about post-Avándaro repression and to draw continuities between censorship in the 1970s and at other times. One week, for instance, Chelico posed a rhetorical question: "Who says no rock was recorded after Avándaro?" He then pulled out a book by Antonio Malacara Palacios, *Catálogo subjetivo y segregacionista del rock mexicano* (Subjective and segregationist catalogue of Mexican rock), and read from it, performatively ad nauseum, a long list of rock LPs and EPs recorded in the early 1970s in Mexico, before concluding that "the labels did not close to rock." When one student objected that perhaps large commercial venues became unavailable to rock in the wake of Avándaro, Chelico responded that this had always been the case. "When did rock have freedom in Mexico?" he asked us one week, answering the question himself: "It had always been prohibited." In this sense, there was an adversarial subtext for the workshop. While Chelico did not deny repression after Avándaro, the journalist sought to put it in context, showing how repression of rock long predated the festival, exploring mass closures of *cafés cantantes* in the 1960s and bans against specific songs in the late 1960s.

This telling of history tended to resonate with and complement students' complex and sometimes conflicting accounts of censorship. "You become aware," one said, "that repression [of rock] always existed." While this participant felt that censorship of the genre had declined ("there's not so much censorship now"), they and others also drew attention to what they perceived as present-day censorship, consisting of venue closures, media control over the cultural sphere, the overall impact of corporate power in popular music, religion, and the continued legacy of single-party rule.[40] For another, present-day expression was limited by *sesgo mediático*—media bias—and by the closing of spaces and platforms to artists not signed to major labels.[41] Another participant stated that in the present one could face reprisals for criticism of the government—opening up the conversation beyond the creative industries.[42]

In turn, Chelico frequently told rock history in ways that mattered for present-day attitudes, on several occasions drawing a comparison between past generations' experiences of rock and the status of reggaetón in the present. While the genre is among the most popular in Mexico, there have been continuous official attempts to censor reggaetón in the country.[43] This censorship has occasionally come from rock fans themselves. Like rock in the past, reggaetón was subject to fierce social criticism and occasional censorship. Moreover, most people judged its sexual politics to be unacceptable. And, just like rock, Chelico observed, reggaetón was seen to be musically uninteresting, monotonous, and harmonically limited. Yet the rockers of the past had gone on to be professional workers such as teachers and doctors, Chelico said, predicting that something similar would occur with reggaetón performers and fans.

The ways that histories of rock censorship were constructed thus made them consequential for the present. If the genre was taken to have been banned outright by the government in the wake of Avándaro, it could be safely distanced from contemporary reggaetón: after all, reggaetón had never been subject to a similar ban in Mexico. However, the idea that rock had been censored in a more horizontal fashion, at the conjuncture of several different sectors of Mexican society, raised more unsettling, provocative questions about present-day attitudes. One student in the workshop, for instance, told me that she participated in a radio show open to play music of any genre, except for reggaetón. A similar formula, as seen in Chapter 5, was repeated across the independent music scene: self-managed spaces, whose identity was tied to the principle of curatorial eclecticism, often excluded reggaetón, in many cases explicitly. Famously, the reggaetón group Calle 13 was booed offstage at Vive Latino in 2011. I have gotten to know politically engaged rappers whose music was subject to censorship on online streaming services. They complained not only about the censorship itself, but about the fact that reggaetón artists seemed to get away with far worse—thus seemingly endorsing censorship while denouncing perceived hypocrisy.

The value of taking a critical and reflective approach to rock history here came to the fore. A comparative decentering of the story of rock censorship in Mexico from Avándaro and the Dirty War had the effect of highlighting an unrecognized but prevalent form of censorship across the city which aligned with patterns of class and ethnic discrimination.[44] The workshop's emphasis on journalistic subjectivities was intertwined with a refusal to view music censorship as bound by genre or linear time. Censorship here was opened, liberated from processual, teleological assumptions consigning it to the despotic past.

International Flows of Knowledge

Such educational activity, and the reopening of closed knowledge that it tends to entail, ought not be taken for granted. The existence of these courses in rock journalism is precarious; they are threatened by marginalization, austerity, and modes of neoliberal governance that have persisted in Mexico even after being rejected at the ballot box in 2018.[45] David Cortés's 2018 course in Multiforo Cultural Alicia was not repeated the following year. Throughout the time that I studied with Chelico, the city's Secretariat of Culture had its budget withheld as part of a government program of austerity—and therefore the salaries of many of its teaching staff were held up for several months. Throughout this period, Chelico complained of a wave of resignations among administrators charged with running Faro de Oriente, obliging him to develop professional relationships and understanding with new personnel. When asked whether he might want to use his public platform to condemn mismanagement at the Faros, he told us that to be *juez y parte* (judge and defendant) would be a violation of journalistic ethics. I opened this chapter by describing the fundamental imbrication of rock journalism with action—the ability, among members of this scene, to advocate for the existence of their creative practice. Yet it is clear that, for many, Mexico's historically closed "transition"—a seemingly endless neoliberal turn—is experienced as a threat to this activity.

On the other hand, there is another, more ambivalent version of this articulation between rock history and action, one that is less responsive to local experience and that foregrounds, at least in part, a colonial dynamic in which Western scholarship "is an unmarked site of general theory, while the non-West is marked and minoritized as the locus of the particular and of empirical detail."[46] One version of Mexican rock history resonates with teleological, "end-of-history" accounts of Mexican democratization. Here the democratic transition is intertwined with the supremacy of neoliberal economics, which came to dominate after the "exhaustion" of developmentalism in Mexico.[47] The single-party regime is positioned as the overriding antagonist; PRI control within Mexico is understood as so complete that the government needed to be weakened by concessions to international (market) forces and the country thus forced toward democracy. Regardless of neoliberalism's wholesale failings in Mexico—for instance, poor economic growth, ballooning inequality, stagnant life expectancy, and the unleashing of a pattern of brutal violence—one does not achieve multiparty democracy without it, or so the story goes.[48] This story exists within a broader, global metanarrative that took hold in the 1990s and early 2000s in which neoliberal capitalism was understood as a necessary condition for democracy to flourish, the most (in)famous account of which was Francis Fukuyama's "end of history" thesis.[49]

This account overlooks the messiness of history. A number of recent accounts of PRI single-party rule revise the long-held notion of the PRI as the "perfect dictatorship"—dominant, stable, and entrenched in power. For instance, historians have demonstrated that the PRI did not straightforwardly control labor unions but engaged in complex negotiations with the same, that the PRI made continuous concessions to the middle classes, and that PRI power was exerted through political violence, which was experienced more intensely in cities than in the countryside.[50] Smith has shown how in the 1960s and 1970s the PRI began to exert control, unevenly, over the press by manipulating paper prices—using tools developed decades earlier in order to promote the development of a robust print media.[51] Across several different spheres, then, the PRI bargained for its continuation in power with a plurality of groups within Mexico, rather than enjoying uncontested control. The democratic reforms brought forward by the authoritarian regimes of Luis Echeverría Álvarez and José López Portillo are good examples of such bargaining. These reforms helped to pave the way toward meaningful multiparty democracy but in themselves they constituted concessions to the student movement.[52] López Portillo's reforms resulted in the PAN winning several seats in the Chamber of Deputies in 1979 and several peaceful transitions of power at the local level in the early 1980s.

Therefore, another account of democratization in Mexico, one that has a strong foothold in the independent music scene that is the focus of this book, is agonistic and open. Informed by radical social movements such as Zapatismo, it tends to perceive continuities between dictatorship and democracy, such as the continuation of clientelistic politics by political parties competing with the PRI after 2000.[53] It emphasizes democratization as a bottom-up process, driven by social movements and grassroots organizations within Mexico.[54] It is skeptical about the impact of institutional changes supporting a constrained multiparty democracy on most people's everyday lives, especially in a context of deep economic inequality.[55] As such, it is harder to narrate in straightforward historical terms; it is more likely to invoke discrete, patchwork histories of struggle among specific activist groups; and it depends on an intuitive, felt sense of freedom and autonomy. The diverse, multidisciplinary tools on offer within the independent music scene discussed here—tools for creative expression and for knowledge production—are highly suited to the task of making this narrative live.

In this intellectual context, it is worth asking: What are the intellectual tools bequeathed to us to make sense of the censorship of Mexican rock? Do they suggest openness or closure? Zolov, for instance, foregrounds cultural nationalism and the Revolutionary Family—both of which are closely related to the paternalistic statecraft of Mexico's single-party regime—as key drivers of repression against youth.[56] Likewise, the history of Avándaro, and the post-Avándaro "lost generation," is at times simplified into the following version: rock was suppressed during the Dirty War period as part of the single-party regime's clampdown against youth organization. The opening given to rock in the late 1980s and early 1990s allowed the genre to enter the transnational creative industries; the rock "boom" thus resulted from a broader weakening of state power by international capital, which undermined the PRI government's hegemony over "national" culture. The PRI, its hand forced and its cultural legitimacy undermined, acceded to multiparty democracy; end of story.

Occasionally, such a historically closed narrative about music aligns with teleological accounts of transition that implicitly perform intellectual work for the ongoing neoliberal economic policy disaster imposed since the early 1980s.[57] For instance, in a book chapter on *rock en español* in Mexico, Corona valorizes the "boom" in Mexican rock in ways that resonate with several wider acts of neoliberal mythmaking.[58] While there is little space to explore Corona's argument in full within these pages, I will start by analyzing his portrayal of economic and political history before exploring how it relates to music. To begin with, Corona relates that a "neoliberal restructuring" took place "*in response to* the disastrous *década perdida* (the lost decade) of the 1980s."[59] This is a contentious account of events, especially when applied to the case of Mexico. Although some contend that Mexico's public debt was the direct cause of stagnation, there is very robust evidence that the lost decade *resulted* from the neoliberal economic policies imposed in response to Mexico's debt crisis, starting with the regime of Miguel de la Madrid (1982–1988).[60] It is then asserted, without reference, that there were "new civil liberties brought about by neoliberalism," although we are not told which ones.[61] Corona also claims—again without providing details—that neoliberal economic policies freed up financial resources with which "the state was better able to support new organisms for the promotion of culture."⁶² He falls short, nonetheless, of stating that *net* state investment in culture or the arts rose during this period.⁶³ Very little evidence exists to demonstrate that the proceeds of privatization of state-run organisms—whose justification was to pay off government debts—were diverted toward other sectors of government during a time when public spending dropped precipitously. In general, the principal beneficiaries of privatization were the buyers of formerly state-owned businesses, at the expense of state workers and unions.⁶⁴

Mexican rock is here incorporated within broader narratives painting globalization as a dynamic force for stylistic innovation. The decrepit cultural nationalism of the PRI is contrasted with the internationalist creative impulses of Mexican *rock en español* artists themselves, who have produced musical hybrids in defiance of national boundaries. "It is globalization," Corona asserts, "that makes it possible for some Latin Americans to embrace rock in both English and Spanish."⁶⁵ This account skirts over experiences both historical and contemporary. Rock bands' engagement with Mexican and Latin American musical tradition goes back at least to the 1970s, with Peace and Love's "Latin Feeling," Nuevo México's incorporation of mariachi and son influences within their music, and Pájaro Alberto's use of *huapango*-style fiddle playing on his 1974 song "Ven a verme," which anticipates by two decades Café Tacuba's deployment of a similar style in their cover of Juan Luis Guerra's "Ojalá que llueva café en el campo." (None of these bands are mentioned in the chapter: they are instead submerged within a black hole of "repression, censorship, and marginalization" imputed to the 1970s.)⁶⁶ It also ignores the fact that rock journalists have frequently aired anxieties about the stagnation of the rock scene since 2000, highlighting a lack of contemporary competition for the stadium rock acts that emerged in the 1980s and 1990s.⁶⁷ The repression of the past thus stands vanquished by bands who have successfully entered transnational flows—simultaneously of capital and of music. Indeed, the chapter presents a northward trajectory: the artist whose innovative genre-hopping and multilingualism is seen to epitomize this trend, Lila Downs, happens to be one who has emigrated to the United States. Popular music history thus comes to work in service of a gesture of postnational, and implicitly US-centric, historical closure.

My intention is not to engage in a full critique of the research of a single scholar seeking to widen the understanding of an underexplored topic, but rather to draw attention to the ambivalent ends that histories of rock censorship may enact. What is needed in response, I would contend, is not an alternative grand narrative—certainly not one with a possible beginning or end.

Rather, as scholars engaging reflexively with the ways that knowledge acts, we need frames through which we are able to recognize and call out music censorship in all of its multiplicity. For these purposes, it is important to decenter grand historical metanarratives. The idea of Mexico's "democratic transition" as a historical event or single process may prevent us from seeing repressive acts carried out by leaders elected through democratic means. The conceptual entanglement of democratization and neoliberal economics may keep us from identifying repressive acts, documented here, carried out in the name of musical commoditization. These more recent blindnesses compete with other metanarratives, long embedded within modern disciplinary governmentality. Thus the notion that people, especially young people, and especially Mexicans, are unable to self-organize peacefully is the most pernicious and long-standing threat to rockers' expressive rights that is discussed in this book. Yet this idea traverses different historical times and physical locations; while often seen as characteristic of authoritarianism, it also characterizes democratic governance post-2000, and it has frequently been endorsed by participants within the very music scenes targeted for censorship. This endorsement sometimes comes—implicitly, in a coerced fashion—from those advocating *for* live music.

A corollary of this is that, in order to adequately respond to music censorship, it is especially important to let go of top-down historical narratives. As observed at the beginning of this book, censorship rarely happens by decree. The only exception documented here, Espinosa Villareal's prohibition of open-air rock in Mexico City in the 1990s, was a failure; drawn in overly literal terms, it engendered resistance. By contrast, the governmentality circumscribing live rock for security reasons had broad societal backing for most of the late twentieth century and was even endorsed within the rock scene itself. Avándaro was being invoked as proof that rock threatened security and civility more than twenty years after the event. When it comes to music censorship, in the words of Timothy Morton, it is helpful to consider that "the whole [might be] weirdly less than the sum of its parts."[68] This is the lens through which, I submit, we might best understand the ways that rock journalists structure knowledge in their work; it most clearly calls us to understand, for example, what it means to write a story invoking the authoritarian past in response to a venue closure in the present.

I want to conclude by describing my engagement with a collective that I began to collaborate with over the course of the research that led to this book. Called ColectivaMente (a name with a double meaning that connotes both "collectively" and "collective mind"), this group was founded in early 2021 by a group of journalists, musicians, organizers, and academics. ColectivaMente systematizes information on Mexican rock and makes it publicly accessible. It comprises various different projects and activities, central to which is a so-called Observatory of Mexican Rock, which manages a publicly accessible database of Mexican rock, and a project to preserve and digitize rare recordings. ColectivaMente also supports an ongoing project to create a dedicated rock museum in Mexico City. The participants in this growing project have sought to overcome the fragmentation of information about rock in Mexico by including several members with extensive private collections.

The work of ColectivaMente has, importantly, been framed and valued in relation to received histories of music censorship. One of the group's stated aims, "to disseminate and promote the memory of Mexican rock and the culture which it has generated," is explicitly understood in response to historical censorship, intended "to guarantee equality among the various cultures which are part of Mexican heritage, and which have traditionally been censored, proscribed and attacked by the State and the media." Some of the work undertaken by the collective, especially the digitization of physical archives, is painstaking.[69] In turn, since the value of this physically tiring work is understood in relation to the historically marginalized and repressed status of *rock nacional*, such documentary labor is symbiotically related to the agonistic intellectual work of narrating censorship and, therefore, to both defining censorship and establishing the boundaries of the political.

This has sometimes generated heated disagreements. On one occasion, a debate broke out after one comparatively young member objected to conversations of an allegedly "political" nature being held within the group. This both provoked controversy and allowed an opportunity for the work of ColectivaMente to be reinserted within Mexican rock's histories of censorship. Older members of the group replied that this was both political and postpolitical terrain: it was political because it related to a complex history of censorship and repression, and it was postpolitical because opposition to authoritarian rule transcended, or ought to transcend, affiliation with political parties. Thus, foundational conversations about the group's purpose have continually circled back to questions about how to define censorship to begin with. At the same time, a fixed definition of censorship has remained elusive: as a member of the organization put it during one meeting, censorship could refer to almost anything, including physical comportment and the formation of bodies.

There have been times at which this circular dialogue has appeared to me a frustrating one, hamstrung by a shared liberationist and antiauthoritarian inheritance easily exploited by illiberal styles of politics. In 2022 and 2023, the Mexico City live music scene was shocked by a series of concerts by neo-Nazi metal bands from both Mexico and abroad; at the beginning of 2023, Multiforo Cultural Alicia was vandalized with swastikas. Voices within the independent scene, and members of ColectivaMente, were caught between the impulse to oppose these groups and the instinct that any move to deplatform them constituted unacceptable censorship. These tensions between competing viewpoints came to a head when the Mexico City mayor Claudia Sheinbaum issued an official letter to an independent venue instructing them to cancel a booked appearance by a Finnish black metal outfit, on the grounds of incitement to hatred.[70] Equally, the dilemmas (such as the claimed need for intolerance toward intolerance) and competing histories (of fascist mass murder and of piecemeal local government repression against independent venues) that emerge within such a contentious moment underline the need to maintain an intellectually light-footed conversation about censorship.

As shown throughout this book, censorship is radically dependent on certain orderings of the political, such as the strict private-public divide typical in liberal democracies, through which acts of censorship may be filtered. By the same token, the recognition that censorship is ideologically embedded does not remove or diminish the ethical responsibility to recognize and call out acts of censorship when they occur. This combination of perspectives can result in a cosmological nomadism, or hopping across registers, as we both seek to shed light on those orderings of the political through which censorship is justified and look to challenge these orderings themselves from a sound epistemological footing. I have attempted to engage this task by identifying a disciplinary governmentality with racist connotations through which restrictions against rock have been justified, and which traverses the culture of *rock nacional* and the *escena independiente*. I have also highlighted ways that this trope has been critiqued by journalists challenging the idea that episodes of disorder were especially common at live rock events, and blaming overzealous security measures themselves for leading to disorder. Vital, too, is the story of how journalists organized in order to express these critiques to begin with. Though the book's argument, I have aimed to distance stories of music censorship in Mexico from metanarratives implying a sense of historical closure, especially those relating to Mexico's transition.

To play us out, I present a brief anecdote showing that I'm not alone in this. It's Mexico City in August 2022, and two collaborators within Colectiva-Mente, journalist Miriam Canales and musician and scholar José Hernández Riwes Cruz, are giving a detailed presentation on New Wave in Mexico in the 1980s, covering dozens of bands that operated from the very beginning of the decade. While the details of these acts are too extensive to describe here, my attention is drawn in particular to the way the pair's research is framed: as a response to the ways the "official history" of rock in Mexico "jumps from Avándaro to 1985," with the consequence that New Wave groups such as Size, Syntoma, Silueta Pálida, and Escuadrón del Ritmo are "invisibilized." During questions after their presentation, the pair clarify the reason for this historical erasure: the official history, as encountered in a documentary such as *Break It All*, includes only those bands with corporate representation.

In the wake of the talk, I eat with several attendees and collaborators of the group. The group includes academics, students, promoters, journalists, musicians, and venue organizers, with many kinds of relationships to institutionalized knowledge. During the course of the conversation, many histories about censorship are intertwined and contrasted across genres and contexts: *foros culturales*, the industrialization of live music, metal, electronic music, punk. These experiences and career trajectories, when taken together, articulate a task in common for those researching music censorship: to resist closure. Here, as we talk, eat, and make connections, participants in the Mexico City rock scene in which I am a fortunate interloper take ownership of their own histories, and these histories—at once overlapping and contrasting, producing incommensuralities and complex resonances—start to feel radically, excitingly open.

NOTES

INTRODUCTION

1. This quotation circulated on Facebook and, without attribution, on Monitor Informativo, an online news website. The original story no longer appears on this website, perhaps for legal reasons, but the organization tweeted the story here: https://twitter.com/InformaMonitor/status/997899767496790016, accessed February 8, 2024. The allegation was also challenged online: a Twitter account named Mitófago (whose description gave their role as "Devouring the lies about Mexican history that cause Mexicans a complex") dismissed the rumor as *"chairos* [supporters of Morena] lying to you." https://twitter.com/Mitofago/status/997550756210163712, accessed February 12, 2019. All translations are the author's unless otherwise stated.
2. This documentary, directed by Miguel Hernández, is available to view on YouTube: "Documental el rock no tiene la culpa (Versión A)," posted by El Rock No Tiene La Culpa, September 12, 2013, https://www.youtube.com/watch?v=U1PI7uuHSSs.
3. I use the phrases *rock mexicano* and *rock nacional* interchangeably with "Mexican rock" throughout this book. Importantly, this book covers a timespan over which the emic terminology to describe Mexican rock often changed. In the 1960s and early 1970s, *la onda chicana, rocanrol,* and *rock chicano* were commonly used. The phrase *rock nacional* superseded these terms from the mid-1970s, and continues to be employed today; *rock mexicano* has also endured throughout this period, for obvious reasons. It is notable that the phrase *rock nacional* would have been familiar to Mexican rockers prior to the mid-1970s, as it has been used to denote Argentinian rock—and its stylistic specificities—since the 1960s. See Pablo Vila, "Argentina's 'Rock Nacional': The Struggle for Meaning," *Latin American Music Review / Revista de Música Latinoamericana* 10, no. 1 (1989): 1–28. This term's rise to prominence in mid-1970s Mexico is worthy of further inquiry, but it appears to have reflected responses to contemporary

anxieties about the dismissal of rock as "cultural imperialism." The use of the phrase *rock nacional* in journalism coincided with calls for the "nationalization" of rock—that is, a turn toward Mexican musical traditions in rock composition and a rejection of cultural imports. See the editorial in *Conecte*, no. 23, August 15, 1976, 3.

4. This is the case for a 2019 online survey of thirty-four thousand global music consumers carried out by the International Federation of the Phonographic Industry: *Music Listening 2019*, https://www.ifpi.org/wp-content/uploads/2020/07/Music-Listening-2019-1.pdf. Indeed, on this survey rock ranked first, followed by pop; "metal" and "alternative/indie" ranked ninth and tenth respectively, suggesting that rock's popularity could be even higher, depending on genre categorizations. A telephone survey of six hundred respondents in 2022 produced the same result, although here rock's popularity was outstripped by that of *banda*, *norteño*, and *regional mexicano*, if aggregated together: A. Guttman, "Favorite Music Genres in Mexico as of July 2023," Statistica, June 6, 2024, https://www.statista.com/statistics/521707/mexico-preferred-music-genres. Notably, rock is significantly less popular in streaming data from Mexico than it is in these surveys. This discrepancy could be explained by generational differences in music format (that is, older generations opting not to stream), or by a postulated gap between the kinds of music Mexicans habitually listen to and the music they hold in esteem, or would go to see live.

5. José Xavier Návar, "50 años de Avándaro," *El Universal*, September 10, 2021, https://www.eluniversal.com.mx/opinion/jose-xavier-navar/50-anos-de-avanadaro.

6. Eric Zolov, *Refried Elvis: The Rise of the Mexican Counterculture* (Berkeley: University of California Press, 1999), 15–16.

7. Will Straw, "Cultural Scenes," *Loisir et société / Society and Leisure* 27, no. 2 (2014): 411–22; Will Straw, "Some Things a Scene Might Be: Postface," *Cultural Studies* 29, no. 3 (2015): 476–85; Andy Bennett and Richard A. Peterson, eds., *Music Scenes: Local, Translocal and Virtual* (Nashville, TN: Vanderbilt University Press, 2004).

8. Amitai Etzioni, "Should We Privatize Censorship?," *Issues in Science and Technology* 36, no. 1 (2019): 19–22.

9. Isaiah Berlin, *Four Essays on Liberty* (Oxford: Oxford University Press, 1969). Also see Ed Wallis, "Bittersweet Symphony," *Index on Censorship* 43, no. 1 (2014): 162–65.

10. Nick Tochka, *Audible States: Socialist Politics and Popular Music in Albania* (New York: Oxford University Press, 2016), 107. Also see Reuben M. Chirambo, "Traditional and Popular Music, Hegemonic Power and Censorship in Malawi:

1964–1994," in *Popular Music Censorship in Africa*, ed. Michael Drewett and Martin Cloonan (London: Routledge, 2016), 109–25.
11. Matei Candea, "Silencing Oneself, Silencing Others. Rethinking Censorship Comparatively (Introduction)," *Terrain: Anthropologie & sciences humaines* 72 (2019): 2–3; Robert Post, "Censorship and Silencing," in *Censorship and Silencing: Practices of Cultural Regulation*, ed. Robert Post (Los Angeles: Getty Research Institute, 1998), 4.
12. Beate Müller, ed., *Censorship and Cultural Regulation in the Modern Age* (New York: Rodopi, 2004); Matthew Bunn, "Reimagining Repression: New Censorship Theory and After," *History and Theory* 54, no. 1 (2015): 25–44.
13. Müller, *Censorship and Cultural Regulation*, 4; Bunn, "Reimagining Repression," 43.
14. Judith Butler, *Excitable Speech: A Politics of the Performative* (New York: Routledge, 1997); Michael Holquist, "Introduction. Corrupt Originals: The Paradox of Censorship," *Publications of the Modern Language Association of America* 109, no. 1 (1994): 14–25; Helen Freshwater, "Towards a Redefinition of Censorship," in *Censorship and Cultural Regulation in the Modern Age*, ed. Beate Müller (New York: Rodopi, 2004), 217–37.
15. Butler, *Excitable Speech*, p.128.
16. Candea, "Silencing Oneself, Silencing Others," 7; Holquist, "Corrupt Originals"; Jacques Derrida, *Eyes of the University: Right to Philosophy 2*, trans. Jan Plug (Stanford, CA: Stanford University Press, 2004).
17. See, for instance, Marie Korpe, ed., *Shoot the Singer! Music Censorship Today* (London: Zed Books, 2004); Michael Drewett and Martin Cloonan, eds. *Popular Music Censorship in Africa* (Aldershot: Ashgate, 2006); Patricia Hall, ed. *The Oxford Handbook of Music Censorship* (Oxford: Oxford University Press, 2015); Annemette Kirkegaard, Helmi Jarviluoma, Jan Sverre Knudsen, and Jonas Otterbeck, eds. *Researching Music Censorship* (Newcastle-upon-Tyne: Cambridge Scholars, 2017).
18. Martin Scherzinger, "Double Voices of Musical Censorship after 9/11," in *Music in the Post-9/11 World*, ed. Jonathan Ritter and J. Martin Daughtry (London: Routledge, 2007), 91–122.
19. Eric Nuzum, "Crash into Me, Baby: America's Implicit Music Censorship since 11 September," in Korpe, *Shoot the Singer!*, 149–59.
20. Matt Stahl, *Unfree Masters: Recording Artists and the Politics of Work* (Durham, NC: Duke University Press, 2013).
21. Jonathan Gingerich, "Is Spotify Bad for Democracy?: Artificial Intelligence, Cultural Democracy, and Law," *Yale Journal of Law and Technology* 24 (2022): 227–316.
22. John Street, *Music and Politics* (Cambridge: Polity, 2012), 6.

23. Candea, "Silencing Oneself, Silencing Others," 3, italics in original.
24. See Martin Cloonan, "Popular Music Censorship in Africa: An Overview," in *Popular Music Censorship in Africa*, ed. Michael Drewett and Martin Cloonan (London: Routledge, 2006), 3–21.
25. Elijah Wald, "Mexico: Drug Ballads and Censorship Today," in Korpe, *Shoot the Singer!*, 170–74; Helena Simonett, César Burgos Dávila, and David Moreno Candil, "State Censorship and the Controversy Surrounding the Narcocorrido Genre in Mexico," in *Pop—Power—Positions: Globale Beziehungen und populäre Musik*, ed. Anja Brunner and Hannes Liechti (Berlin: IASPM D-A-CH, 2020), 129–53.
26. Jonathan Ilan, "Digital Street Culture Decoded: Why Criminalizing Drill Music Is Street Illiterate and Counterproductive," *British Journal of Criminology* 60, no. 4 (2020): 994–1013.
27. Mariano Sánchez-Talanquer and Kenneth Greene, "Is Mexico Falling into the Authoritarian Trap?," *Journal of Democracy* 32, no. 4 (2021): 56–71; María Inclán, *The Zapatista Movement and Mexico's Democratic Transition: Mobilization, Success, and Survival* (New York: Oxford University Press, 2018).
28. On the PRI as a perfect dictatorship, see Gilbert M. Joseph and Jurgen Buchenau, *Mexico's Once and Future Revolution: Social Upheaval and the Challenge of Rule since the Late Nineteenth Century* (Durham, NC: Duke University Press, 2013). For the PRI regime as a *dictablanda*, see Paul Gillingham and Benjamin T. Smith, eds. *Dictablanda: Politics, Work, and Culture in Mexico, 1938–1968* (Durham, NC: Duke University Press, 2014). And for the PRI regime as a violent militarized system, see Jaime M. Pensado and Enrique C. Ochoa, "Introduction," in *México beyond 1968: Revolutionaries, Radicals, and Repression during the Global Sixties and Subversive Seventies*, ed. Jaime M. Pensado and Enrique C. Ochoa (Tucson: University of Arizona Press, 2018), 3–16.
29. Interview, Ignacio Pineda, June 2018.
30. Interview, Foro Ricardo Flores Magón, July 2018.
31. Interview, La Otra Rima, August 2019.
32. Zolov, *Refried Elvis*.
33. Eric Zolov, *Rebeldes con causa: La contracultura mexicana y la crisis del Estado patriarcal* (Mexico City: Grupo Editorial Norma, 2002).
34. Stuart Hall and Tony Jefferson, *Resistance through Rituals: Youth Subcultures in Post-War Britain*, 2nd ed. (New York: Routledge, 2006); Dick Hebdige, *Subculture: The Meaning of Style* (New York: Routledge, 1979).
35. Stuart Hall, "Encoding/Decoding," in *Media Studies: A Reader*, ed. Sue Thornham, Caroline Bassett, and Paul Marris (New York: New York University Press, 2009), 51–61.

36. See for example Martin Lamotte, "Rebels without a Pause: Hip–Hop and Resistance in the City," *International Journal of Urban and Regional Research* 38, no. 2 (2014): 686–94.
37. One may allude, for instance, to Tochka's observation that a binary contrast between "artistic subjectivity dependent on complicity versus resistance to political-economic orders" was not recognizable to musicians who had lived through socialism and post-socialism in Albania. Tochka, *Audible States*, 16–17.
38. Laudan Nooshin, "Whose Liberation? Iranian Popular Music and the Fetishization of Resistance," *Popular Communication* 15, no. 3 (2017): 163–91.
39. Guillermo O'Donnell and Phillipe C. Schmitter, *Transitions from Authoritarian Rule* (Baltimore: Johns Hopkins University Press, 1986).
40. A similar approach to translating *libertaria* is taken in Maurice Magaña, *Cartographies of Youth Resistance: Hip-Hop, Punk, and Urban Autonomy in Mexico* (Berkeley: University of California Press, 2020); and in Josh Kun, "The Aesthetics of *Allá*: Listening like a Sonidero," in *Audible Empire: Music, Global Politics, Critique*, ed. Ronald Radano and Tejumola Olaniyan (Durham, NC: Duke University Press, 2016), 95–115.
41. For instance, Zolov describes "broader appropriation of rock and roll culture by urban youth as a vehicle for their own rebellious outlook." Eric Zolov, "Rebeldismo in the Revolutionary Family: Rock 'n' Roll's Early Challenges to State and Society in Mexico," *Journal of Latin American Cultural Studies* 6, no. 2 (1997): 214). This depiction is especially notable for imputing to young people an *inherent* rebelliousness existing outside rock, but expressed through it. Elsewhere, he contends that "the containment of *rocanrol* restrained musicians from developing a more explicitly radical critique of patriarchal authority and of the government's oppressive nationalism that a more independent rock 'n' roll movement might have achieved." Eric Zolov, "La Onda Chicana: Mexico's Forgotten Rock Subculture," in *Rockin' las Américas: The Global Politics of Rock in Latin/o America*, ed. Deborah Pacini Hernandez, Hector Fernández l'Hoeste, and Eric Zolov (Pittsburgh, PA: University of Pittsburgh Press, 2004), 27. The counterfactual in this statement reveals an underlying liberal presupposition: to the extent that rock may have failed to live up to its rebellious potential, it is because of government repression; individuals want to be free, and governments stop them.
42. Michel Foucault, *Security, Territory, Population: Lectures at the Collège de France, 1977–78*, trans. Graham Burchell (New York: Palgrave Macmillan, 2009), 108.
43. Claudio Lomnitz, *Exits from the Labyrinth: Culture and Ideology in the Mexican National Space* (Berkeley: University of California Press, 1992), 2.

44. A similar pretext for censorship has also emerged in other postcolonial contexts, such as in restrictions on film in India. See William Mazzarella, *Censorium: Cinema and the Open Edge of Mass Publicity* (Durham, NC: Duke University Press, 2013).
45. Chris Anderton, *Music Festivals in the UK: Beyond the Carnivalesque* (New York: Routledge, 2018), 10; Roxy Robinson, *Music Festivals and the Politics of Participation* (New York: Routledge, 2016), 16–17.
46. Patricia Vega, "Decidió RTC cambiar la sede de la bienal de video," *La Jornada*, September 3, 1990, 33.
47. Claudio Lomnitz, "Modes of Citizenship in Mexico," *Public Culture* 11, no. 1 (1999): 272–73.
48. Street, *Music and Politics*, 12.
49. Pablo Espinosa, "Molotov ingresa al elenco del Hard Rock Live," *La Jornada*, February 10, 1998, 27. It is nonetheless notable that these performances intervene in affective and media flows that are out of these groups' control; thus in 2020 Molotov found themselves subject to renewed social media outrage about the contents of *¿Donde jugarán las niñas?*, with many defending the album on the basis that it was subversive and provocative. See "Pretenden 'cancelar' a Molotov por álbum de hace 23 años," *Yosoitú*, July 24, 2020, archived at https://web.archive.org/web/20220805152901/https://www.yosoitu.com/gente/espectaculos/pretenden-cancelar-a-molotov-por-album-de-hace-23-anos/416768.
50. Mark Mattern, *Acting in Concert: Music, Community, and Political Action* (New Brunswick: Rutgers University Press, 1998).
51. Zolov, *Refried Elvis*, 187–88.
52. "A book is a true mental journey, a fascinating experience. . . . From culture is born an intelligent person . . . who will always be more intelligent than somebody who doesn't read. . . . If a musician is cultured they will be more creative, their music will have more quality . . . and an audience that reads will be more demanding [with] better judgement." Roberto Vazquez V., "Lectura y cultura," *Conecte*, no. 66, January 2, 1978, 41.
53. "The first thing I published was poetry and short stories, that's the territory I come from, my background is literary and until the present I consider myself more connected to literature to journalism." Patricia Peñaloza, "La subjetividad, interpretación literaria de los hechos," in *El rock también se escribe*, ed. David Cortés and Alejandro González Castillo (Monterrey: Universidad Autónoma de Nuevo León, 2020), 93–97.
54. Benjamin T. Smith, *The Mexican Press and Civil Society, 1940–1976: Stories from the Newsroom, Stories from the Street* (Chapel Hill: University of North Carolina

Press, 2018); Vanessa Freije, *Citizens of Scandal: Journalism, Secrecy, and the Politics of Reckoning in Mexico* (Durham, NC: Duke University Press, 2020); Paul Gillingham, Michael Lettieri, and Benjamin T. Smith, eds. *Journalism, Satire, and Censorship in Mexico* (Albuquerque: University of New Mexico Press, 2018).
55. Nick Couldry, *Why Voice Matters: Culture and Politics after Neoliberalism* (London: Sage, 2010).
56. On the rise of neoliberal technocracy and its implications for political expression, see Nick Couldry, *Why Voice Matters: Culture and Politics after Neoliberalism* (London: Sage, 2010). On states of exception, see Giorgio Agamben, *State of Exception*, trans. Kevin Attell (Chicago: University of Chicago Press, 2005).
57. Agamben, *State of Exception*; Achille Mbembe, *Necropolitics* (Durham, NC: Duke University Press, 2019); Onur Ulas Ince, *Colonial Capitalism and the Dilemmas of Liberalism* (New York: Oxford University Press, 2018).
58. James C. Scott, *The Art of Not Being Governed: An Anarchist History of Upland Southeast Asia* (New Haven, CT: Yale University Press, 2009), 4. Also see James C. Scott, *Seeing Like a State: How Certain Schemes to Improve the Human Condition Have Failed* (New Haven, CT: Yale University Press, 1998). Notably, Scott's arguments have recently been complicated by Graeber and Wengrow, who are suspicious of the ways writers such as Scott tend to reify "the state" and thus pave the way for the kinds of celebratory narratives depicting state dominance as the teleological endpoint of a series of development stages found in popular science books by writers like Steven Pinker. In reality, as these authors show, "the state" has far less consistency across the broad swathe of history than Scott tends to admit. David Graeber and David Wengrow, *The Dawn of Everything: A New History of Humanity* (London: Allen Lane, 2021).
59. Adam D. Morton, "Change within Continuity: The Political Economy of Democratic Transition in Mexico." *New Political Economy* 10, no. 2 (2005): 181–202.
60. See, for example, a series of polls carried out periodically by the Secretaria de Gobernación in Mexico since 2001, entitled the Encuesta Nacional Sobre Cultura Política y Prácticas Ciudadanas (National Poll of Political Culture and Citizen Practice, ENCUP): http://fomentocivico.segob.gob.mx/es/FomentoCivico/ENCUP. These conclusions are drawn from the most recent of these polls, carried out in 2005, 2008, and 2012.
61. O'Donnell and Schmitter, *Transitions from Authoritarian Rule*.
62. Smith, *Mexican Press and Civil Society*, 281.
63. John Baily, *Can You Stop the Birds Singing?: The Censorship of Music in Afghanistan* (Copenhagen: Freemuse, 2001), 39–42. Timothy W. Ryback, *Rock around the Bloc: A History of Rock Music in Eastern Europe and the Soviet Union* (Oxford:

Oxford University Press, 1990); Jeff Hayton, "Crosstown Traffic: Punk Rock, Space and the Porosity of the Berlin Wall in the 1980s," *Contemporary European History* 26, no. 2 (2017): 353–77; Sabrina P. Ramet, *Rocking the State: Rock Music and Politics in Eastern Europe and Russia* (Boulder, CO: Westview, 1994). Pekacz argues as follows: "Rock was not inherently anti-Communist (neither were rock musicians inherently anti-Communists); rock in many cases profited from Communist state patronage; the state (being more pragmatic than dogmatic) succeeded in the domestication of rock; relationships between the socialist state and rock were more often symbiotic than contradictory, hence many rock musicians were more interested in 'adapting' to the status quo, rather than in destroying it." Jolanta Pekacz, "Did Rock Smash the Wall?: The Role of Rock in Political Transition," *Popular Music* 13, no. 1 (1994): 48.

64. Deborah Pacini Hernández, Héctor Fernández l'Hoeste, and Eric Zolov, eds. *Rockin' las Américas: The Global Politics of Rock in Latin/o America* (Pittsburgh, PA: University of Pittsburgh Press, 2004), 1.

65. Pacini Hernández, l'Hoeste, and Zolov, *Rockin' las Américas*, 16, 2.

66. See Paul Cooney, "Argentina's Quarter Century Experiment with Neoliberalism: From Dictatorship to Depression," *Revista de economía contemporánea* 11, no. 1 (2007): 7–37; Kurt Weyland, "Neoliberalism and Democracy in Latin America: A Mixed Record," *Latin American Politics and Society* 46, no. 1 (2004): 135–57. In the case of Argentina, neoliberalism is often associated with the democratically elected presidency of Carlos Menem (1989–1999). The roots for Menem's neoliberal transition were nonetheless laid by the Argentinian junta, which both received support from the International Monetary Fund and implemented a neoliberal economic program of tariff reductions, reductions in subsidies, encouragement of foreign direct investment and rejection of "import substitution," and removal of labor rights. See Tomás Undurraga, "Neoliberalism in Argentina and Chile: Common Antecedents, Divergent Paths," *Revista de Sociologia e Política* 23, no. 5 (2015): 11–34.

67. Claude Lefort, *Democracy and Political Theory*, trans. David Macey (Cambridge: Polity, 1988), 11.

68. Scott, *Art of Not Being Governed*, x.

69. Zolov, *Refried Elvis*; José Agustín, *La contracultura en México: La historia y el significado de los rebeldes sin causa, los jipitecas, los punks y las bandas* (Mexico City: Editorial Grijalbo, 1996); Maritza Urteaga, *Por los territorios de rock: Identidades juveniles y rock mexicano* (Mexico City: NCA, Colección Joven, 1998).

70. Agustín, *La contracultura en México*, 58–59.

71. See, for example, Jon Shefner and Julie Stewart, "Neoliberalism, Grievances, and Democratization: An Exploration of the Role of Material Hardships in

Shaping Mexico's Democratic Transition," *Journal of World-Systems Research* 17, no. 2 (2011): 353–78.

CHAPTER 1

1. Roberto Ponce, "'Rompen' en México a Gustavo Santaolalla y su documental," *Proceso*, December 23, 2020.
2. Andrea Quintana, "Rompan todo: Las grandes bandas mexicanas ausentes en el nuevo documental de Netflix sobre rock en América Latina," *Pólvora*, December 2, 2020; Paola Sánchez Castro, "Rompan Todo en Netflix: Las ausencias mexicanas que no se perdonan," *El Heraldo de México*, December 21, 2020.
3. Jon Pareles, "Rebeldía, genio y represión: 'Rompan todo' el documental que explora el legado del rock latino," *New York Times*, December 25, 2020.
4. Pensado and Ochoa, "Introduction."
5. Pensado and Ochoa, "Introduction," 8. Katia E. Monroy, "Avándaro y las juventudes en México: Miradas múltiples en torno a un festival." *Revista oficial de historia e interdisciplina* 10 (2019): 115–32.
6. Susana Draper, *1968 Mexico: Constellations of Freedom and Democracy* (Durham, NC: Duke University Press, 2018), 11.
7. Francisco Valenzuela, "Rompan Todo y el mito de la censura en el rock," *Revés*, December 21, 2020.
8. Julián Woodside, "Carientismos: Cuestionemos las historias oficiales," *Indierocks*, January 4, 2021.
9. Zolov, *Refried Elvis*; Urteaga, *Por los territorios de rock*; Federico Rubli, *Estremécete y rueda: Loco por el rock and roll* (Mexico City: Chiapa Ediciones, 2007); Teresa Estrada, *Sirenas al ataque: Historia de las mujeres rockeras mexicanas, 1956–2006* (Mexico City: Editorial Océano de México, 2008); José Rodrigo Moreno-Elizondo, "Crisis contracultural y rock en la Ciudad de México: Relaciones de producción, reproducción viva y sociabilidad, 1972–1977," *Historia y sociedad* 38 (2020): 205–28.
10. Urteaga states that Mexican rock suffered a "long night" from Avándaro to the mid-1980s (Urteaga, *Por los territorios de rock*, 230); in the second edition of his memoir *Guaraches de ante azul*, Federico Arana writes that after the 1971 Avándaro Festival rock "was practically prohibited," to be "decriminalized" only in the 1990s (Arana, *Guaraches de ante azul*, 2nd ed. [Mexico City: María Enea, 2002], 395); and Roura wrote that "rock was shut down simultaneously" in the wake of this festival (cited in Zolov, *Refried Elvis*, 223). The "hard" account of post-Avándaro censorship also appears in more general accounts of Mexican popular music. For instance, Josh Kun, alluding to the long-night idea in his

influential book *Audiotopia*, makes the exaggerated claim that Mexican rock was "once outlawed." Josh Kun, *Audiotopia: Music, Race, and America* (Berkeley: University of California Press, 2005), 185.
11. Zolov, *Refried Elvis*, 223. See David Cortés, *El otro rock mexicano* (Mexico City: Grupo Editorial Tomo, 1999).
12. Good examples of this tendency are found in Zolov, *Refried Elvis*; Rubli, *Estremécete y rueda*; and Estrada, *Sirenas al ataque*. I highlight these contributions both because of their attention to detail and because they highlight the social aspects of censorship. Rubli's account in *Estremécete y rueda* takes into consideration multiple possible narratives about post-Avándaro censorship, including an especially compelling story in which the scandal over the festival was orchestrated in order to embarrass Hank González, then a figurehead of the PRI's leftist contingent. Since Estrada's *Sirenas al ataque* highlights the experience of women rockers, its account of censorship is especially attentive to the ways that censorship may be effected through social institutions.
13. Zolov, *Refried Elvis*, 218. In early 1972 it was written that "radio coverage has been stopped [*frenado*] because of what happened at Avándaro." Armando Molina, "Rock Chicano 71," *Pop*, no. 82, January 14, 1972, 8–10. An interview with Three Souls from December 1972 in *Pop* has a member complain that "on the radio they don't want to play anything from the Onda Chicana." Miguel Morales and Vivianne Klein, "Three Souls in My Mind," *Pop*, no. 101, December 18, 1972, 10–11. In *México Canta* in January 1973, the band Tequila complained that radio stations "are removing programmes dedicated to Mexican bands . . . ah, but they do have hours for Credence [Clearwater Revival], Grand Funk, The Doors . . . it's all for the foreigner, but we're in Mexico, now, the TV, forget it." José Luis [Pluma], "Denuncia: Protesta de Los Tequila contra los abusos," *Conecte*, no. 408, January 19, 1973, 18–21.

In the early 1970s Mexican rock is noted as having featured, often as part of regular specialized programming, in a variety of radio broadcasts, such as on a Radio Juventud program called *¿Cual es la onda?* (Daniel Toscano, *Pop*, no. 82, January 14, 1972, 18); on Radio Moderna (Vivianne Klein, "Onda Rocanrolera," *Pop*, no. 91, July 24, 1972, 30–31); on Radio Éxitos and Radio Mil (José Luis Pluma, "Acuario," *México Canta*, no. 452, 1973, 4–5); on Radio Universidad (Miguel Morales, "Radio: Rock en Radio Universidad," *Conecte*, no. 3, February 1975, 15); on XEO (Celia G., "Que onda con . . . Three Souls in My Mind," *Conecte*, no. 14, November 1975, 7); and on Radio 590 (Morales and Klein, "Three Souls in My Mind").
14. Armando Molina, "Rock Chicano 71."
15. Zolov, "La Onda Chicana," 40.

16. "Television: Los programas musicales," *Conecte*, no. 3, February 1975, 15; "'Rock en la cultura': Única plataforma de lanzamiento para grupos mexicanos," *Conecte*, no. 8, June 1975, 8. The latter article provides a useful albeit nonexhaustive list of the bands that had performed on this show to date: "Nahuatl, Peace and Love, Three Souls in My Mind, Enigma, Tequila, Dug Dug's, Bandido, Pájaro Alberto y Sacrosaurio, Luz y Fuerza, David y Goliath, Árbol, Nuevo México, etc."
17. For instance, one Three Souls in My Mind concert held in late 1972 at Sala Chopin was broadcast live on Radio 590, filmed for the television program Alta Tensión, and attended by journalists from *Excélsior, Novedades*, and *El Heraldo de México*, alongside luminaries such as actors Valerie Jodorowsky, Juan Ferrara, Octavio Galindo, Pablo Leder, and Ana de Sade. Morales and Klein, "Three Souls in My Mind." Despite the common notion that mentioning Avándaro on the radio had been banned at this time, the event featured a rendition of the band's new song "La Encuerada de Avándaro" (The Naked Girl of Avándaro). A similar scene was painted for a 1972 concert given to promote the band Tinta Blanca in the newly inaugurated Poliforum, located in the historic center of Mexico City; this event was attended by staff from Polydor, journalists, and "one model after another." Vivianne Klein, "Concierto en el Poliforum de la TINTA BLANCA," *Pop*, no. 92, August 28, 1972, 24–25.
18. Although it is impossible to fit restrictions into any straightforward timeline, repression was likely hardened after 1973, when PRI official Manuel Alvírez wrote in national newspaper *Excélsior* that "all live sessions, permits, *tardeadas* and everything that smelt of rock" were to be banned on the basis that rock "incited youth to excess and drug use." This gesture was interpreted by *México Canta* not as a targeted effort to silence rock but as a misguided attempt to shut down any form of collective action in the wake of student protests. José Luis Pluma, "Acuario," *México Canta*, no. 413, November 23, 1973, 4–5.
19. A 1973 attempt to integrate rock with a series of movie screenings in a cinema in Ciudad Satélite, to the north-west of Mexico City, was denied a permit on technical grounds, after press coverage painted the event as a second Avándaro (José Luis Pluma, "Acuario," *México Canta*, no. 435, July 27, 1973, 4–5), and a 1976 effort that "sought to repeat Avándaro 71" was denied a permit (Arturo Castelazo, "Ahí se va," *Conecte*, no. 20, July 1, 1976, 6). A cultural festival planned in the Valle de Bravo in April 1976, to feature a variety of music including rock alongside jazz and classical music and counting on the support of the Casa de la Cultura of the government of Estado de México, was branded as "Avándaro II" by rock journalists; while it is unclear whether this represented the organizers' intentions, the authorities apparently balked at the association

and refused to grant a permit (Arturo Castelazo, "Ahí se va," *Conecte*, no. 17, April 1976, 6; Arturo Castelazo, "Ahí se va," *Conecte*, no. 20, July 1, 1976, 6). Even ten years afterward, a concert known as "Avandarito," planned in September 1981 to celebrate Avándaro's tenth anniversary, attracted police reprisals. One editor, writing two months later, recalled having raised concerns "that it was a little risky having mentioned the name of Avándaro" in promotional posters (José Luis Pluma, "Avandarito: Otro Apañon para no variar," *Conecte*, no. 236 [precise date not visible, likely end of October 1981], 12–13). The event did not go to plan: although the organizers expected three thousand attendees at most, ten thousand showed up on the day, overwhelming security at the venue. Further, Avandarito was scheduled for a venue close to a newly created police academy. Avandarito ended up being suspended amid riots and police violence (Jorge Álvarez Astudillo, "¡10 años después de Avándaro es increíble que suceda lo mismo!" *Conecte*, no. 237, November 1981, 28–29).

20. Daniel Toscano, "Conexión," *Pop*, no. 101, December 18, 1972, 42. "Acuario," *México Canta*, no. 451, 1973, 4–5.
21. Ricardo Morales, "El Festival Congregación 75," *México Canta*, no. 494, [1975], 10–11.
22. Victor Roura, *Apuntes de rock: Por las calles del mundo* (Mexico City: Ediciones Nuevomar, 1985).
23. Estrada, *Sirenas al ataque*, 100.
24. Celia G., "Que onda con . . . Three Souls in My Mind," *Conecte*, no. 14, November 1975, 7. Also see Estrada, *Sirenas al ataque*, 117–18.
25. Moreno-Elizondo, "Crisis contracultural." Also see Louise E. Walker, *Waking from the Dream: Mexico's Middle Classes after 1968* (Stanford, CA: Stanford University Press, 2013), 32–33; and Zolov, "La Onda Chicana," 31–39.
26. Three Souls in My Mind became El Tri in 1985, after a legal struggle over the band's name with their drummer, Carlos Hauptvogel. Throughout the 1970s, their music openly criticized the government and police brutality, and discussed the gritty realities of Mexico City; it thus maintained a vital connection with the experiences of the capital's poorer classes. Unlike their contemporaries, El Tri has gone on to national and international recognition. Zolov, *Refried Elvis*, 250–51. Zolov, "La Onda Chicana"; Ignacio Corona, "The Politics of Language, Class, and Nation in Mexico's Rock en Español Movement," in *Song and Social Change in Latin America*, ed. Lauren Shaw (New York: Lexington Books, 2013), 91–119.
27. Moreno-Elizondo, "Crisis contracultural," 222.
28. On the presumed antiauthoritarianism of countercultures, see Theodore Gracyk, *I Wanna Be Me: Rock Music and the Politics of Identity* (Philadelphia,

PA: Temple University Press, 2001); and Carson Holloway, *All Shook Up: Music, Passion, and Politics* (Dallas: Spence, 2001). On the combining of libertarian and communitarian influences in the US counterculture, see Michael J. Kramer, *The Republic of Rock: Music and Citizenship in the Sixties Counterculture* (Oxford: Oxford University Press, 2013); Andy Bennett, "Reappraising 'Counterculture,'" *Volume! La revue des musiques populaires* 9, no. 1 (2012): 20–31.

29. Zolov's *Refried Elvis* makes no mention of *Conecte*, although he does discuss *México Canta*, *Pop*, and *Piedra Rodante*. José-Rodrigo Moreno-Elizondo's account, however, relies heavily on *Conecte* on the basis that it constituted something like a publication of record for this scene, as does David Cortés. Moreno-Elizondo, "Crisis contracultural"; Cortés, *El otro rock mexicano*.
30. Jeffrey Alexander, *The Meanings of Social Life: A Cultural Sociology* (New York: Oxford University Press, 2013), 27–84, 155–77.
31. See for example Draper, *1968 Mexico*, 12.
32. Interview, Antonio Malacara Palacios, January 2022.
33. Tony Harcup, "'I'm Doing This to Change the World': Journalism in Alternative and Mainstream Media," *Journalism Studies* 6, no. 3 (2005): 361–74.
34. See Monroy, "Avándaro y las juventudes en México," 121–22.
35. Rubli argues that the media outrage over Avándaro was orchestrated by conservative factions of the PRI to embarrass the then governor of Estado de México, Hank González, a leader of the developmentalist old guard. Rubli, *Estremécete y rueda*, 477–502. Rock journalists have also repeatedly portrayed Avándaro as a failed stitch-up, permitted by the government in order to create a pretext to repress young people after anticipated disturbances at the festival. This account serves to square the circle between government repression of rock after Avándaro and the practical support for the festival provided by the government of Estado de México and the presidency. The president, Luis Echeverría Álvarez, reportedly sent three hundred buses to aid with transportation at the festival, provoking cries of "a toke for Echeverría" (Eligio Calderón, Vicente Anaya, Carla Zenzes, and José Luis Fernández, *Avándaro: ¿Aliviane o movida?* (Mexico City: Editorial Extemporáneos, 33).
36. "Diez años después: 11 de septiembre de 1971," *Conecte*, no. 229, September 1981, 6.
37. Ruvalcaba, *Nosotros*, 10.
38. Interview, Víctor Manuel Alatorre, May 2020.
39. Víctor Manuel Alatorre, personal communication, January 2021.
40. Smith, *Mexican Press and Civil Society*.
41. "Editorial," *Conecte*, no. 1, December 1974, 3.
42. Interview, Víctor Manuel Alatorre, May 2020.

43. Interview, Walter Schmidt, October 2020; Interview, Víctor Manuel Alatorre, May 2020; Interview, Antonio Malacara Palacios, January 2022. One respondent even ridiculed the writer Federico Rubli's claim that the editor of *México Canta* had requested that he refrain from writing about Mexican rock.
44. Interview, Víctor Manuel Alatorre, January 2022.
45. Interview, Walter Schmidt, October 2020.
46. Although short-lived, *Piedra Rodante* was significant as a publication that was willing to discuss largely taboo topics relating to the consumption of hallucinogens and changing sexual preferences. It is discussed in detail in Luis González-Reimann and Eric Zolov, "Digital Resources: Piedra Rodante (Mexico's Rolling Stone Magazine)," in *Oxford Research Encyclopedia of Latin American History* (New York: Oxford University Press, 2021).
47. Interview, Óscar Sarquiz, January 2022.
48. On the lack of work for rock musicians, the opening to a January 1973 issue of *México Canta* states that "every day there are more groups and fewer sources of work" ("Acuario," *México Canta*, no. 406, January 5, 1973, 5). Later in the same issue, Federico Rubli writes that "one of the greatest problems of the Mexican musician is finding sources of work"; Rubli puts this down to a purported post-Avándaro ban on festivals. Federico Rubli, "A un año de Avándaro el rock ha retrocedido," *México Canta*, no. 406, January 5, 1973, 16–17. *México Canta* documents a protest, in March 1973, held by Mexican rock musicians at the offices of the Sindicato de Músicos (Musicians' Union) in order to highlight the "lack of work for *rocanroleros*." Venus Rey, the head of the union, came down to talk to the protesters and agreed to fight for their opportunities to work. "Acuario," *México Canta*, no. 414, March 2, 1973, 4–5. Regarding internal conflicts: Arturo Castelazo, writing in *Conecte* in August 1975, condemned a recent event in Arena México, a venue that could hold sixteen thousand and that had advertised the band Nahuatl was down to play, without letting the band know. Arturo Castelazo, "Ahí se va," *Conecte*, no. 11, August 1975, 4. Regarding the lack of work ethic, note that through the 1970s and early 1980s, there were continual comments in *México Canta* and *Conecte* about the need for professionalism and unity. In January 1981, after an Alice Cooper concert in Monterrey occurred without incident, a note from the editor reflected that Mexican audiences might finally be ready for rock: "we are removing the infantile, which will benefit the movement a great deal. Professionalism in all things." "Editorial," Conecte, no. 197, January 1981, 4. An editorial in April 1985 declared, tentatively, that "*rock nacional* is taking on the features of professionalism, ever since a few months ago." "Editorial," *Conecte*, no. 404, April 1985, 3.

49. Regarding disorderly behavior during live concerts, Ricardo Morales, reporting on a festival held in Arena México, "El Festival Congregación 75," stated that "the behaviour of the youth left much to be desired, demonstrating that they lack a great deal of maturity for large festivals." Ricardo Morales, "El Festival Congregación 75," *México Canta*, no. 494, 1975, 10–11. Regarding payola schemes, in a June 1975 interview with Carlos Mata from the band Nuevo México, the singer complains that "there exists a mafia in radio where everything's done on the basis of money" and states that, in response, the band were planning "a series of concerts outside radio stations to put pressure on them." Arturo Castelazo, "Carlos Mata de Nuevo México declara," *Conecte*, no. 8, June 1975, 9. An editorial from February 1976 states that "We all know that radio stations don't play the albums of Mexican groups [*grupos nacionales*]." "Editorial," *Conecte*, no. 16, February 1976, 3. Another editorial from July of the same year condemns the practice of payola, accusing radio stations of receiving "large amounts of money to play certain songs 30 or 40 times a day, to turn them into hits." "Editorial," *Conecte*, no. 21, July 15, 1976, 3.
50. "Chava Ex Love Army," *México Canta*, no. 455, 1973, 20–21. The latter critique was concretized in music at this time in the often-noted case of Three Souls' "Abuso de Autoridad" (Abuse of Authority)—a song that has been perhaps misleadingly taken as representative of contemporary attitudes in Mexican rock. For example, see Janet Sturman, *The Course of Mexican Music* (New York: Routledge, 2015), 244. In July 1975, Mexican band Decibel told *Conecte* in an interview that "we didn't know that Mexican rock existed . . . nobody has created true Mexican rock. Rock is revolution, not a copy." "Decibel: Un nuevo grupo mexicano," *Conecte*, no. 9, July 1975, 9. The following month, radio programmer Rafael Martiarena blamed Mexican bands' lack of success on their obsession with credibility over accessibility and asked rock bands to ensure "that their albums are accessible for people." "Entrevista con un programador de radio," *Conecte*, no. 11, August 1975, 9. This message had been taken to heart by long-standing outfit Los Dug Dug's, who told *Conecte* writer Felipe Guadarrama in July 1975 that "they don't play us on the radio because we make heavy music," and that they were "producing something more accessible, general and commercial, for everyone to listen to." Felipe Guadarrama, "Conectentrevista con Los Dug Dug's," *Conecte*, no. 9, July 1975, 20.
51. "¿Qué ha sucedido con el rock a diez años de Avándaro?" *Conecte*, no. 229, September 1981, 3.
52. Estrada, *Sirenas al ataque*, 109; Zolov, "La Onda Chicana," 32.
53. These terms also held connotations from elsewhere in the Americas: for example, the "Cordobazo" of 1969, a civil uprising in the city of Córdoba

against the Argentine military dictatorship in 1969; and the "Rosariazo" of the same year, an antidictatorship protest and strike movement in the Argentinian city of Rosario that lasted several months.

54. Letter by Manuel García, *Conecte*, no. 234, October 1981, 33.
55. *Conecte* shared many writers with the magazine *México Canta* and, indeed, may be considered a kind of extension of the same, although the latter publication persevered until the middle of the decade.
56. Interview, Óscar Sarquiz, January 2022. Also see Estrada, *Sirenas al ataque*, 100–102.
57. The inflation caused by the economic crisis was reflected in *Conecte*'s prices: the cost of the magazine rose from five pesos for its first issue to six hundred pesos by the end of 1987.
58. A reader called Luis de Ocampo Barredo, writing from Mérida in 1980, ascribed the problem to humanity, rather than any particular system: "Tell me: does the capitalist system alienate its youth less?" The technological advances of capitalism, this reader objected, were tempered by their appropriation by the elite classes. For this reader, Baca "should not write in a rock magazine like *Conecte*." Another reader, Ernesto Márquez Rodríguez from Iztapalapa, Mexico City, wrote in defense of socialism in the same issue: "The bases upon which the SOCIALIST System is built, are its exterior politics, and freedom. . . . The idea that there is no ROCK in Cuba, this is false." Readers' letters, *Conecte*, no. 185, September 1980, 32–33. Indeed, this reader's objection was later reflected in a *Conecte* report from Cuba in February 1982, concerning a tour of Mexican avant-garde rocker Guillermo Briseño in the country: "With this," asserted writer Antonio Malacara Palacios, "we can bury one of the most ambiguous and ridiculous arguments of rock's detractors, something like: this music is nothing more than an interventionist weapon of capitalist imperialism." Antonio Malacara Palacios, "Entre paréntesis: México," *Conecte*, no. 247, February 1982, 8–9.
59. Enrique Marroquín, "Dios quiere que llueva para unirnos," *Piedra Rodante*, no. 6, October 30, 1971, 10–12.
60. Arturo Castelazo, "Adiós a los 70s, 10 años de crisis, pero no de muerte," *Conecte*, no. 159, February 1980, 12–14.
61. See Jeffrey W. Rubin, "Contextualizing the Regime: What 1938–68 Tells Us about Mexico, Power, and Latin America's Twentieth Century," in *Dictablanda: Politics, Work, and Culture in Mexico, 1938–1968*, ed. Paul Gillingham and Benjamin T. Smith (Durham, NC: Duke University Press, 2014), 391.
62. Matthew Karush, *Musicians in Transit: Argentina and the Globalization of Popular Music* (Durham, NC: Duke University Press, 2017), 199.

63. Estrada, *Sirenas al ataque*, 33.
64. Antidisco politics were not informed, as in the United States, by racism; disco in Mexico shed the association with Black identity that the genre held north of the border.
65. Daniel Toscano, "Conexión," *Pop*, no. 101, December 18, 1972, 42.
66. Miguel Morales, "Entrevista con Tinta Blanca," *Pop*, no. 105, February 15, 1973, 14–15.
67. "Acuario," *México Canta*, no. 414, March 2, 1973, 4–5.
68. "Editorial," *Conecte*, no. 20, July 1, 1976, 3.
69. "De ahora en adelante el sindicato de músicos organizará los conciertos de rock," *Conecte*, no. 33, February 15, 1977, 7.
70. "Editorial," *Conecte*, no. 55, October 16, 1977, 3. It seems likely that "discotheque" in this context does not refer to disco as a genre.
71. Arturo Castelazo, "Las desilusionantes tocadas de Mexico City," *Conecte*, no. 7, May 1975, 6.
72. "Editor," *Conecte*, no. 142, September 1979, 5.
73. Castelazo, "Las desilusionantes tocadas."
74. Salvador Sánchez G, "Como te comunicas?," *Conecte*, no. 3, February 1975, 22.
75. "The word, the concept of communication was still being debated at this time, and about the media. . . . Most are information media, not communication media. Communication has to be back and forth." Interview, Antonio Malacara Palacios, January 2022. "Experimental communication" in the United States counterculture is also discussed in Kramer, *Republic of Rock*, 63–69.
76. "Editorial," *Conecte*, no. 77, March 20, 1978, 3; Víctor Roura, "Pablo Cancer," *México Canta*, no. 451, 1973, 13–14.
77. José Luis Pluma, "Entrevista con Tinta Blanca," *México Canta*, no. 424, May 11, 1973, 31–32. Bonnie Adams, "La verdad desnuda y la música sacra," *Pop*, no. 82, January 14, 1972, 42–43.
78. Armando Molina, "Rock Chicano 71." The later idea that until the 1980s Mexican rock was dominated by Spanish-language covers of English songs, or poorly written English lyrics is incorrect. See, for example, Estrada, *Sirenas al ataque*, 53.
79. Moreno-Elizondo explores these claims about rock and communication, but tends to take them at face value as a straightforward description of live events, rather than critically seeking to place them in cultural context. Moreno-Elizondo, "Crisis contracultural," 221–22.
80. Antonio Malacara Alonso, "Rock Sobre Ruedas," *Pop*, November 14, 1972, 24–25.
81. See James Carey, *Communication As Culture: Essays on Media and Society*, rev. ed. (New York: Routledge, 2008).

82. "Editorial," *Conecte*, no. 74, February 27, 1978, 3.
83. For instance, Alex Lora, the lead singer of Three Souls in My Mind, met the band's future manager after *México Canta* published his phone number; they eventually married. Estrada, *Sirenas al ataque*, 109.
84. José Luis Pluma, "Acuario," *México Canta*, no. 452, 1973, 4–5.
85. "Editorial," *Conecte*, no. 3, February 1975, 3.
86. José Luis Pluma, "Acuario," *México Canta*, no. 416, March 16, 1973, 4–5.
87. For more on debates about freedom of expression and communication within the hippie counterculture in the United States, see Kramer, *Republic of Rock*, 210.
88. Draper, *1968 Mexico*, 22.
89. Arturo Castelazo, "Las desilusionantes tocadas de Mexico City," *Conecte*, no. 7, May 1975, 6.
90. Vladimir Hernández, "Carteles," *Conecte*, no. 117, January 13, 1979.
91. Arturo Castelazo, "El rock hacia los 80s," *Conecte*, no. 142, September 1979, 14–16.
92. La Bruja. "La función de un hoyo funkie," *Conecte*, no. 143, September 1979, 14–15.
93. Arturo Castelazo, "El rock hacia los 80s," *Conecte*, no. 123, February 1979, 8–10.
94. By now, many scholars have complicated the simplistic opposition between attentive listening and nonattentive hearing. See, for example, Ruth Herbert, *Everyday Music Listening: Absorption, Dissociation and Trancing* (New York: Routledge, 2016).
95. *Conecte*, no. 15, January 1976, 6. In fact, there had been consistent family ties between presidents and the rock scene. Famously, the son of Gustavo Díaz Ordaz (1964–1970) was a rock fan. During an interview with Armando Blanco, the owner of the record store and live music venue Hip 70, which took place at Blanco's home in Mexico City, he told me that most of the furniture in the room had once belonged to the family of Luis Echeverría, before he had bartered for it with the president's daughters, with whom he studied at university.
96. *Conecte*, no. 15, January 1976, 8. "Extraordinaria demanda de localidades!"
97. Arturo Castelazo, "Júntense, júntense," *Conecte*, no. 15, January 1976, 3.
98. "Lo que dijeron los periódicos," *Conecte*, no. 15, January 1976, 4.
99. Castelazo, "Júntense, júntense."
100. This term is used in a 1981 *Conecte* retrospective on Avándaro in order to argue that rock in Mexico and other "Third World countries" would inevitably be behind the curve. Vladimir Hernández, "Avándaro, ¿te acuerdas tú?," *Conecte*, no. 230, September 1981, 31–33.

101. For instance, the editor of *Conecte* speculated that Kiss may have cancelled a Mexico City concert planned to be held in 1980 "because [the audience] behaved like animals as they left the Deep Purple concert" earlier that year. "Editorial," *Conecte*, no. 182, August 1980, 4.
102. Arturo Castelazo, "En Tlatelolco . . . un nuevo comportamiento del rock-escucha," *Conecte*, no. 128, April 1979, 8.
103. Antonio Malacara Alonso, "Consecuencia Inadvertida de un crítico de paso," *Conecte*, no. 66, January 2, 1978, 12–13.
104. Antonio Malacara Alonso, "Olvidémonos de ser super estrellas," *Conecte*, no. 69, January 23, 1978, 32–33.
105. Antonio Malacara Alonso, "Los Alivianados Rocanroleros! ¿Pos Cuales?," *Conecte*, no. 67, January 9, 1978, 32–33.
106. A *Conecte* editorial in September 1976 decries a lack of creative activity, anticipating the emergence of *rock en español*: "We ought not to publish more pointless nonsense which will only help to follow the same abysmal path that Mexican rockers have followed until now. It's about progress, renewal, finding a style, making rock in Spanish." "Editorial," *Conecte*, no. 24, September 1, 1976, 3. An article by Antonio Malacara Alonso in January 1979 described progressive rock as "a consequence of a musical and ideological awakening." Antonio Malacara Alonso, "Rock progresivo: consecuencia de un despertar ideológico y musical," *Conecte*, no. 116, January 2, 1979, 30–31. In February 1977 *Conecte* ran a feature on progressive rock band Nahuatl that put this band in the context of "an avalanche of young musicians, better educated and with the acquired experiences of their ancestors, flooding the scene in our country, impregnating it with a sincere love for music and an intellectual progression that will revolutionize the system." "Nahuatl," *Conecte*, no. 33, February 15, 1977, 34–35. On the need to increase professionalism, see "Editorial," *Conecte*, no. 124, March 1979, 7. On transcending "mediocrity," see a *Conecte* editorial in April 1979 stating that "we are all hoping that national rock leaves behind the mediocrity in which it has been stuck for more than 15 years." "Editorial," *Conecte*, no. 128, April 1979, 7. One from July 1975 decried the "same mediocrity as ever" in the Mexican rock scene. "Editorial," *Conecte*, no. 10, July 1975, 3. In the latter issue, there is also an interview with Carlos Mata from the band Nuevo México bemoaning the "degraded level in which rock and roll music in our country finds itself." Castelazo, "Carlos Mata de Nuevo México declara."
107. Arturo Castelazo, "El rock nacional hacía los 80s," *Conecte*, no. 142, September 1979, 14–16. Note that these are the rules for entry for the second iteration of the competition.
108. "Editorial," *Conecte*, no. 117, January 13, 1979, 7.

109. Antonio Malacara Alonso, "Un exitoso músico de rock," *Conecte*, no. 117, January 13, 1979, 20–21.
110. Antonio Malacara Alonso, "Un exitoso músico de rock, 2ª parte," *Conecte*, no. 118, January 1979, 16–17.
111. Alonso, "Un exitoso músico de rock, 2ª parte."
112. "Editor," *Conecte*, no. 132, June 1979, 5.
113. Antonio Malacara Alonso, "Notas," *Conecte*, no. 126, April 1979, 32–33. In the same interview, Trevilla states that he spent five years, between music school and conservatory training, "searching for new musical sensations." At his conservatory, he complained of "a series of setbacks in composition" due to the fact that "the staff have a very conservative style of teaching."
114. Arturo Castelazo, "80s," *Conecte*, no. 126, April 1979, 8–14.
115. "Antonio Malacara Palacios, "Azzor," *Conecte*, no. 172, May 1980, 8–9.
116. Jorge Reyes, "Un dialogo con Jorge Pantoja," *Conecte*, no. 180, July 1980, 8–9, 34.
117. Moreno-Elizondo, "Crisis contracultural," 223.

CHAPTER 2

1. Fernando Ortega Pizarro, "Intolerancia de autoridades al prohibir un concurso de rock ya autorizado," *Proceso*, no. 588, February 8, 1988, 54–55.
2. Latin America's "Lost Decade" of economic stagnation during the 1980s followed a regional debt crisis triggered by successive oil price shocks in the 1970s. As the Bretton Woods institutions became involved in servicing government debts, Latin American governments were coerced into imposing draconian spending cuts on public services such as health and education; many have argued that these cuts damaged regional economic growth in the long term, in addition to their immediate human cost. In Mexico, where neoliberal economic restructuring was especially deep, the decade was experienced as a period of rapidly accelerating inflation, increased poverty, and widening economic equality. See José Antonio Ocampo, "The Latin American Debt Crisis in Historical Perspective," in *Life after Debt: The Origins and Resolutions of Debt Crisis*, ed. Joseph Stiglitz and Daniel Heymann (London: Palgrave Macmillan, 2014), 87–115; Enrique R. Carrasco, "The 1980s: The Debt Crisis and the Lost Decade of Development," *Transnational Law and Contemporary Problems*, no. 9 (1999): 116–26; and Graciela L. Kaminsky and Alfredo Pereira, "The Debt Crisis: Lessons of the 1980s for the 1990s," *Journal of Development Economics* 50, no. 1 (1996): 1–24. In studying the rock scene of the 1980s and 1990s, information about this crisis is often helpful in dating publications: important: when the date of a particular issue is unclear, one can relatively accurately estimate the date by its price.

3. *Colectivo Cambio Radical Fuerza Positiva*, no. 3, June 1988.
4. "Siguen presos en Querétaro siete *chavos-banda* del Distrito Federal," *Colectivo Cambio Radical Fuerza Positiva*, no. 3, June 1988, 1.
5. Zolov, "La Onda Chicana," 40.
6. See José Hernández Riwes Cruz, *Jumping Someone Else's Train REMIX: Una reflexión sobre el revival Post-Punk en la CDMX* (Mexico City: Venas Rotas, 2021); and Marcos Hassan, "6 Electronic Pioneers That Helped Mexico Become an Avant-Garde Haven," *Remezcla*, November 18, 2021.
7. See Raymond A. Patton, *Punk Crisis: The Global Punk Rock Revolution* (Oxford: Oxford University Press, 2018).
8. José Luis Paredes Pacho, "Un país invisible: Escenarios independientes: Autogestión, colectivos, cooperativas, microempresas y cultura alternativa," in *Cultura mexicana: revisión y prospectiva*, ed. Francisco Toledo, Enrique Florescano, and José Woldenberg (Mexico City: Taurus, 2008), 140–73.
9. Urteaga, *Por los territorios de rock*, 114–16.
10. Fraser and Gordon trace the shifting meanings of the notions of "dependence" and "independence," reaching back to their usage in preindustrial Europe, when "dependence" was seen favorably and linked to social hierarchy. "Independence" became especially prized, they show, during neoliberalization in the postindustrial West in the late twentieth century. See Nancy Fraser and Linda Gordon, "A Genealogy of Dependency: Tracing a Keyword of the US Welfare State," *Signs: Journal of Women in Culture and Society* 19, no. 2 (1994): 309–36.
11. The earliest reference I have encountered in the rock press to being "independent" comes from 1973, when the band Three Souls in My Mind stated they preferred to be "independent. . . . Three coordinate better than many, because there are different ways of thinking." Here "independence" sat within a broadly libertarian viewpoint that contrasted individual authenticity with collective conformity. La Bruja, interview with Three Souls, *México Canta*, no. 427, June 1, 1973, 32–33.
12. José Luis Pluma, "Todo lo que sucede es una necesidad del rock: Syntoma, 'se está creando una infraestructura,'" *Conecte*, no. 360, [July] 1984, 34–35.
13. For example, see John Street's response to Martin Cloonan in *Music and Politics*, 16–18.
14. Arturo Castelazo, "El rock hacia los 80s," *Conecte*, no. 142, September 1979, 14–16.
15. Zolov, "La Onda Chicana," 39.
16. The perception that rock was recorded by inexperienced producers was reinforced in an interview with newly hired Polydor producer Rafael Guadarrama, who while working with the latest equipment looked to make up for his lack

of experience with multitrack consoles with "enthusiasm." Vivianne Klein, "Cotorreando con las grabadoras," *Pop*, no. 82, January 14, 1972, 44–46. There were, however, also those who implied that complaints about the quality of recording may have distracted from bands' own technical deficiencies; looking back on the country's first wave of rock acts, José Luis Pluma reflected that "for me, the recordings that those groups made in that era sound better than those made now. And note, they only had two channels and poor equipment." José Luis Pluma, "Acuario," *México Canta*, no. 451, 1973, 4–5.

17. Estrada, *Sirenas al ataque*, 113.
18. Castelazo, "Carlos Mata de Nuevo México declara."
19. José Luis Pluma, "México en concierto," *Conecte*, no. 4, March 1975, 15. José Luis Pluma, "La raza: Una compañía, más que una banda de rock," *Pop*, no. 406, January 5, 1973, 30–31. Arturo Castelazo, "La Semilla del Amor," *Conecte*, no. 28, November 15, 1976, 16–17.
20. "Un Segundo Estudio de Mr Loco," *Conecte*, no. 77, March 20, 1978, 40. Several of Mister Loco's songs have since reached international fame, due to their prominent inclusion in the 2006 Jack Black comedy *Nacho Libre*. The group also won the World Popular Song Festival in Tokyo in 1975.
21. "El Studio 88 sigue apoyando al Rock Mexicano," *Conecte*, no. 200, February 1981, 3.
22. Jorge Reyes, "La propia producción de discos: Única alternativa de los grupos mexicanos, 2da parte," *Conecte*, no. 132, June 1979, 30–31. Gendered language in original.
23. Jorge Reyes, "La propia producción de discos, única alternativa de los grupos mexicanos, III," *Conecte*, no. 143, September 1979, 21, 28. Reyes appears to be unaware of the exploitative nature of the contracts Virgin Records actually signed with even its highest-profile artists. See David Hesmondhalgh, "Post-Punk's Attempt to Democratise the Music Industry: the Success and Failure of Rough Trade," *Popular Music* 16, no. 3 (1998): 257.
24. Jorge Reyes, "La propia producción de discos V," *Conecte*, no. 145, September 1979, 22–23; Jorge Reyes, "La propia producción de discos VI," *Conecte*, no. 146, October 1979, 16–17.
25. Reyes, "La propia producción de discos V"; Reyes, "La propia producción de discos VI." The fifth and sixth installments presume that readers would record in a studio called Estudios Arcoiris, which was equipped with a four-track recorder. This studio was apparently founded by Carlos Mata of the band Nuevo México as an offshoot of a promotional company he announced in the pages of *Conecte* in 1975. See Castelazo, "Carlos Mata de Nuevo México declara."
26. Arturo Castelazo, "Independencia . . .," *Conecte*, no. 149, October 1979, 12.

27. Antonio Malacara Palacios, "Dug Dug's: Una producción independiente," *Conecte*, no. 177, June 1980, 22. I have been unable to find proof that this album was in fact recorded.
28. Jorge Alvarez Estudillo, "La manera de hacer un disco... de rock independiente?" *Conecte*, no. 207, 1981, 28–29. See "Various—Rock Nacional 1981," Discogs, https://www.discogs.com/release/15551578-Various-Rock-Nacional-1981.
29. The author does, however, mention musicians' preexisting contracts with labels as an obstacle to participation. It would appear from the article that musicians were not paid for their contributions, though the article does not state this directly.
30. For instance, in June 1980 José Luis Pluma argued that participants in the rock scene had a duty to support "the mass-scale rock concerts that are being organized in Mexico City... since, independently of carrying out the function of providing a spectacle for the youth, it strengthens the rock movement that is still alive in our country." José Luis Pluma, "La importancia de los conciertos en México," *Conecte*, no. 177, June 1980, 3.
31. "Editor," *Conecte*, no. 149, October 1979, 5.
32. Estrada, *Sirenas al ataque*, 112–17.
33. Felipe Guadarrama, "México Rock," *Conecte*, no. 9, July 1975, 15.
34. See "Editorial," *Conecte*, no. 342, 1984, 3: "*Rock nacional* is seeing new alternatives, but more than that, new opportunities. Each day that passes, we've seen the opening of new forums for projection for rockers. And it's not an illusion. Radio Éxitos has opened up completely, along with the labels. Cafés are starting to feature rock. Even the TV has big plans." LUCC is an acronym of "La Última Carcajada de la Cumbancha" (The Last Guffaw of the Rampage), a line drawn from Agustín Lara's song "La Cumbancha." "Foros, clubes y discotheques: ¿Hubo lugares para el rock en la ciudad de México?," *Conecte*, no. 435, December 1985, 31–33.
35. Agustín, *La contracultura en México*, 160. Guillermo Castillo Ramírez, Julie Anne Boudreau, and Adriana Ávila Farfán, "Tianguis del Chopo: Espacio urbano de regulación/transgresión," *Revista mexicana de sociología* 82, no. 3 (2020): 557–85.
36. Interview, Tony Mendez, May 2020.
37. Interview, Danny Yerna, June 2019.
38. Édgar Corona, "Tutti Frutti, un documental que ya queremos ver," *Atómika*, February 9, 2019, https://atomika.home.blog/2019/02/09/tutti-frutti-el-templo-del-underground-un-documental-que-ya-queremos-ver.
39. Interview, Eduardo Barajas, November 2021.
40. Antonio Malacara Palacios, "Juan Navarro: El primer aniversario de Comrock," *Conecte*, no. 428, 1985, 22–25.

41. The labels were Discos Rosenbach and Trópico Digital, both established in 1983. See Rafael González, *60 años del rock mexicano*, vol. 2, *1980–1989* (Mexico City: Ediciones B, 2016), 25, 155.
42. Long-standing local independent labels also organized live events as the scene grew; Discos Peerless, for instance, announced a rock festival in 1983, with a recording contract as the first prize. Jorge Álvarez Astudillo, "1er Festival de Rock Juvenil de Discos Peerless," *Conecte*, no. 319, September 1983, 32–33.
43. "Editorial," *Conecte*, no. 299, May 1983, 3. Antonio Malacara Alonso, "Las producciones discograficas y el rock," *Conecte*, no. 299, May 1983, 14.
44. Pluma, "Todo lo que sucede es una necesidad del rock."
45. Comrock is a portmanteau of "company" and "rock," but is elsewhere jokingly described as an acronym of "Representative and Organizing Company of Kilometric Ensembles." Palacios, "Juan Navarro."
46. Palacios, "Juan Navarro."
47. "We can't complain. We have five albums on the market, all five are selling very well. Concretely, the El Tri album is a hit. We're going to end the year with more than a hundred thousand copies sold between all the albums we've released." Palacios, "Juan Navarro."
48. Braniff also later complained that Venus Rey and SUTM blocked them from recording acts with synthesizers, based on the allegation that electronic instruments "displaced" professional musicians. See "Chela Braniff," Espacio de COMROCK85, August 16, 2008, https://soy69tremendo.wordpress.com/2008/08/16/chela-braniff/.
49. Palacios, "Juan Navarro."
50. Antonio Malacara Palacios, "Ricardo Ochoa," *Conecte*, no. 485, 1987, 20–21.
51. An editorial in 1983 noted a recent expansion of "semi-professional and almost home-run" *tardeadas* (afternoon concerts), which were welcomed as an indication of the "needs of the youth for rock music, for communication for its own sake," but accompanied by the hope that "this movement might reach higher levels of professionalism." "Editorial," *Conecte*, no. 304, June 1983, 3.
52. Urteaga, *Por los territorios de rock*, 114.
53. For critical perspectives on the reification of "independence" and "do-it-yourself" in punk culture, see Pete Dale, "It Was Easy, It Was Cheap, So What? Reconsidering The DIY Principle of Punk and Indie Music," *Popular Music History* 3, no. 2 (2008): 171–93; and Matthew Bannister, "'Loaded': Indie Guitar Rock, Canonism, White Masculinities," *Popular Music* 25, no. 1 (2006): 77–95.
54. Indeed, as late as 1983 the editors of *Conecte* indicated that "independent" production could have been perceived as autochthonous to Mexico when

they wrote: "The phenomenon of carrying out recordings in an independent manner, on the part of rock bands that are ignored by the major labels, is not only occurring in Mexico, but in the whole world." "Editorial," *Conecte*, no. 302, June 1983, 3.

55. On punk as a "refreshing" addition to the rock movement, see Vladimir Hernández, "El punk: Trae frescura el rock y le impregnarán sentido neto y real," *Conecte*, no. 74, February 27, 1978, 42–43.

56. Arturo Castelazo, "Dangerous Rhythm: Un dramático rompimiento con el pasado," *Conecte*, no. 122, February 1979, 6–11.

57. "Editor," *Conecte*, no. 123, February 1979, 7.

58. For distinct perspectives and historical vantage points on the 1978–1979 Winter of Discontent that brought down the Labour government of James Callaghan, see William Rodgers, "Government under Stress: Britain's Winter of Discontent, 1979," *Political Quarterly* 55, no. 2 (1984): 171–79; and Colin Hay, "The Winter of Discontent Thirty Years On," *Political Quarterly* 80, no. 4 (2009): 545–52. The 1970s continue to be invoked on the political right of the United Kingdom as a period of self-inflicted crisis brought on by economic mismanagement. By contrast, Hay asserts that the United Kingdom's economic problems had the same cause as the global debt crisis that triggered Latin America's Lost Decade: "The real story of the 1970s is one of the rise and attempted management of a condition of simultaneously rising inflation and unemployment—'stagflation'—following the steep rise in oil prices associated with the Yom Kippur War." Hay, "Winter of Discontent," 549.

59. Carlos Baca, "Las disertaciones filosóficas de Rocky Prex," *Conecte*, no. 223, [month obscured] 1981, 24–25.

60. Baca, "Las disertaciones filosóficas . . . "

61. "Editorial," *Conecte*, no. 43, July 5, 1977, 3.

62. Agustín, *La contracultura en México*, 164.

63. "Editor," *Conecte*, no. 154, December 1979, 5.

64. Jorge Reyes, "La prensa y el punk," *Conecte*, no. 154, December 1979, 12.

65. "La verdad verdadera," *CHAPS (Chavas Activas Punks)*, year 1, no. 3, 1989.

66. *Colectivo Cambio Radical Fuerza Positiva*, no. 3, June 1988.

67. "Editorial," *Conecte*, no. 494, [October?] 1987, 1.

68. See Rogelio Marcial, "Políticas públicas de juventud en México: Discursos, acciones e instituciones," *Ixaya: Revista Universitaria de Desarrollo Social* 3 (2012): 9–49.

69. Homero Campa, "Las bandas, respuesta de marginados al fallido proyecto del capitalismo," *Proceso*, no. 464, September 1985.

70. Homero Campa, "Campechano Ramírez Garrido comió con chavos banda: Los muchachos piden respeto pero no creen en promesas de policías," *Proceso*, no. 524, November 1986, 25–27.
71. Fernando Ortega Pizarro, "Perderá su carga explosiva, dicen los independientes," *Proceso*, no. 571, October 1987, 63–65.
72. Ortega Pizarro, "Perderá su carga."
73. "¿Qué le han hecho al rock?" *La Kaza, publicación muy ocasional y casi independiente*, no. 3. [1989?], 16.
74. Urteaga, *Por los territorios de rock*, 46.
75. José Luis Pluma, Interview with Herbe Pompeyo, *Conecte*, no. 342, 1984, 35–37.
76. Ciudad Nezahualcóyotl is a poor, very highly populated district of Estado de México, to the east of Mexico City.
77. José Luis Pluma, Interview with Herbe Pompeyo.
78. Ortega Pizarro. "Perderá su carga."
79. Ortega Pizarro. "Perderá su carga."
80. Ortega Pizarro. "Perderá su carga."
81. Víctor Roura, "El camino del rock no memorizable," *La Jornada*, October 20, 1987, 27.
82. "3 muertos al caer un graderío en el Palacio de los Deportes." *La Jornada*, September 1, 1987, 13.
83. "Sólo 12 policías en el festival del Palacio de los Deportes: Llamarán a declarar a los organizadores," *La Jornada*, September 2, 1987, 14.
84. *La Jornada*, for instance, published only two brief notes about the deaths, which identified neither the artists nor the company that organized the event. The tragedy was also covered, in little depth, by the newspaper *Unomásuno* ("4 muertos y 50 heridos en un concierto juvenil en el Palacio de los Deportes," *Unomásuno*, October 2, 1987, 12). To a small extent the tragedy also made it into the international news (e.g., "Mexico Press Briefs," *United Press International*, October 2, 1987).
85. There is a cursory description, for example, in Carlos Tomasini, "Un símbolo chilango: La historia del Palacio de los Deportes," *Revista Chilango*, December 3, 2015, https://www.chilango.com/ciudad/nota/2015/12/31/la-historia-del-palacio-de-los-deportes.
86. Roura, "El camino del rock no memorizable."
87. Alejandro Islas, "A la víbora de la mar," *Unomásuno*, October 9, 1987, 24.
88. "A diez años de Nacimiento del Rock Rupestre Habla el Cineasta . . . Sergio García," *Conecte*, no. 654, March 1994, 3–5. Notably, similar discourses had been prevalent since the 1960s in Argentine rock culture, where bands deemed to

be overly commercial would be called *complacientes* ("complacent"). Laura Lunardelli, *Alternatividad, divino tesoro: El rock argentino en los 90* (Buenos Aires: Editorial Biblos, 2002), 31–32.
89. Fernando Ortega Pizarro, "Rock disidente, el de 'maldita vecindad.' Es otro que se arriesga en el disco commercial," *Proceso*, no. 611, July 18, 1988, 60.
90. There is an interesting—if less subtle—analogue to this resistance against societal paternalism in Televisa-backed act Flans' 1985 hit "No Controles."
91. For example, Corona, "Politics of Language, Class, and Nation"—also see the discussion at the end of this chapter.
92. Roberto Ponce, "Rock y TLC," *Proceso*, no. 794, 1992, 83–84. The article also reports that a competing Free Art Treaty was signed in San Francisco, among figureheads from the musical, theatrical, and artistic communities across North America.
93. José Luis Paredes Pacho, *Rock mexicano: Sonidos de la calle* (Mexico City: Pesebre, 1992), 35–43.
94. Paredes Pacho, *Rock mexicano*, 85.
95. Paredes Pacho, *Rock mexicano*, 13.
96. Paredes Pacho, *Rock mexicano*, 60.
97. Paredes Pacho, *Rock mexicano*, 54–59.
98. Paredes Pacho, *Rock mexicano*, 59–60.
99. Paredes Pacho, *Rock mexicano*, 106, 82.
100. Paredes Pacho, *Rock mexicano*, 85.
101. Paredes Pacho, *Rock mexicano*, 106.
102. Corona, "Politics of Language, Class, and Nation."
103. Zolov, "La Onda Chicana," 41.

CHAPTER 3

1. A video of this transmission is available to view online here: "Banda Bostik - Tlatelolco '68 / Viajero [Vive Latino XV - 2014]," YouTube video, posted by LU1S 2, March 29, 2014, https://www.youtube.com/watch?v=7b5RN6zcVV8.
2. "Metal Fest, cancelado; cunde decepción entre metaleros," Aristegui Noticias, March 13, 2014, https://aristeguinoticias.com/1303/kiosko/metal-fest-cancelado-cunde-decepcion-entre-metaleros/.
3. Indeed, in a live performance broadcast on online radio in 2017, Guadaña dedicated the same song "to the dog President we've had the whole damn time since the Porfiriato," inviting listeners to shout *chinga su madre* at Peña Nieto "to your heart's content." Here, he undermined mainstream narratives about democratic transition by drawing a historical continuity between present-day

governments and the dictatorship of Porfirio Díaz (1877–1911). "Banda Bostik Tlatelolco 68 Grupo Radio Clin Tv," YouTube video, posted by Grupo Radio Clin, November 23, 2017, https://www.youtube.com/watch?v=ateRhk9hes8.
4. Interview, Luis Jasso, August 2018.
5. Interview, Luis Jasso, August 2018.
6. For instance, in 2009 the company allegedly threatened to veto the businesses providing sound and security to an independent festival entitled Festival Goliath, which had chosen to sell tickets directly rather than via the OCESA subsidiary Ticketmaster. This case was mentioned to me by one interviewee, who I choose not to identify; it was also discussed in Patricia Peñaloza, "Ruta sonora," *La Jornada*, December 10, 2009; and Vicente Gutiérrez Lagos, "Goliath Festival," *Ruidos y susurros*, October 14, 2009, https://ruidosysusurros.blogspot.com/2009/10/goliath-festival.html. The latter features an interview with the organizer, who states that he took great precautions to reveal the headliners (Pitbull and Black Eyed Peas) slowly in advance of the festival in order to avoid the competition stealing these acts. See, for instance, a case in 2014 in which OCESA organized a festival entitled Electric Daisy Carnival on the same day as the long-standing independent electronic music festival Electric Planet. This led the organizer of the Electric Planet to take the festival to San Luis Potosí. The organizer, Pedro Moctezuma, painted OCESA as a threat to freedom of expression, complaining that "they always tell me to say nothing, but I will not remain silent." See "Empresarios vs. monopolio OCESA," *Revista Negocios*, August 27, 2017, http://www.revistanegocios.mx/texto-diario/mostrar/791791/empresarios-vs-monopolio-ocesa.
7. Gustavo Silva, "Realizan giras para ganar dinero," *El Universal*, April 16, 2008, https://archivo.eluniversal.com.mx/espectaculos/82646.html. This point obscures constant price increases for OCESA tickets, resulting from a lack of competition.
8. Maricarmen Cortés, "CIE, acuerdo con Cofece," *Dinero en imagen*, October 23, 2018, https://www.dineroenimagen.com/maricarmen-cortes/cie-acuerdo-con-cofece/104148.
9. Interview, Jorge Caballero, January 2022.
10. Octavio Paz, "The Philanthropic Ogre," *Dissent* 26, no.1 (1979): 43-52.
11. The company is not mentioned, for instance, in Zolov, *Refried Elvis*; Pacini Hernández, l'Hoeste, and Zolov, *Rockin' las Americas*; Alejandro Madrid, *Transnational Encounters: Music and Performance at the US-Mexico Border* (Oxford: Oxford University Press, 2011); or Mark Pedelty, *Musical Ritual in Mexico City: from the Aztec to NAFTA* (Austin: University of Texas Press, 2004).

12. Timothy Taylor, "The Commodification of Music at the Dawn of the Era of Mechanical Music," *Ethnomusicology* 51, no. 2 (2007): 281–305; David Arditi, *Getting Signed: Record Contracts, Musicians, and Power in Society* (New York: Palgrave Macmillan, 2020).
13. Zolov, *Refried Elvis*, 62–92.
14. Arturo García Hernández, "La buena onda marcó al concierto de rock más concurrido que se ha hecho en México," *La Jornada*, November 15, 1992, 20.
15. Federico Campbell, "Vargas Llosa y la experiencia de la libertad," *La Jornada*, September 2, 1990, 37.
16. Hermann Bellinghausen, "¿Renacimiento de qué?," *La Jornada*, November 30, 1992, 24; Jorge Alberto Manrique, "Intolerancia, otra vez," *La Jornada*, April 22, 1992.
17. Gabriel Peña Rico, "The Wall: Berlin 1990," *La Jornada*, August 19, 1990, 31.
18. Vive Latino features mostly artists from Mexico and Latin America. Success at Vive Latino continues to be a key factor in bands' ability to attract interest from record labels and from OCESA itself; to book a band for one of its large-scale venues, OCESA needs to show that the band can attract an audience of ten thousand people paying four hundred pesos each. Interview, Raymundo Gabriel, October 2020.
19. García Hernández, "La buena onda."
20. Televisa and CIE, "Grupo Televisa and CIE Form Strategic Alliance for Live Entertainment in Mexico," press release, October 18, 2002, https://www.televisair.com/~/media/Files/T/Televisa-IR/press-releases/english/10-18-2002/tv-cie-eng.pdf.
21. It was pointed out at the time that OCESA's rise was facilitated by state subsidies. See Renato Ravelo, "La floreciente industria de conciertos de rock, subsidiada por el publico," *La Jornada*, July 13, 1993, 23.
22. Roberto Ponce, "Los empresarios de Ocesa y su manejo del Palacio de los Deportes: Vendrá Sinatra," *Proceso*, no. 756, April 1991, 76–78; Raúl Monge, "Que se mantengan solos DDF," *Proceso*, no. 807, April 1992, 26–28.
23. Interview, Eduardo Barajas, November 2021.
24. As noted earlier, LUCC is an acronym for "The Last Guffaw of the Rampage," a phrase taken from a song by the *bolerista* Agustín Lara.
25. Interview, Eduardo Barajas, November 2021.
26. Interview, Eduardo Barajas, November 2021.
27. Roberto Ponce, "Explican los dueños de LUCC el fracaso de publico en Rola 92 en el Palacio de los Deportes," *Proceso*, no. 818, July 1992, 82–83; Roberto Ponce, "La delegacion Tlalpan suspende permisos para el foro cultural Arteria:

Nos quieren ahorcar, dice su coordinador Eduardo Barajas," *Proceso*, no. 937, October 1994, 130–31. LUCC closed its doors at the end of 1992, after five years of operation. The venue had been shut by authorities roughly twenty times during its five-year existence, mostly following complaints from neighbors—some of whom accused the venue of hosting Satanic rituals. In early 1992 its owners made an agreement with the authorities that they would close the venue for good in December, so long as they could avoid closures for the duration of the year.

28. See Roberto Ponce, "Los festivales de blues y jazz en el Auditorio caros y sin artistas mexicanos pero necesarios coinciden los músicos," *Proceso*, no. 831, October 1992, 2–3. This feature on a jazz and blues festival also highlighted issues of language: it was called "Mexico City Jazz & Blues (that's right—in English)."
29. Renato Ravelo, "La ola de conciertos masivos de rock rebasa a nuestros críticos y músicos. Hoy inicia U2 sus presentaciones en el Palacio de los Deportes," *La Jornada*, November 25, 1992, 25.
30. Roberto Ponce, "Artistas, disqueras, promotores, representantes: Pese a las limitaciones, ya hay un mercado," *Proceso*, no. 1020, May 1996, 36–40.
31. Ponce, "Los empresarios de Ocesa y su manejo del Palacio de los Deportes."
32. This quote was attributed to Camacho Solís by the organizers of LUCC. Ponce, "Explican los dueños de LUCC."
33. See Ponce, "La delegacion Tlalpan suspende permisos para el foro cultural Arteria." In response, the venue organizers appealed to the authorities to uphold their commercial and legal rights to run events in the venue.
34. Sergio Monsalvo, "La dinamita de Iron Maiden devino chinampina en concierto," *La Jornada*, October 3, 1992, 40. This message provoked one journalist to write, angrily, that the message should be broadcast in the offices of promotors and police officers, since rock audiences would not create public disorder "with good treatment by organizers and security." Nonetheless, this was a rare open challenge to the premise that the unruly rock public was at fault for disorder and could be legitimately censored if not appropriately disciplined.
35. Ponce, "Los empresarios de Ocesa y su manejo del Palacio de los Deportes." Anxieties about the sanitization of rock were also reflected in sardonic reviews of mainstream or international acts performing in OCESA venues, such as one describing the Canadian band Green Day "destroying their instruments in an educated, orderly fashion, throwing the remains behind them so as to avoid an accident in the distinguished crowd." José Homero, "Las artes sin musa," *La Jornada*, January 10, 1999.

36. Ponce, "Los empresarios de Ocesa y su manejo del Palacio de los Deportes." This logic, of course, adapts the repressive, paternalistic logic of the "Revolutionary Family" into the mainstream commercial sphere. See Zolov, *Refried Elvis*.
37. Ravelo, "La floreciente industria de conciertos de rock, subsidiada por el publico."
38. For instance, the security for the OCESA-run Corona Capital festival was noted in *La Jornada* to have numbered 800 private security agents and 150 auxiliary police in 2015. Jorge Caballero, "Todo listo, para recibir a los 100 mil asistentes al Corona Capital," *La Jornada*, November 21, 2015. In 2017, security was estimated at 745 private security agents alongside 425 auxiliary police and 60 riot police. "Corona Capital promete ser más que un banquete musical," *La Jornada*, November 8, 2017, 7. The fact that a major newspaper habitually publishes such figures indicates that security at festivals continues to be a major concern.
39. Markus-Michael Müller, *The Punitive City: Privatized Policing and Protection in Neoliberal Mexico* (London: Bloomsbury, 2016).
40. Roberto Ponce, "Detrás del temor que provocan, están 500 jovenes preparados para proteger al publico," *Proceso*, no. 1129, June 1998, 106–9.
41. Ravelo, "La floreciente industria de conciertos de rock, subsidiada por el público."
42. Interview, Ileana Gordillo, January 2022.
43. Claudia Herrera Beltrán, "Dos horas de luz sónica," *La Jornada*, February 8, 1998. It is arguable that the principle that a private company is responsible for security at its own events is still not fully established in the present-day scene. For instance, after a spate of robberies at an OCESA festival in 2016, one journalist argued that "as this is a private event, OCESA assumes co-responsibility and needs to respond to this crimewave; it is being called upon to energetically reinforce its security measures." Patricia Peñaloza, "Ruta Sonora," *La Jornada*, November 25, 2016. In many live music contexts, this would be stating the obvious; that this point is considered worth mentioning reveals the comparative novelty of the privatization of security at live rock events in Mexico.
44. Salvador Quiauhtlazollin, "Black Sabbath, ni dioses ni diablos; solo ruido infernal," *La Jornada*, November 10, 1992, 26.
45. Renato Ravelo, "Caifanes, concierto de catequismo sobre la fe en el rock nacional. Conquistó para México el Palacio de los Deportes," *La Jornada*, May 2, 1993, 59.

46. Renato Ravelo, "La floreciente industria de conciertos de rock, subsidiada por el publico."
47. Chava Rock, "Ska-P dice adiós con una fiesta que desbordó energía y talento," *La Jornada*, October 7, 2005.
48. This was the case for a Sisters of Mercy concert in 1999, as *La Jornada* reported: "An hour and a quarter of the gig had passed, at 9:45, when almost one hundred goths [*darkies*] attempted a *portazo*. The security . . . was overwhelmed, but on being reinforced by riot police, [they] took advantage to take fire extinguishers and dampen the euphoria of the dark mass before them [that is, they sprayed the crowd]. . . . One goth lay on the ground, having hurt their leg in the attempted *portazo*, imploring a [private security guard]: 'let me in, they already beat me, go on, let me in,' but they ignored him." Jorge Caballero, "Sisters of Mercy cambió su neblina inglesa por el smog chilango, pero chafeó el sonido," *La Jornada*, October 25, 1999.
49. "Personal de Ocesa golpeó a joven, acusa," Letter by Erika Cruz Guillén, published in *La Jornada*, June 2, 2002. OCESA security operatives have also been associated with violence outside of a live music context, for instance when they were accused of assaulting an elderly jogger running through the sports complex in which Palacio de los Deportes is located. See Susana González, "Protesta vecinal contra la presencia de Ocesa en la Magdalena Mixhuca," *La Jornada*, January 4, 2005.
50. "Ataque de Lobos en el Metropólitan," *La mosca en la pared*, no. 20, February 1998, 7.
51. Roberto Ponce, "Detrás del temor que provocan, están 500 jóvenes preparados para proteger al público," *Proceso*, no. 1129, June 1998, 106–9.
52. See Francisco Valenzuela, "Ricardo Robles: El empresario detrás del Woodstock Morelia," *El Sol de Morelia*, July 30, 2020. The festival was entitled Woodstock Morelia, and it took place in a sports stadium in the city of Morelia; its lineup featured many members of the old guard of United States rock, most notably an ensemble formed of the surviving members of The Doors. While part of the eventual failure of the festival was blamed on political obstruction (its sponsor, Ricardo Robles, was the son of the founder of the leftist opposition party PRD and had organized fundraisers for the party), OCESA's alleged dirty tricks campaign led to the festival attracting an audience of less than a fifth of capacity. Speaking to *El Sol de Morelia* in 2020, the organizer Salvador Munguia (a journalist better known by his pen name, Chava Rock) stated that OCESA had "boycotted us; they pushed the rumor that it was a fraud, and they even managed to get [national newspapers] *El Universal* and *Excélsior* to

publish that the event was cancelled." See Francisco Valenzuela, "Woodstock en Morelia, un festival fracasado," *El Sol de Morelia*, December 28, 2019.
53. Interview, "Mariano," August 2018.
54. Interview, Jorge Caballero, January 2022.
55. Interview, "Mariano," August 2018.
56. Francisco Zamudio, "Los periodistas del rock mexicano y su entorno a partir de la época dorada para los medios especializados: Encuentros y desencuentros," in Cortés and González Castillo, *El rock también se escribe*, 66–75.
57. "Lo que callamos los periodistas de rock," Peperock, March 29, 2017, http://peperock.com/2017/03/29/lo-que-callamos-los-periodistas-de-rock/.
58. Brenda Marín, "Billy Joel: Rock, abusos y prepotencia," *La Banda Rockera* 89 ([March 1992?]): 13. This story is a reprint from the magazine *La Afición*.
59. For an account of the spread of the so-called *Reforma* style across Mexico City newspapers, see Sallie Hughes, *Newsrooms in Conflict: Journalism and the Democratization of Mexico* (Pittsburgh, PA: University of Pittsburgh Press, 2006).
60. Interview, "Jeremy," January 2022.
61. For instance, from April 1994, *La Jornada* ran two full-page features on Pink Floyd in the days preceding the band's concerts at the Autodromo Hermanos Rodríguez; in January 1994 Aerosmith's performance at Palacio de los Deportes was announced the week prior in an article covering almost a whole page; a week and a half before Sting was due to perform at Palacio de los Deportes he earned a full-page feature in *La Jornada* containing a brief interview in which the singer stated his desire to visit Chiapas in the wake of the 1994 Zapatista uprising. Meanwhile, the Rolling Stones' January 1995 performance at the Autódromo Hermanos Rodríguez was announced in a full-page feature three months prior, in October 1994.
62. "From pop, reggae, jazz and rock, Mexico experienced a catharsis of exquisite musical genres. OCESA . . . was the number one promoter of Anglo-Saxon [that is, rock] concerts in all Latin America. In our country alone, they presented more than 100 concerts to more than one million spectators." "Ocesa presentó más de 100 conciertos este año," *La Jornada*, December 19, 2002.
63. Fernando Figueroa, "La Ley de Herodes," *La Jornada*, June 13, 1999.
64. Roberto Ponce, "Artistas, disqueras, promotores, representantes: pese a las limitaciones, ya hay un mercado," *Proceso*, no. 1020, 1996, 36–40.
65. Ponce, "Los empresarios de Ocesa."
66. Ponce, "Los empresarios de Ocesa."
67. "A 27 años de Avándaro, dos conciertos de la promotora Ocesa," *La Jornada*, August 29, 1998.

68. "Editorial: Ante la negativa del DDF y el temor de la UNAM a organizar los conciertos Salinas convenció a Zedillo y dieron el sí final a los Rolling Stones," *Proceso*, no. 949, January 1995, 93–96.
69. Roberto Ponce, "Ante 17000 jóvenes en el Palacio de los Deportes," *Proceso*, no. 1090, September 1997, 100–2.
70. Erika Duarte, "Muere una menor de edad durante el concierto," *La Jornada*, October 7, 2005.
71. Interview, "León," August 2018.
72. Zamudio, "Los periodistas del rock mexicano."
73. Müller, *The Punitive City*; Jenny Pearce, "Perverse State Formation and Securitized Democracy in Latin America," *Democratization* 17, no. 2 (2010): 286–306.

CHAPTER 4

1. The activities of this organization are described in Jorge H. Velasco García, *El canto de la tribu*, 2nd ed. (Mexico City: CONACULTA, 2013), 109–12.
2. See Neil Harvey, *The Chiapas Rebellion: The Struggle for Land and Democracy* (Durham, NC: Duke University Press, 1998); and Richard Stahler-Sholk, "Resisting Neoliberal Homogenization: The Zapatista Autonomy Movement," *Latin American Perspectives*, 34, no. 2 (2007): 48–63.
3. See Thomas Olesen, *International Zapatismo: The Construction of Solidarity in the Age of Globalization* (London: Zed Books, 2005); Niels Barmeyer, *Developing Zapatista Autonomy: Conflict and NGO Involvement in Rebel Chiapas* (Albuquerque: University of New Mexico Press, 2009); and Chris Gilbreth and Gerardo Otero, "Democratization in Mexico: The Zapatista Uprising and Civil Society," *Latin American Perspectives* 28, no. 4 (2001): 7–29.
4. An active performer in the rock scene since the 1970s, Guillermo Briseño began his career performing with the funk-inflected band Cosa Nostra before embarking on a solo career. His music has incorporated influences from a range of genres, especially progressive rock and blues.
5. Paredes Pacho, "Un país invisible."
6. Wayne A. Cornelius, "Mexico: Salinas and the PRI at the Crossroads," *Journal of Democracy* 1, no. 3 (1990): 61–70.
7. "Condena a la guerra en medio de rock, blues y rechiflas," *La Jornada*, January 23, 1991. The event reportedly featured the shout "viva Hussein!"
8. Subcomandante Marcos, "Palabras del Sup para la mesa redonda 'De la cultura subterránea a la cultura de la resistencia.'" Multiforo Cultural Alicia, October 26, 1999, https://enlacezapatista.ezln.org.mx/1999/10/26/palabras-del-sup-para-la-mesa-redonda-de-la-cultura-subterranea-a-la-cultura-de-la-resistencia/.

9. See Marco Tavanti, *Las Abejas: Pacifist Resistance and Syncretic Identities in a Globalizing Chiapas* (New York: Routledge, 2013).
10. See Jonathan Fox, Carlos García Jiménez, and Libby Haight, "Rural Democratisation in Mexico's Deep South: Grassroots Right-To-Know Campaigns in Guerrero," *Journal of Peasant Studies* 36, no. 2 (2009): 271–98.
11. See Magaña, *Cartographies of Youth Resistance*.
12. For example, Zolov, *Refried Elvis*; Pedelty, *Musical Ritual*; and Madrid, *Transnational Encounters*.
13. Hughes, *Newsrooms in Conflict*, 13, 142.
14. Alan O'Connor, "Punk and Globalization: Mexico City and Toronto," in *Communities across Borders*, ed. Paul Kennedy and Victor Roudometof (New York: Routledge, 2002), 159–71.
15. "Más artistas en el acto del Angel," letter published in *La Jornada*, February 20, 1995, 2.
16. These caravans included Chicano musicians from Los Angeles, such as Rage Against the Machine frontman Zack de la Rocha and Yaotl Mazahua, the lead singer of rap metal outfit Aztlán Underground.
17. Elio Henríquez, "Concluye el foro americano contra el neoliberalismo," *La Jornada*, April 9, 1996.
18. This was explained by Rita Guerrero and Poncho Figueroa, of the band Santa Sabina, in comments made to *La Jornada* in 1998: "Perhaps at a concert we can't give all the information, but we can awaken the impulse for them to inform themselves about what's really happening, given that the media in our country are so deficient," Guerrero said. Figueroa added that "we're concerned with informing people, because we know that young people are victims of the misinformation project of the federal government." Ángel Vargas, "La Bola se encargará de poner música al pecado el viernes," *La Jornada*, November 12, 1998.
19. A detailed account of rock after the Zapatista uprising is provided in Benjamin Anaya, *Neozapatismo y rock mexicano* (Mexico City: Ediciones La Cuadrilla de la Langosta, 1999).
20. Interview, Paco Barrios "El Mastuerzo," January 2013.
21. See Álvaro García, "El caótico concierto de Caifanes en la Del. Venustiano Carranza," *Rock en México*, April 21, 2020, http://www.rockenmexico.com/historias/el-caotico-concierto-de-caifanes-en-la-del-venustiano-carranza/.
22. Víctor Ballinas and Ricardo Olayo, "Prohibe el DDF conciertos de rock y espectáculos de masas al aire libre," *La Jornada*, February 21, 1995, 60, 43.
23. Raúl Monge, "Le dicen la 'Ley Espinosa' y nadie se ha salvado: golpizas a choferes, colonos, comerciantes, reporteros, y ahora, a los maestros. El regente de la capital convierte a las 'fuerzas de disuasión' en fuerzas de choque,"

Proceso, no. 1021, May 27, 1996, 12–17; Ballinas and Olayo, "Prohibe el DDF"; Roberto Ponce, "Grupos, foros, proyectos: El PRD debate du oferte cultural para el DF en medio del hermetismo," *Proceso*, no. 1096, November 2, 1997, 60–67.

24. Ricardo Olayo and Miriam Posada, "Hubo provocadores en el concierto de Caifanes, asegura el Delegado," *La Jornada*, February 22, 1995, 40.
25. As contemporary reporting makes clear, this prohibition occurred within a broader repressive context. Espinosa Villareal took an intolerant approach to popular protest in the capital and presided over a number of cases of the violent suppression of peaceful civil society actions by riot police. See Monge, "Le dicen la 'Ley Espinosa' y nadie se ha salvado."
26. Ballinas and Olayo, "Prohibe el DDF."
27. Patricia Peñaloza, "Ruta Sonora," *La Jornada*, May 12, 2006. Monge, "Le dicen la 'Ley Espinosa' y nadie se ha salvado."
28. Interview, Poncho Figueroa, June 2019.
29. Erik Carranza, "Las células que (ya no) explotan," *Arquine*, February 19, 2019, https://www.arquine.com/las-celulas-que-ya-no-explotan.
30. Interview, Rafael González, July 2018.
31. Interview, Poncho Figueroa, June 2019.
32. Maldita Vecindad, "El derecho a la fiesta," *La Jornada*, March 4, 1995, 26.
33. "Maratón artístico por Chiapas en el estadio de prácticas de Ciudad Universitaria, 'aunque se oponga la UNAM,'" editorial in *Proceso*, no. 967, 1995, 109–10.
34. Interview, Rafael González, July 2018.
35. "Invitan a participar en la despedida de la Caravana a Chiapas," letter published in *La Jornada*, March 23, 1995, 59.
36. "Bandas roqueras se suman a la marcha independiente," letter published in *La Jornada*, April 30, 1995, 2.
37. Adriana Díaz Enciso, "Rock por la paz y la tolerancia," *La Jornada*, 4 March 1995, 25.
38. Peñaloza, "Ruta Sonora."
39. Gavin O'Toole, *The Reinvention of Mexico: National Ideology in a Neoliberal Era* (Liverpool: Liverpool University Press, 2010).
40. O'Toole, *Reinvention of Mexico*, 46, 60.
41. Monge, "Que se mantengan solos DDF."
42. See, for example, a 1995 article by the novelist Carlos Fuentes, who contended that "the impulse toward political reform comes from below, from civil society and its organizations, from culture and its manifestations." Carlos Fuentes, "El fin del sistema mexicano," *Proceso*, no. 997, December 1995, 2–8. Indeed, "civil society" and "culture" came to be associated so closely during

the neoliberal era that the former could be invoked as a pretext for cuts to cultural funding. In 1998 the former federal subsecretary of Finance, Francisco Gil Díaz, called for tax reductions for businesses to be paid for by cuts in cultural spending: "There are artistic events, like symphonic concerts, operas, and plays, that the government doesn't have to support. The people who want to see them will pay for them, those who have a cosmopolitan culture. Civil society can take care of that." Fernando Ortega Pizarro, "Dignas de Ripley, las medidas fiscales para 1999, dice Gil Díaz, exsubsecretario de Ingresos y ahora empresario," *Proceso*, no. 1155, December 1998, 36–37.

43. Adriana Díaz Enciso, "Rock por la paz y la tolerancia," *La Jornada*, March 4, 1995, 25.
44. Díaz Enciso, "Rock por la paz."
45. Ángel Vargas, "La Bola se encargará de poner música al pecado el viernes," *La Jornada*, November 12, 1998.
46. See, for instance, the following opening to a 1993 review of a live concert in Mexico City in 1993: "Slam a dense breath slam buffalo slam slam a clash of legs and plexuses slam acid criticism slam it's not partying slam pasty bolo slam sweat slam a clash of legs and forearms . . . slam music coming out of bodies slam thud slam surf over the bodies slam a dive from the stage to the audience slam cannon fodder slam tumbles slam frenzy slam slam slam slam slam slam slam. Obsessive circular dustup [*madrificación*]." Pablo Espinosa, "Y se desató el slam en el Gimnasio Juan de la Barrera," *La Jornada*, July 4, 1993, 23.
47. Pablo Espinosa, "El escenario, un perol de slam y mucha adrenalina enardecida," *La Jornada*, May 5, 1996, 26.
48. Díaz Enciso, "Rock por la paz."
49. "Maratón artístico," *Proceso*, no. 967, May 1995.
50. Octavio Rodríguez Araujo, "Pide explicación sobre una controvertible decisión de la Rectoría de la UNAM," letter published in *La Jornada*, June 26, 1997, 2.
51. José Gil Olmos, "Que Barnes retire la suspensión a Inti Muñoz, ordena un juez," *La Jornada*, July 10, 1997, 40.
52. "The record companies told us, or the managers told us 'don't talk' [about the EZLN], 'it's a war,' 'they're indigenous, they're bad vibes' right? All this misinformation about everything that was going on." Interview, Ileana Gordillo, January 2022.
53. Julio Aguilar, "Los jóvenes y el PRD," *Unomásuno*, June 19, 1997, 13; Sergio Wals, "El voto joven, decisivo. Podría determinar la elección," *Unomásuno*, June 9, 1997, 1, 8.
54. Taibo II's proposals for "cultural revolution" and "democratization" within culture were met with public pushback from some intellectuals. For instance,

Carlos Monsiváis aired suspicion about a supposed shift toward populism, arguing that government support for rock ought to "depend on the quality of the groups," and Javier Sicilia linked "cultural revolution" to Maoism, criticizing it as a leftist, dangerously ideological idea. José Alberto Castro, "Rascón, Monsiváis, Domínguez y Sicilia, entre el asombro y el malestar, refutan la 'revolución cultural' de Taibo II," *Proceso*, no. 1096, November 2, 1997, 62–63.
55. Ponce, "Grupos, foros, proyectos."
56. Ponce, "Grupos, foros, proyectos."
57. Ponce, "Grupos, foros, proyectos."
58. Ponce, "Grupos, foros, proyectos."
59. Interview, Gabino Palomares, December 2020.
60. "DFiesta" is a portmanteau of the Spanish for "party" and the official title of the capital at that time (Distrito Federal, or DF). Radical Mestizo was a concert series created and directed by José Luis Paredes Pacho. See Tania Molina Ramírez, "Radical Mestizo, música sin fronteras: Lo marginal toca en el centro," *La Jornada*, April 14, 2002.
61. Peñaloza, "Ruta Sonora."
62. See Gustavo Coutiño Soriano, "Rebeldía, música y consumo cultural: De los conciertos solidarios al Vive Latino," in *Etnorock: Los rostros de una música global en el sur de México*, ed. Martín de la Cruz López Moya, Efraín Ascencio Cedillo, and Juan Pablo Zebadúa Carbonell (Mexico: Universidad de Ciencias y Artes de Chiapas, 2014), 143–55; and Julián Woodside, "Sobre la festivalización o 'festivalitis' en México: Vive Latino y Corona Capital como manifestaciones contemporáneas de mestizofilia y anglofilia," *Revista argentina de musicología* 21, no. 2 (2020): 107–27.
63. There are also links between the broader corporatization of rock and a situation in which spontaneous performances at protests are no longer possible. In the wake of the earthquake in September 2017 that killed 228 in Mexico City, rockers found that efforts to hold fundraising concerts for the *damnificados* made homeless by the earthquake were undermined by the fact that major artists had signed exclusivity contracts for performances in the city. Interview, Armando Vega Gil, August 2018.
64. Interview, Poncho Figueroa, June 2019. See Joselo, "Vive Latino, 20 años," *Excélsior*, May 2018.; Myrna Martínez, "Vive Latino se consolida como patrimonio urbano," *El Financiero*, March 27 2014.
65. Interview, Raymundo Gabriel, October 2020.
66. Interview, Ileana Gordillo, January 2022.
67. "Vibra Zócalo con La Maldita," *Metro*, April 22, 2002.

68. "Llena la plancha del Zócalo concierto 'Radical Mestizo,'" *El Universal*, April 21, 2002.
69. Hugo García Michel, "Ojo de Mosca," *La mosca en la pared*, no. 58, May 2002.
70. See Andrew Green, "Activist Musicianship, Sound, the 'Other Campaign' and the Limits of Public Space in Mexico City," *Ethnomusicology Forum* 25, no. 3 (2016): 345–66.

CHAPTER 5

1. Gerardo Jímenez, "New's Divine: Drogas, mentiras y videos," *Proceso*, June 19, 2009.
2. Interview, Akil Ammar, August 2018.
3. "Akil Ammar - 20 DE JUNIO," YouTube video, posted by Akil Ammar, June 17, 2009, https://www.youtube.com/watch?v=sAOk6hNcPxI.
4. "Akil Ammar—'Reverso' Censurado Por El Universal 17/06/09," YouTube video, posted by 2packali, June 18, 2009, https://www.youtube.com/watch?v=6amIdusQNI.
5. Comment posted by Thesongsoffreedom on "Akil Ammar—'Reverso' Censurado Por El Universal 17/06/09," YouTube video.
6. Although the term *foro cultural* may be applied to venues not featuring music, all of the spaces studied here are music venues.
7. For instance, in March 1999 the organizers of Multiforo Cultural Alicia denounced the forcible entrance of a group of forty masked paramilitaries, armed with high-calibre weapons, in unmarked uniforms and vehicles without registration plates, into the venue during a concert, where they assaulted several members of staff and audience members. See "Denuncian agresión de grupo paramilitar en el Multiforo Alicia," letter published in *La Jornada*, April 2, 1999.
8. See María Teresa López Flamarique, *Alicia en el espejo: Historias del Multiforo Cultural Alicia* (Mexico City: Ediciones Alicia, 2010); Abril Schmucler, dir., *Alicia mas allá del abismo* (CONACULTA, 2015).
9. See, for example, Fernanda Pesce, "Historic Mexico City Rock and Counterculture Hub Closes," *AP News*, April 10, 2023, https://apnews.com/article/mexico-historic-venue-alicia-nightclub-closed-a0f0e5146640304c1bd42cae90e46be1.
10. See, for example, César Becerra, "Multiforo Alicia regresa con nueva sede y ya hay fecha para el primer concierto," *El Heraldo de México*, March 1, 2024, https://heraldodemexico.com.mx/tendencias/2024/3/1/multiforo-alicia-regresa-con-nueva-sede-ya-hay-fecha-para-el-primer-concierto-582418.html.
11. The space was named as such in honor of both *Alice in Wonderland* and the Italian independent radio station Radio Alice.

12. Ángel Rama, *The Lettered City* (Durham, NC: Duke University Press, 1996).
13. Jorge Caballero, "El Alicia, buen ejemplo de autogestión y autonomía," *La Jornada*, January 13, 2012.
14. For instance, the now-famous ska outfit Panteón Rococó stated in a 2004 interview that "many [bands] were born in Multiforo Cultural Alicia, like us." Arturo Cruz Bárcenas, "Panteón Rococó: Volvimos a ganar el Zócalo; hagamos un domingo chido," *La Jornada*, June 12, 2004.
15. In most of Mexico the smallest branch of government is called the municipality (*municipio*); however, Mexico City was divided into a series of delegations (*delegaciones*) until 2016, when these districts were renamed mayorships (*alcaldías*). For clarity, I will use the phrase "local government" alongside these terms.
16. See "El Multiforo Alicia . . . a la verga . . . !!! ¿Se pierde algo?" Peperock, June 6, 2015, archived at https://web.archive.org/web/20220521014949/https://peperock.com/2015/06/06/el-multiforo-alicia-a-la-verga-se-pierde-algo/.
17. Rosalía Vergara, "Monreal detecta red de corrupción que operaba en la delegación Cuauhtémoc," *Proceso*, July 20, 2015. As Lomnitz points out, a culture of corruption in Mexican governance is rooted in poverty and the weakness of the state, which lends bureaucrats a great deal of "discretionary power"; so long as these conditions persist, so too will corruption. Claudio Lomnitz, *Deep Mexico, Silent Mexico: An Anthropology of Nationalism* (Minneapolis: University of Minnesota Press, 2001), 60–61.
18. Interview with anonymous respondent, June 2019.
19. David Graeber, *Direct Action: An Ethnography* (Chico: AK Press, 2009), 282–83.
20. Graeber, *Direct Action*, 284.
21. Scott, *Art of Not Being Governed*.
22. The following blog post explicitly attacks Multiforo Cultural Alicia: "Such crybaby statements, such as those given by mister Nacho Pineda, the owner of Alicia (yes indeed, the collective, libertarian, cultural, self-managed space has an owner, believe it or not . . .) are laughable, at least they make me think that despite the fact that this is all a BUSINESS, nobody ever had the vision for it to evolve as such." Peperock, "El Multiforo Alicia . . . a la verga . . . !!! ¿Se pierde algo?"
23. Interview, Abigail Morgado, December 2018.
24. Interview, Ignacio Pineda, June 2018.
25. See Paredes Pacho, "Un país invisible."
26. Paredes Pacho, "Un país invisible."
27. Holly Kruse, "Subcultural Identity in Alternative Music Culture," *Popular Music* 12, no. 1 (1993): 33–41; Keir Keightley, "Reconsidering Rock," in *The Cambridge*

Companion to Pop and Rock, ed. Simon Frith, Will Straw, and John Street (Cambridge: Cambridge University Press, 2001), 109–42.
28. Interview, Ignacio Pineda, July 2018.
29. Hip-hop's early growth in Mexico City was found in rock venues, and some of the most famous early exponents of hip-hop in Mexico, such as Molotov and Control Machete, mix the genre with rock.
30. Paredes Pacho, "Un país invisible."
31. Interview, Talía, August 2019.
32. Some of the clauses added to the contract related to health concerns—for instance, one responded to an incident at the venue in which a death metal band had used out-of-date animal blood during a live set.
33. Indeed, some other foros culturales have followed a similar path during the pandemic, with some lending increasing priority to cover acts as a way to make ends meet.
34. One venue had several very prominent signs up prohibiting drugs. Its owner told me: "the people who come . . . and drugs are found on them, we throw them out, we warn them to go and throw away what they have, and if they don't do that, we have to throw them out. We're very strict that there's no drugs in the venue."
35. Interview, Dimitri, July 2018.
36. Peperock, "El Multiforo Alicia . . . a la verga . . . !!! ¿Se pierde algo?"
37. Paredes Pacho, "Un país invisible."
38. Luis Hernández Navarro, "Víctima del Covid, el Foro Alicia definirá su suerte en 2022: Pineda," *La Jornada*, November 27, 2021.
39. Interview, Fernando, June 2019.
40. See Emma Felton, Christy Collis, and Phil Graham, "Making Connections: Creative Industries Networks in Outer-Suburban Locations," *Australian Geographer* 41, no. 1 (2010): 57–70; Shannon Garland, "Amiguismo: capitalism, Sociality, and the Sustainability of Indie Music in Santiago, Chile," *Ethnomusicology Forum* 28, no. 1 (2019): 26–44.
41. Hernández Navarro, "Víctima del Covid, el Foro Alicia definirá su suerte en 2022."
42. "Faro" is an acronym for "Fábrica de Artes y Oficios"; a perhaps idiosyncratic translation for this phrase, but one that reflects the reality of the "Faros" program, is "Arts and Trades Hub." The word "Faro" itself means "lighthouse." "Pilares" is an acronym for "Puntos de Innovación, Libertad, Arte, Educación y Saberes" (Points of Innovation, Freedom, Art, Education and Knowledges).
43. Tomás Ejea has written critically about the creation of Fonca (National Fund for Culture and the Arts) and CONACULTA (National Council for Culture and

the Arts, which subsequently became the national Secretary of Culture) by the PRI regime to gain legitimacy in the wake of the 1988 electoral fraud. See Tomás Ejea, *Poder y creación artística en México: Un análisis del Fondo Nacional para la Cultura y las Artes (Fonca)* (Mexico City: Universidad Autónoma Metropolitana Azcapotzalco, 2011).

44. Eduardo Vázquez Martín, "La cultura: Espacio de la libertad," talk given at the Primer Congreso Internacional Cultura y Desarrollo, La Habana, Cuba, 2001, republished in *Políticas culturales en la Ciudad de México 1997–2005*, ed. Benjamin González (Mexico City: Ediciones del Basurero, 2006), 24–26.
45. Eduardo Vázquez Martín, "Experiencias culturales del primer gobierno democrático de la Ciudad de México," in *Políticas culturales en la Ciudad de México 1997–2005*, ed. Benjamin González (Mexico City: Ediciones del Basurero, 2006), 49.
46. Vázquez Martín, "Experiencias culturales," 53.
47. This was the case, for example, with Centro Cultural La Pirámide, Teatro Benito Juarez, Teatro Sergio Magaña, and Casa Refugio Citlaltépetl, all of which were run independently before being appropriated by the city government after the turn of the millennium. Centro Cultural El Rule, located in the capital's historic center, is an especially interesting case: constructed in the early twentieth century, it was badly damaged in the 1985 earthquake and was scheduled for demolition before a group of writers that included Gabriel García Márquez began to use and maintain it as a cultural center; their efforts included occupying the building in 1992. It was later appropriated by the city government and renovated in 2017 in a public-private initiative supported by billionaire Carlos Slim Helú. See Merry MacMasters, "Rescatan el edificio El Rule; se convierte en centro cultural interdisciplinario," *La Jornada*, June 17, 2017.
48. Interview, Baltazar Padilla, July 2019. It just so happened that, on the day that we held an interview, Baltazar had planned to raise this issue with the PT's representatives in the local government.
49. Technically, Benito Juarez has been an *alcaldía* (mayorship) since the city became Ciudad de México in 2016, having previously been a *delegación*; I use the term "local government" here for simplicity.
50. In Mexico, a civil association (*asociación civil*) is the equivalent of a nonprofit organization.
51. Interview, José Luis, June 2019.
52. Interview, José Luis, June 2019.
53. Equally, a trajectory toward administration is seen across the arts in many spheres, beyond self-managed or community spaces.

54. Interview, José Luis, June 2019.
55. Interview, José Luis, June 2019.
56. See "Protesta de miembros del Centro Cultural La Piramide," Vimeo video, posted by Alejandro Meléndez, September 19, 2012, https://vimeo.com/49801085.
57. Pablo Reyes, "En riesgo proyecto autónomo del Centro Cultural la Pirámide en la Ciudad de México," *Desinformémonos*, March 5, 2015, https://desinformemonos.org/en-riesgo-proyecto-autonomo-del-centro-cultural-la-piramide-en-la-ciudad-de-mexico/.
58. "Vida CDMX - Centro Cultural 'La Piramide,'" YouTube video, posted by Capital 21, September 3, 2018, https://www.youtube.com/watch?v=qQnXE9-WaDw. The closest this report got to describing any struggle between activists and the government over CCLP was mentioning its "struggle to remain relevant"; however, it hints at this contentious history as it depicts artwork from the space in solidarity with the Zapatista movement and as it shows the CCLP logo—a pyramid with a clenched fist rising from the top.
59. Interview, José Luis, June 2019.
60. Alida Piñón, "Artistas llevan 8 meses sin pago de Cultura CDMX," *El Universal*, November 27, 2019. In any event, the Secretariat of Culture did direct more resources into the space later, at the end of the Covid-19 pandemic, so that it could make repairs and install a new lighting system. José Luis, personal communication, July 2023.
61. David Graeber, *Bullshit Jobs: A Theory* (New York: Simon and Schuster, 2018).
62. Interview, José Luis, June 2019.
63. Derrida, *Eyes of the University*, 63.
64. Interview, Ignacio Pineda, August 2018.
65. Francisco Alanís, "El Multiforo Cultural Alicia bajo amenaza de clausura," *Sopitas.com*, June 3, 2015, https://www.sopitas.com/noticias/el-multiforo-cultural-alicia-bajo-amenaza-de-clausura.
66. See Juan José Olivares, "'Un poco político,' el cierre del Alicia, afirma Ignacio Pineda," *La Jornada*, August 16, 2015, 6.
67. Laura Gómez Flores, "La clausura del Multiforo Alicia 'no es cuestión política ni ataque a la cultura,'" *La Jornada*, August 17, 2015, 39.
68. See Patricia Peñaloza, "Ruta Sonora: El Alicia vive, la lucha sigue," *La Jornada*, August 21, 2015.
69. "three souls in my mind ABUSO DE AUTORIDAD #NoAlCierreDelAlicia," posted on Twitter by @jah_kahoz, June 7, 2015, https://twitter.com/jah_kahoz/status/607557058141888512.
70. *Rock rupestre* (prehistoric rock) is a musical movement with its origins in 1980s Mexico City, with a stripped-down acoustic sound and descriptive,

gritty, detailed lyrics. Its most well-known exponent is Rockdrigo González (1950–1985). See Jorge Pantoja, ed., *Rupestre: El libro* (Mexico City: Ediciones Imposible, 2013).

71. León Chávez Teixeiro (1936–) is a singer and songwriter whose artistic profile emerged in the context of the 1968 protests and workers' movements more generally. His music is mostly orchestrated for acoustic instruments; much of it describes the gritty realities of city life and of participation in protest movements. Alberto Isordia, or "Pájaro Alberto," is a rock singer from Tijuana who has performed solo, as well as in the bands Love Army and Tijuana Five.

72. This song resulted from firsthand experience of Rock Sobre Ruedas that Catana recounted to the newspaper *Milenio*. Catana stated: "Once I saw a truck with musicians arrive to a park, connect to electricity, and they started to play.... After a while someone shouted that the police were coming and it was 'disconnect, let's get out of here.'" David Cortés, "Rafael Catana: La vida en el Terregal," *Milenio*, December 1, 2016, https://www.milenio.com/blogs/qrr/rafael-catana-la-vida-en-el-terregal.

73. Although this phrase is difficult to translate, I use the term "corny" here due to the resonances between corn and Mexican identity, especially relating to indigeneity.

74. This song is based on the popular Andrea Lagunes song "La balada del vagabundo."

75. Here it is noteworthy that one member of the group briefly directed the Secretariat of Culture of the Tlalpan *alcaldía* under the Morena administration.

76. According to AMLO's schema, the first transformation was Mexican independence, the second was Benito Juarez's movement for liberal reform, and the third was the Revolution from 1910 to 1920.

77. The concept of "anarchist miracles" is used by Graham Benton to analyze the book as a whole. See Graham Benton, "Unruly Narratives: The Anarchist Dimension in the Novels of Thomas Pynchon" (PhD diss., Rutgers University, 2002).

78. Thomas Pynchon, *The Crying of Lot 49* (New York: Vintage Classics, 1996), 120.

79. Pynchon, *Crying of Lot 49*, 120.

80. Pynchon, *Crying of Lot 49*, 120.

CHAPTER 6

1. Jorge Caballero, "Miguel Ángel Mancera debería voltear a ver la escena cultural independiente," *La Jornada*, January 17, 2013; Jorge Caballero, "Ante el monopolio cultural, El Alicia no cierra: Nacho Pineda," *La Jornada*, August 17, 2012.

2. Sergio Meyer, "La cultura no es un lujo sino una necesidad y un derecho humano," Cámara de diputados, LXV Legislatura, press release, May 20,

2020, http://www5.diputados.gob.mx/index.php/esl/Comunicacion/Agencia-de-Noticias/2020/Mayo/20/5149-La-cultura-no-es-un-lujo-sino-una-necesidad-y-un-derecho-humano-Sergio-Mayer.

3. Prior to the administrative changes of 1997, each *delegación* was ruled by a "delegate" directly nominated by the president.

4. Antonio Rovira, "Derecho a la cultura," *El País*, March 10, 2017; Laura Bellver Carsí, "Por el derecho a la cultura para todos sin exclusión," *El País*, December 21, 2020; Abril Becerra, "Organizaciones convocan a un encuentro para debatir sobre el lugar de los derechos culturales en la nueva Constitución," *diarioUchile*, July 25, 2021, https://radio.uchile.cl/2021/07/25/organizaciones-convocan-a-un-encuentro-para-debatir-sobre-el-lugar-de-los-derechos-culturales-en-la-nueva-constitucion/.

5. See "Ley 2176, Derechos Culturales," Law passed by Legislatura de la Ciudad Autónoma de Buenos Aires, November 26, 2006, https://buenosaires.gob.ar/sites/default/files/media/document/2021/02/25/29303c62278a44476233eb6f677dd5 2e81256ccc.pdf; and Gabriel Enrique Arjona Pachón, *Derechos culturales en el mundo, Colombia y Bogotá* (Bogotá: Secretaría Distrital de Cultura, Recreación y Deporte, December 2011), https://ant.culturarecreacionydeporte.gov.co/sites/default/files/derechos_culturales_en_el_mundo_colombia_y_bogota.pdf.

6. Arjona Pachón, "Derechos culturales en el mundo."

7. Frédéric Mégret, "Where Does the Critique of International Human Rights Stand?: An Exploration in 18 Vignettes," in *New Approaches to International Law*, ed. José María Beneyto and David Kennedy (The Hague: TMC Asser, 2012), 6.

8. Celina Romany, "Women as Aliens: A Feminist Critique of the Public/Private Distinction in International Human Rights Law," *Harvard Human Rights Journal* 6, no. 6 (1993): 87; Douglas Sanders, "Getting Lesbian and Gay Issues on the International Human Rights Agenda," *Human Rights Quarterly* 18 (1996): 67–106; Michael Ashley Stein, "Disability Human Rights," in *Nussbaum and Law*, ed. Robin West, (London: Routledge, 2015), 3–49.

9. Mégret, "Where Does the Critique of International Human Rights Stand?"; Klisala Harrison, *Music Downtown Eastside: Human Rights and Capability Development through Music in Urban Poverty* (New York: Oxford University Press, 2020).

10. See Mégret, "Where Does the Critique of International Human Rights Stand?," 12; Makau wa Mutua, "The Ideology of Human Rights," *Virginia Journal of International Law* 36 (1995): 595.

11. Jonathan Gross and Nick Wilson, "Cultural Democracy: An Ecological and Capabilities Approach," *International Journal of Cultural Policy* 26, no. 3 (2020): 328–43.

12. See Butler, *Excitable Speech*; Bunn, "Reimagining Repression."

13. See Ejea, *Poder y creación artística en México*.
14. Vázquez Martín, "La cultura: Espacio de la libertad," 32.
15. "Coinciden PRI, PAN y PRD en sustituir Socicultur por un Instituto de Cultura para el Distrito Federal," *Unomásuno*, June 3, 1997, 24. Vázquez Martín, "La cultura: Espacio de la libertad," 40.
16. Carlos Monsiváis, speaking in 1993, stated that "There's talk . . . of legislating the right to culture, and when they start to talk about the details, the PRI politicians allege: it's about protecting the rights of the Indian peoples. . . . The right to culture is also the right to sufficient libraries in the whole country [and] high-quality entertainment at an accessible price." Ana María González, "Avance de la sociedad civil, punto clave en el futuro de la cultura: Monsiváis," *La Jornada*, May 15, 1993, 25. Equally, the idea of the right to culture in Mexico City can also be traced back to urban social movements in the capital's margins. See Sian Hunter Dodsworth, "Prácticas culturales, memoria e identidad colectiva: El caso de Acapatzingo" (MA thesis, Centro de Investigaciones y Estudios Superiores en Antropología Social, 2020).
17. See Gemma Van der Haar, "The Zapatista Uprising and the Struggle for Indigenous Autonomy," *European Review of Latin American and Caribbean Studies* 76 (2004): 99–108.
18. Andrea Becerril, "Plantea Payán elevar el derecho a la cultura a rango constitucional," *La Jornada*, April 28, 2000.
19. Lomnitz, *Deep Mexico, Silent Mexico*, 35ff.
20. As discussed by Brian Massumi, *Ontopower: War, Powers, and the State of Perception* (Durham, NC: Duke University Press, 2015).
21. Zolov, *Refried Elvis*.
22. "In Rock, all of us who are in it in one form or another, should be interested in learning a little more, because whisper it or shout it from the rooftops, Rock is really learned, not anyone can understand it straight away." Roberto Vázquez, "Lectura y cultura."
23. Vázquez Martín, "La cultura: Espacio de la libertad."
24. Vázquez Martín, "Experiencias culturales."
25. Vázquez Martín, "Experiencias culturales," 38.
26. It is important to note that, while the focus here is music venues, the "right to culture" drive built on the mobilization of cultural actors of many different kinds. A vital organization in this drive was the Network of Organized Independent Cultural Spaces (RECIO), which represented mostly theater venues. The ways that such organizations contributed to the "right to culture" policy initiatives is beyond the scope of this book.

27. Patricia Peñaloza, "Ruta Sonora," *La Jornada*, June 29, 2001.
28. Fabrizio León and Jorge Caballero, "Definen hoy la realización del Tecnogeist," *La Jornada*, April 2, 2002. Circo Volador is discussed in detail in Héctor Castillo Berthier, "My Generation: Rock and La Banda's Forced Survival opposite the Mexican State," in *Rockin' las Américas: The Global Politics of Rock in Latin/o America*, ed. Deborah Pacini Hernandez, Hector Fernández l'Hoeste, and Eric Zolov (Pittsburgh, PA: University of Pittsburgh Press, 2004), 241–60; and in Kelley Tatro, *Love and Rage: Autonomy in Mexico City's Punk Scene* (Middletown, CT: Wesleyan University Press, 2022). As with many independent venues, it was created in an abandoned building—in this case a former cinema. It was closed by the municipal government between 2000 and 2002 over parking requirements. Circo Volador continues to operate as a significant community arts space with a broad cultural offering.
29. Paredes Pacho, "Un país invisible."
30. Paredes Pacho, "Un país invisible."
31. Paredes Pacho, "Un país invisible."
32. "Ley para el funcionamiento de establecimientos mercantiles del Distrito Federal," *Gaceta Oficial del Distrito Federal*, February 28, 2002, no. 28, https://docs.mexico.justia.com/estatales/distrito-federal/ley-para-el-funcionamiento-de-establecimientos-mercantiles-del-distrito-federal.pdf; "Ley para el Funcionamiento de Establecimientos Mercantiles en el Distrito Federal," decree issued May 20, 1996, SEGOB: Diario oficial de la federación, http://www.dof.gob.mx/nota_detalle.php?codigo=4886471&fecha=29/05/1996.
33. Paredes Pacho, "Un país invisible"; "Ley de fomento cultural del Distrito Federal," *Gaceta oficial del Distrito Federal*, October 14, 2003, https://mexico.justia.com/estados/cdmx/leyes/ley-de-fomento-cultural-del-distrito-federal/.
34. Jesús Ramírez Cuevas, "La política cultural de la ciudad a debate: Foros alternativos bajo amenaza," *La Jornada*, September 25, 2005.
35. CECI does differ in some ways from RECIA: it does not include venues that receive government support or are partly administered by local governments. Interview, Ignacio Pineda, August 2018.
36. See CECI's Facebook page, https://www.facebook.com/pg/laC3C1/about/?ref=page_internal. Note that the group's initial name presented it as "Coordinator" rather than "Collective" of independent cultural spaces.
37. Jesús Ramírez Cuevas, "Foros alternativos bajo amenaza."
38. "El Correo Illustrado," *La Jornada*, August 16, 2016.
39. Fabrizio León and Jorge Caballero, "Definen hoy la realización del Tecnogeist," *La Jornada*, April 2, 2022.
40. Jesús Ramírez Cuevas, "La fiesta no es para todos," *La Jornada*, May 27, 2001.

41. Ramírez Cuevas, "Foros alternativos bajo amenaza."
42. Jorge Caballero, "Ante el monopolio cultural, El Alicia no cierra: Nacho Pineda," *La Jornada*, August 17, 2012.
43. Interview, Fernando Beristán, June 2019.
44. In recent years, this kind of information has also been shared more widely among local businesses through shared WhatsApp groups. Interview, Talía, December 2021.
45. López Flamarique, *Alicia en el espejo*, 148–49.
46. Jorge Ricardo, "Clausuraron 'sin notificación previa'' el espacio Dada X," *La Jornada*, April 19, 2007.
47. Patricia Peñaloza, "Ruta Sonora: Arcade Fire, Whitey, Baile por la libertad," *La Jornada*, April 20, 2007.
48. Interview with anonymous respondent, June 2019.
49. For instance, one poster created by Multiforo Cultural Alicia under the government of Felipe Calderón Hinojosa (2006–2012) reads "Stop the Bullets: Our Proposal—Culture and Education."
50. See *Plan nacional de desarrollo, 2019–2024* (Mexico City: Presidencia de la República, 2019), https://lopezobrador.org.mx/wp-content/uploads/2019/05/PLAN-NACIONAL-DE-DESARROLLO-2019-2024.pdf.
51. "Buscan promover la inclusión y el derecho a la cultura," *24horas*, March 12, 2019, https://www.24-horas.mx/2019/03/12/buscan-promover-la-inclusion-y-el-derecho-a-la-cultura/.
52. For instance, at the 2019 Reunión Nacional de Cultura [National Meeting of Culture] Frausto sought "a country which constructs each day, through culture, peace." Gerardo León, "Buscan lograr la paz en México a través de la cultura," *El Sol de México*, November 28, 2019. https://www.elsoldemexico.com.mx/cultura/buscan-lograr-la-paz-en-mexico-a-traves-de-la-cultura-4513227.html. "Concretar el derecho humano a la cultura, mi objetivo: Frausto," *La Jornada*, February 11, 2019.
53. Mónica Mateos-Vega, "La cultura nunca más volverá a ser un adorno: Alejandra Frausto," *La Jornada*, December 4, 2018.
54. This came about, in part, as a response to CECI's previous demands for a working group to address problems with the licensing regime. "El Correo Illustrado," *La Jornada*, August 16, 2016.
55. Various authors, "Declaración de principios para una ley de cultura en México," *Diario de Campo* 4, no. 1 (2017): 124.
56. See Eckhart Boege, "El patrimonio biocultural y los derechos culturales de los pueblos indígenas, comunidades locales y equiparables," *Diario de Campo*

4, no. 1 (2017): 39–70; and Maya Lorena Pérez Ruiz, "¿Cómo Pasó? Reflexiones sobre la reconfiguración del campo cultural en México," *Diario de Campo* 4, no. 1 (2017): 7–38.

57. "Presentan iniciativa de Ley de Cultura para la CDMX," *El Universal*, August 29, 2017, https://www.eluniversal.com.mx/cultura/patrimonio/presentan-iniciativa-de-ley-de-cultura-para-la-cdmx.

58. "Ley de Cultura garantiza los derechos de residentes y visitantes de la Ciudad de México: Suárez del Real," *MugsNoticias*, December 21, 2017, https://www.mugsnoticias.com.mx/cultura/ley-de-cultura-garantiza-los-derechos-de-residentes-y-visitantes-de-la-ciudad-de-mexico-suarez-del-real/.

59. Lomnitz, *Deep Mexico, Silent Mexico*, 82–83.

60. One participant, however, felt that the consultation was included too many participants in cultural scenes without requisite experience or expertise. Interview, Juliet Fontana, August 2019. It is notable that many of the earlier protagonists of the right to culture, including some of the most prominent members of CECI, did not participate in the consultations.

61. Interview, Laura Mishelle Muñoz, December 2021.

62. Interview, Laura Mishelle Muñoz, August 2019.

63. Interview, Laura Mishelle Muñoz, August 2019.

64. Michael Herzfeld, *The Social Production of Indifference: Exploring the Symbolic Roots of Western Bureaucracy* (New York: Routledge, 2021).

65. Interview, Talía Chavira, December 2021.

66. Interview, Laura Mishelle Muñoz, December 2021.

67. Interview, Talía Chavira, December 2021.

68. Interview, Laura Mishelle Muñoz, December 2021.

69. See "#EnVivo | Foro: Renovación de la Ley para la realización de espectáculos," Facebook video, posted by Congreso TV, August 5, 2022, https://www.facebook.com/CongresoTv/videos/620191872749514. Accessed on August 13, 2024.

70. Interview, Laura Mishelle Muñoz, December 2021.

71. For example, one commenter under the following video feature made by the Secretariat of Culture on the reopening writes: "what happened to anarchy?" "¡Regresa El Alicia! Con más de 27 años de trayectoria, el #MultiforoCulturalAlicia reabre sus puertas a finales del mes de marzo de este año," Facebook video, posted by Secretaría de Cultura Ciudad de México, March 1, 2024, https://www.facebook.com/Cultura.Ciudad.de.Mexico/videos/766579558753569.

72. On the affective politics of threat, see Massumi, *Ontopower*, 3–19.

73. Lomnitz, *Deep Mexico, Silent Mexico*, 35–36.

74. Lomnitz, *Deep Mexico, Silent Mexico*, 56.

75. Interview, Laura Mishelle Muñoz, August 2019.
76. Interview, Laura Mishelle Muñoz, July 2022.

CHAPTER 7

1. Cortés's book was published in 2012 by Grupo Editorial Tomo.
2. Rafael González, *60 años del rock mexicano*, vol. 3, *1990–2016* (Mexico City: Sr González Producciones, 2019), 461.
3. Lydia Goehr, *The Imaginary Museum of Musical Works: An Essay in the Philosophy of Music* (Oxford: Clarendon Press, 1992).
4. See Arjun Appadurai, ed., *The Social Life of Things: Commodities in Cultural Perspective* (Cambridge: Cambridge University Press, 1988).
5. Lomnitz, *Deep Mexico, Silent Mexico*, 218–20.
6. See Keith Jenkins, *Refiguring History: New Thoughts on an Old Discipline* (London: Routledge, 2003); Alun Munslow, *The New History* (New York: Routledge, 2016); and Mark Mason, "Deconstructing History," in *Derrida and the Future of the Liberal Arts: Professions of Faith*, ed. Mary Caputi and Vincent J. Del Casino Jr. (London: Bloomsbury, 2013), 93–121.
7. Stephen D. Reese, "The New Geography of Journalism Research: Levels and Spaces," *Digital Journalism* 4, no. 7 (2016): 816–26.
8. Ricardo Bravo, "Ser partícipes, no sólo cronistas," in Cortés and González Castillo, *El rock también se escribe*, 59–65.
9. Alejandro González Castillo, "José Luis Pluma y la odisea de la revista *Conecte*," in Cortés and González Castillo, *El rock también se escribe*, 126–37.
10. Salcedo, "El rock no está peleado con el pop ni con nadie." By contrast, Salcedo stated that with The Beatles on the front cover, sales would rise by up to 60 percent.
11. Hugo García Michel, "Breve y sucinta historia de La Mosca," in Cortés and González Castillo, *El rock también se escribe*, 55–58.
12. José Xavier Návar, "De los viejos excesos de los sellos disqueros a la era de los sitios patito," in Cortés and González Castillo, *El rock también se escribe*, 22–27.
13. Stories of "social media myths" could be read as a defensive move, something tantamount to "atrocity stories" designed to safeguard the journalist's professional status and lower the status of a rival occupation. See Robert Dingwall, *Essays on Professions* (Aldershot: Ashgate, 2008), 42.
14. Alejandro González Castillo, "José Luis Pluma y la odisea de la revista *Conecte*."
15. Patricia Peñaloza, "La subjetividad, interpretación literaria de los hechos."
16. David Cortés, "Revistas de rock, guías y culpables," in Cortés and González Castillo, *El rock también se escribe*, 48–54. This writer later recalled that he only

got to write in *El Nacional*—the only national newspaper at the time with a section focused on rock, with an impressive roster of established writers—by handing the editor a feature on jazz. See "Prologue" in David Cortés, *Escritos en el tiempo* (Mexico City: Librosampleados, 2019).

17. David Cortés and Alejandro González Castillo, "Presentación," in Cortés and González Castillo, *El rock también se escribe*, 9–11.
18. Andrew Abbott, *The System of Professions: An Essay on the Division of Expert Labor* (Chicago: University of Chicago Press, 1988), 131.
19. See Julia Evetts, "A New Professionalism? Challenges and Opportunities," *Current Sociology* 59, no. 4 (2011): 406–422; and Andrew Green, "Beyond the Crew: Hip-Hop and Professionalization in Mexico City," *Cultural Sociology* 16, no. 1 (2022): 25–44.
20. García Michel, "Breve y sucinta historia de La Mosca."
21. González Castillo, "José Luis Pluma y la odisea de la revista *Conecte*."
22. Federico Rubli, "Rock en México. Un recuento (Todos éramos William Miller)," in Cortés and González Castillo, *El rock también se escribe*, 13–21.
23. Federico Rubli, "Rock en México."
24. González Castillo, "José Luis Pluma."
25. Federico Rubli, "Rock en México."
26. Susana Cato, "Robo, mutilaciones e incumplimiento de los editores debilitan la hemeroteca y la biblioteca de la UNAM," *Proceso*, no. 559, July 20, 1987, 56.
27. José Luis Paredes Pacho, "Fotocopias, grapas y engrudo," in Cortés and González Castillo, *El rock también se escribe*, 40–42.
28. Bravo, "Ser partícipes, no sólo cronistas."
29. Návar, "De los viejos excesos de los sellos disqueros a la era de los sitios patito."
30. Carlos Monsiváis, "Introduction," in *Rock mexicano: Sonidos de la calle*, by José Luis Paredes Pacho (Mexico City: Pesebre, 1992), viii.
31. See Couldry, *Why Voice Matters*.
32. Návar, "50 años de Avándaro."
33. "I believe that the mission of journalists is not to state if [artists] are good or bad, but simply to inform about their existence so that people can form their own judgements." Walter Schmidt, "La audacia del tipo que escribía sobre cosas extrañas," in Cortés and González Castillo, *El rock también se escribe*, 28–32. "I believe in journalism as a means of liberty, because the more we hide information, the less free the citizen is. An important mission of journalism is to incite, give informative elements so that the citizen can decide for themselves and can renew or change their thinking, adapt. Journalism helps to question and to reaffirm convictions." Peñaloza, "La subjetividad, interpretación literaria de los hechos."

34. In 2018, incoming administrators in the Secretariat of Culture were unreceptive to assessment through means of a fanzine, related to its comparative novelty as an assessment format and the perception that it was difficult to measure.
35. Arturo Escobar, *Pluriversal Politics: The Real and the Possible* (Durham, NC: Duke University Press, 2020), xi.
36. Interview, Alexis, May 2019.
37. Chelico gave us one tip to verify that a journalist had, in fact, gone to Avándaro: at one point, a van had caught fire, and those who had attended would know on which side of the stage it was located.
38. Personal communication, Yolanda, June 2019.
39. Interview, Alexis and Adrian, May 2019.
40. Interview, Adrian, May 2019.
41. Interview, Alexis, May 2019.
42. Interview, Paty, May 2019. Multiple participants mentioned the example of the journalist Carmen Aristegui, often celebrated for her critical, independent journalism, who was fired from her radio station in 2011 after insinuating that former president Felipe Calderón Hinojosa had an alcohol problem, having frequently clashed with media owners about her ability to freely discuss political corruption.
43. See, for instance, reports of a legislative attempt to ban reggaetón in the Sinaloa state government by two politicians belonging to the Morena governing party, based on a Finnish study linking reggaetón to "aggressive sexual behaviour, dietary problems, lack of self-esteem, consumption of harmful substances and depression among young people." Daniel Gutiérrez Dieck, "Las veces que el 2019 ha intentado cancelar el reggaetón," *Telehit*, July 16, 2019, https://www.telehit.com/urbano/las-veces-que-el-2019-ha-intentado-cancelar-el-reggaeton.
44. Petra R. Rivera-Rideau, *Remixing Reggaetón: The Cultural Politics of Race in Puerto Rico* (Durham, NC: Duke University Press, 2015); Raquel Z. Rivera, Wayne Marshall, and Deborah Pacini Hernández, eds., *Reggaeton* (Durham, NC: Duke University Press, 2009); Geoffrey Baker, *Buena Vista in the Club: Rap, Reggaetón, and Revolution in Havana* (Durham, NC: Duke University Press, 2011).
45. Andrés Manuel López Obrador attacked neoliberalism during the 2018 campaign, yet doubled down on neoliberal austerity policies after being elected—enacting cuts to public services, including health, alongside headline-grabbing cuts to politicians' salaries and benefits. See David Agren, "AMLO's Mexico Leads to Drastic Cuts to Health System," *Lancet* 393 (2019): 2289–90; and Ramón I. Centeno, "Not a Mexican Pink Tide: The AMLO Administration and the Neoliberal Left," *Latin American Perspectives* 50, no. 2 (2023): 112–29. For critical perspectives on the 2018 elections and the administration of

López Obrador, see Mariano Sánchez-Talanquer, "Mexico 2019: Personalistic Politics and Neoliberalism from the Left," *Revista de Ciencia Política* 40, no.2 (2020): 401–30; and German Petersen and Fernanda Somunao, "Mexican De-Democratization? Pandemic, Hyper-Presidentialism and Attempts to Rebuild a Dominant Party System," *Revista de Ciencia Política* 41, no. 2 (2021): 353–76.

46. Peter A. Jackson, "The Neoliberal University and Global Immobilities of Theory," in *Area Studies at the Crossroads: Knowledge Production at the Mobility Turn*, ed. Katja Mielke and Anna-Katharina Hornidge (New York: Palgrave Macmillan, 2017), 30.

47. See Michel Duquette, *Building New Democracies: Economic and Social Reform in Brazil, Chile, and Mexico* (Toronto: University of Toronto Press, 1999); and Wayne A. Cornelius, "Mexico's Delayed Democratization," *Foreign Policy* 95 (1994): 53–71. The term "exhaustion" does a lot of work within this discourse, obscuring the specific political choices made that led to the crisis of developmentalism, such as OPEC countries coordinating to raise oil prices and the decision of Western banks to raise interest rates sharply at the end of the 1970s. On the other hand, it has been convincingly argued that the mostly US-trained economists behind 1980s structural adjustment in Mexico went further than forced to by the Bretton Woods institutions. See Sarah Babb, *Managing Mexico: Economists from Nationalism to Neoliberalism* (Princeton, NJ: Princeton University Press, 2004). To say that developmentalism was "exhausted" falsely imputes a historical inevitability to the transition to neoliberalism and overlooks the coercive dynamics through which neoliberalism was imposed. The heterodox economist Ha-Joon Chang has convincingly argued that a developmentalist approach was vital to the industrialization of the United States and Europe. He points out that in the nineteenth century, the most protectionist economies in the world were also the most successful—the United States and the United Kingdom. See Ha-Joon Chang, "Rethinking Development Economics: An Introduction," in *Rethinking Development Economics*, ed. Ha-Joon Chang (London: Anthem, 2003), 1–18; and Ha-Joon Chang, *Kicking Away the Ladder: Development Strategy in Historical Perspective* (London: Anthem, 2002).

48. On poor economic growth, see Robert A. Blecker, "Mexico: Unequal Integration and 'Stabilizing Stagnation,'" in *Handbook of Economic Stagnation*, ed. L. Randall Wray and Flavia Dantas (Cambridge, MA: Academic, 2022), 225–49; and Arturo Huerta, "The Stagnation of the Mexican Economy Is Here to Stay," in Wray and Dantas, *Handbook of Economic Stagnation*, 251–71. On ballooning inequality, see Ingrid Bleynat, Amílcar E. Challú, and Paul Segal, "Inequality, Living Standards, and Growth: Two Centuries of Economic Development in Mexico," *Economic History Review* 74, no. 3 (2021): 584–610. On stagnant

life expectancy, see World Bank Group, "Esperanza de vida al nacer, total (años) – Mexico," at https://datos.bancomundial.org/indicador/SP.DYN.LE00.IN?locations=MX. On the pattern of brutal violence, see Dawn Marie Paley, "Cold War, Neoliberal War, and Disappearance: Observations from Mexico," *Latin American Perspectives* 48, no. 1 (2021): 145–62.
49. Francis Fukuyama, *The End of History and the Last Man* (New York: Free Press, 1992).
50. Draper, *1968 Mexico*; Pensado and Ochoa, "Introduction"; Walker, *Waking from the Dream*; Gillingham et al., *Journalism, Satire, and Censorship in Mexico*.
51. Smith, *Mexican Press and Civil Society*.
52. The contents of Echeverría's reforms indicate their intention to shore up the regime's legitimacy in response to the student movement. See González-Reimann and Zolov, "Digital Resources." The voting age was lowered to eighteen, and the age at which one could run for office was reduced. The reforms also reduced the barriers for political competition with the PRI: the percentage of the total vote required for a political party to be represented in the Chamber of Deputies was reduced from 2.5 percent to 1.5 percent; non-PRI political parties were allowed access to broadcast media and were permitted to sit on committees and other government bodies. As the Dirty War raged, these reforms were openly justified by PRI politicians as the "institutionalization of conflicts," incorporating opposition within an electoral system. See Rafael Segovia, "La reforma política: El ejecutivo federal, el PRI y las elecciones de 1973," *Foro internacional* 14, no. 3 (1974): 305–30. Echeverría's political reforms were extended by the regime of López Portillo (1976–1982), which was hit by another legitimacy crisis: the presidential elections of 1976 went uncontested. López Portillo responded by giving the politically liberal Jesús Reyes Heroles the task of further establishing in law the principles of democratic competition. Reforms were introduced in 1977 that made the Federal Electoral Commission (CFE) independent of the PRI; made it easier for political parties to register as such and defined them as "public interest entities" with the right to participate in elections, gain media exposure, and access resources to carry out their activities; extended media access for non-PRI parties; and reduced the amount of time given for electoral results to be processed (thus diminishing the possibilities for fraud to occur).
53. Inclán, *Zapatista Movement*, 6.
54. Gilbreth and Otero, "Democratization in Mexico"; Dolores Trevizo, *Rural Protest and the Making of Democracy in Mexico, 1968–2000* (University Park: Penn State University Press, 2015); Antonio García De León, "From Revolution

to Transition: The Chiapas Rebellion and the Path to Democracy in Mexico," *The Journal of Peasant Studies* 32, nos. 3-4 (2005): 508-27.

55. Claudio A. Holzner, "The Poverty of Democracy: Neoliberal Reforms and Political Participation of the Poor in Mexico," *Latin American Politics and Society* 49, no. 2 (2007): 87-122.

56. Zolov, *Refried Elvis*; Zolov, "La Onda Chicana."

57. Asa Cristina Laurell, "Three Decades of Neoliberalism in Mexico: The Destruction of Society," *International Journal of Health Services* 45, no. 2 (2015): 246-64; Arturo Guillén, "Mexico, an Example of the Anti-Development Policies of the Washington Consensus," *Estudos Avançados* 26 (2012): 57-76.

58. Corona, "Politics of Language, Class, and Nation."

59. Corona, "Politics of Language, Class, and Nation," 94, italics added.

60. See, for example, Ocampo, "Latin American Debt Crisis"; and Kaminsky and Pereira, "Debt Crisis."

61. Corona, "Politics of Language, Class, and Nation," 99. Although it is not stated, this claim may be a reference to the constitutional reforms of 1992, which expanded the private economic right to buy and own property (in particular relating to commonly held *ejido* land) and removed many restrictions placed on religious organizations by the 1917 Constitution. The latter restrictions, however, must be understood in the context of the postcolonial nineteenth-century conflicts between religious conservatives and secular liberals, both in Mexico and across Latin America; indeed, in the context of Mexico they sparked the religious rebellion of the late 1920s known as the Cristero War. The former constitutional reforms sparked protests across Mexican civil society and were widely seen as a key motivation for the Zapatista uprising.

62. Corona, "Politics of Language, Class, and Nation," 98.

63. Let's suppose Corona is referring, here, to the creation of Fonca, an arts funding organization founded in 1989. Given that Fonca was created in the wake of electoral fraud in 1988 as a means to shore up the ruling party's legitimacy, its creation would seem to have more to do with a perverse reaction to the democratization of Mexico's institutions than neoliberal economic policy. See Ejea, *Poder y creación artística en México*.

64. Dag MacLeod, *Downsizing the State: Privatization and the Limits of Neoliberal Reform in Mexico* (University Park, PA: Penn State University Press, 2004).

65. Corona, "Politics of Language, Class, and Nation," 104.

66. Corona, "Politics of Language, Class, and Nation," 96.

67. Many complain that the Mexican bands able to fill large venues in the present are largely the same as those able to do so in the 1990s.

68. Timothy Morton, *Dark Ecology: For a Logic of Future Coexistence* (New York: Columbia University Press, 2016), 12.
69. It is worth noting that ColectivaMente has been able to attract students to complete their *servicio social* (social service), a period of obligatory work prior to graduation, usually carried out with nongovernmental organizations, with the collective.
70. "Reportan que Satanic Warmaster realizó concierto clandestino en México," *Aristegui Noticias*, February 20, 2023, https://aristeguinoticias.com/2002/kiosko/reportan-que-satanic-warmaster-realizo-concierto-clandestino-en-mexico/; "Un grupo neonazi griego celebra dos conciertos secretos en Ciudad de México y Ciudad Juárez," *El País*, January 18, 2023; Juan José Olivares, "Concierto neonazi en la CDMX," *La Jornada*, November 9, 2022.

BIBLIOGRAPHY

Abbott, Andrew. *The System of Professions: An Essay on the Division of Expert Labor.* Chicago: University of Chicago Press, 1988.

Agamben, Giorgio. *State of Exception.* Trans. Kevin Attell. Chicago: University of Chicago Press, 2005.

Agren, David. "AMLO's Mexico Leads to Drastic Cuts to Health System." *Lancet,* no. 393 (2019): 2289-2290.

Agustín, José. *La contracultura en México: La historia y el significado de los rebeldes sin causa, los jipitecas, los punks y las bandas.* Mexico City: Editorial Grijalbo, 1996.

Alexander, Jeffrey. *The Meanings of Social Life: A Cultural Sociology.* New York: Oxford University Press, 2013.

Anaya, Benjamin. *Neozapatismo y rock mexicano.* Mexico City: Ediciones La Cuadrilla de la Langosta, 1999.

Anderton, Chris. *Music Festivals in the UK: Beyond the Carnivalesque.* New York: Routledge, 2018.

Appadurai, Arjun, ed. *The Social Life of Things: Commodities in Cultural Perspective.* Cambridge: Cambridge University Press, 1988.

Arana, Federico. *Guaraches de ante azul.* 2nd edition. Mexico City: María Enea, 2002.

Arditi, David. *Getting Signed: Record Contracts, Musicians, and Power in Society.* New York: Palgrave Macmillan, 2020.

Babb, Sarah. *Managing Mexico: Economists from Nationalism to Neoliberalism.* Princeton, NJ: Princeton University Press, 2004.

Baily, John S. *Can You Stop the Birds Singing? The Censorship of Music in Afghanistan.* Report published by Freemuse, 2001.

Baker, Geoffrey. *Buena Vista in the Club: Rap, Reggaetón, and Revolution in Havana.* Durham, NC: Duke University Press, 2011.

Bannister, Michael. "'Loaded': Indie Guitar Rock, Canonism, White Masculinities." *Popular Music* 25, no. 1 (2006): 77-95.

Barmeyer, Niels. *Developing Zapatista Autonomy: Conflict and NGO Involvement in Rebel Chiapas*. Albuquerque: University of New Mexico Press, 2009.

Bennett, Andy. "Reappraising 'Counterculture.'" *Volume! La revue des musiques populaires* 9, no. 1 (2012): 20–31.

Bennett, Andy, and Richard Peterson, eds. *Music Scenes: Local, Translocal and Virtual*. Nashville, TN: Vanderbilt University Press, 2004.

Benton, Graham. "Unruly Narratives: The Anarchist Dimension in the Novels of Thomas Pynchon." PhD dissertation, Rutgers University, 2002.

Berlin, Isaiah. *Four Essays on Liberty*. Oxford: Oxford University Press, 1969.

Blecker, Robert. "Mexico: Unequal Integration and 'Stabilizing Stagnation.'" In *Handbook of Economic Stagnation*, edited by L. Randall Wray and Flavia Dantas, 225-49. Cambridge, MA: Academic.

Bleynat, Ingrid, Amílcar E. Challú, and Paul Segal. "Inequality, Living Standards, and Growth: Two Centuries of Economic Development in Mexico." *Economic History Review* 74, no. 3 (2021): 584–610.

Boege, Eckhart. "El patrimonio biocultural y los derechos culturales de los pueblos indígenas, comunidades locales y equiparables." *Diario de Campo* 4, no. 1 (2017): 39–70.

Brown, Wendy. *Undoing the Demos: Neoliberalism's Stealth Revolution*. New York: Zone Books, 2015.

Bunn, Matthew. "Reimagining Repression: New Censorship Theory and After." *History and Theory* 54, no.1 (2015): 25–44.

Butler, Judith. *Excitable Speech: A Politics of the Performative*. New York: Routledge, 1997.

Camp, Roderick A. "The Revolution's Second Generation: The Miracle, 1946–1982 and Collapse of the PRI, 1982–2000." In *A Companion to Mexican History and Culture*, edited by William Beezley, 468–79. Oxford: Wiley-Blackwell, 2011.

———. "The Time of the Technocrats and Deconstruction of the Revolution." In *The Oxford History of Mexico*, edited by William Beezley and Michael Meyer, 569–97. Oxford: Oxford University Press, 2000.

Candea, Matei. "Silencing Oneself, Silencing Others: Rethinking Censorship Comparatively (Introduction)." *Terrain: Anthropologie & sciences humaines* 72 (2019).

Carey, James. *Communication As Culture: Essays on Media and Society*. Rev. edition. New York: Routledge, 2008.

Carrasco, Enrique. "The 1980s: The Debt Crisis and the Lost Decade of Development." *Transnational Law and Contemporary Problems* 9 (1999):116–26.

Castillo Berthier, Héctor. "My Generation: Rock and *La Banda*'s Forced Survival opposite the Mexican State." In *Rockin' las Américas: the global politics of rock* in Latin/o America, edited by Deborah Pacini Hernandez, Hector Fernández l'Hoeste, and Eric Zolov, 241–60. Pittsburgh, PA: University of Pittsburgh Press, 2004.

Castillo Ramírez, Guillermo, Julie Anne Boudreau, and Adriana Ávila Farfán. "Tianguis del Chopo: Espacio urbano de regulación/transgresión." *Revista mexicana de sociología* 82, no. 3 (2020): 557–85.

Centeno, Ramón. "Not a Mexican Pink Tide: The AMLO Administration and the Neoliberal Left." *Latin American Perspectives* 50, no. 2 (2023): 112–29.

Chang, Ha-Joon. *Kicking Away the Ladder: Development Strategy in Historical Perspective*. London: Anthem, 2002.

———. "Kicking Away the Ladder: Infant Industry Promotion in Historical Perspective." *Oxford Development Studies* 31, no. 1 (2003): 21–32.

———. "Rethinking Development Economics: An Introduction." In *Rethinking Development Economics*, edited by Ha-Joon Chang, 1–18. London: Anthem, 2003.

Chirambo, Reuben. "Traditional and Popular Music, Hegemonic Power and Censorship in Malawi: 1964–1994." In *Popular Music Censorship in Africa*, edited by Michael Drewett and Martin Cloonan, 109–25. London: Routledge, 2016.

Cloonan, Martin. *Banned: Censorship of Popular Music in Britain, 1967–92*. Aldershot: Arena, 1996.

———. "Popular Music Censorship in Africa: An Overview." *Popular Music Censorship in Africa*, edited by Michael Drewett and Martin Cloonan, 3–21. London: Routledge, 2006.

———. "What Is Music Censorship? Towards a Better Understanding of the Term." In *Shoot The Singer! Music Censorship Today*, edited by Marie Korpe, 3–5. London: Zed Books, 2004.

Cooney, Paul. "Argentina's Quarter Century Experiment with Neoliberalism: From Dictatorship to Depression." *Revista de economía contemporánea* 11, no.1 (2007): 7–37.

Cornelius, Wayne. "Mexico's Delayed Democratization." *Foreign Policy* 95 (1994): 53–71.

———. "Mexico: Salinas and the PRI at the Crossroads." *Journal of Democracy* 1, no. 3 (1990): 61–70.

Corona, Ignacio. "The Politics of Language, Class, and Nation in Mexico's Rock en Español Movement." In *Song and Social Change in Latin America*, edited by Lauren Shaw, 91–119. Lanham, MD: Lexington Books, 2013.

Cortés, David. *El otro rock mexicano*. Mexico City: Grupo Editorial Tomo, 1999.

———. *Escritos en el tiempo*. Mexico City: Librosampleados, 2019.

Cortés, David, and Alejandro González Castillo. *El rock también se escribe*. Monterrey: Universidad Autónoma de Nuevo León, 2020.

Couldry, Nick. *Why Voice Matters: Culture and Politics after Neoliberalism*. London: Sage, 2010.

Coutiño Soriano, Gustavo. "Rebeldía, música y consumo cultural: De los conciertos solidarios al Vive Latino." In *Etnorock: Los rostros de una música global en el sur de México*, edited by Martín de la Cruz López Moya, Efraín Ascencio Cedillo, and Juan Pablo Zebadúa Carbonell, 143–55. Mexico: Universidad de Ciencias y Artes de Chiapas, 2014.

Cross, John. "Street Vendors and Postmodernity: Conflict and Compromise in the Global Economy." *International Journal of Sociology and Social Policy* 20, nos. 1–2 (2000): 29–51.

Dale, Pete. "It Was Easy, It Was Cheap, So What? Reconsidering The DIY Principle of Punk and Indie Music." *Popular Music History* 3, no. 2 (2008): 171–93.

De León, Antonio García. "From Revolution to Transition: The Chiapas Rebellion and the Path to Democracy in Mexico." *Journal of Peasant Studies* 32, nos. 3–4 (2005): 508–27.

Derrida, Jacques. *Eyes of the University: Right to Philosophy 2*. Translated by Jan Plug. Stanford, CA: Stanford University Press, 2004.

Dingwall, Robert. *Essays on Professions*. Aldershot: Ashgate, 2008.

Draper, Susana. *1968 Mexico: Constellations of Freedom and Democracy*. Durham, NC: Duke University Press, 2018.

Drewett, Michael, and Martin Cloonan, eds. *Popular Music Censorship in Africa*. Aldershot: Ashgate, 2006.

Duquette, Michel. *Building New Democracies: Economic and Social Reform in Brazil, Chile, and Mexico*. Toronto: University of Toronto Press, 1999.

Ejea, Tomás. "Hacia una política cultural democrática e incluyente para la Ciudad de México: Retos y perspectivas." In *La Ciudad de México y los retos legislativos actuales*, vol. 2, edited by Karina Ochoa and Jorge Mercado. Mexico City: Asamblea Legislativa del DF.

———. *Poder y creación artística en México: Un análisis del Fondo Nacional para la Cultura y las Artes (Fonca)*. Mexico City: Universidad Autónoma Metropolitana Azcapotzalco, 2011.

Escobar, Arturo. *Pluriversal Politics: The Real and the Possible*. Durham, NC: Duke University Press, 2020.

Estrada, Teresa. *Sirenas al ataque: Historia de las mujeres rockeras mexicanas (1956–2006)*. Mexico City: Editorial Océano de México, 2008.

Etzioni, Amitai. "Should We Privatize Censorship?" *Issues in Science and Technology* 36, no. 1 (2019): 19–22.

Evetts, Julia. "A New Professionalism? Challenges and Opportunities." *Current Sociology* 59, no. 4 (2011): 406–22.

Felton, Emma, Christy Collis, and Phil Graham. "Making Connections: Creative Industries Networks in Outer-Suburban Locations." *Australian Geographer* 41, no. 1 (2010): 57–70.

Foucault, Michel. *Security, Territory, Population: Lectures at the Collège de France, 1977–78*. Translated by Graham Burchell. New York: Palgrave Macmillan, 2009.

Fox, Jonathan, Carlos García Jiménez, and Libby Haight. "Rural Democratisation in Mexico's Deep South: Grassroots Right-to-Know Campaigns in Guerrero." *Journal of Peasant Studies* 36, no. 2 (2009): 271–98.

Fraser, Nancy, and Linda Gordon. "A Genealogy of Dependency: Tracing a Keyword of the US Welfare State." *Signs: Journal of Women in Culture and Society* 19, no. 2 (1994): 309–36.

Freije, Vanessa. *Citizens of Scandal: Journalism, Secrecy, and the Politics of Reckoning in Mexico*. Durham, NC: Duke University Press, 2020.

Freshwater, Helen. "Towards a Redefinition of Censorship." In *Censorship and Cultural Regulation in the Modern Age*, edited by Beate Müller, 217–37. New York: Rodopi, 2004.

Fukuyama, Francis. *The End of History and the Last Man*. New York: Free Press, 1992.

García Michel, Hugo. "Breve y sucinta historia de La Mosca." In Cortés and González Castillo, *El rock también se escribe*, 55–58.

Garland, Shannon. "Amiguismo: Capitalism, Sociality, and the Sustainability of Indie Music in Santiago, Chile." *Ethnomusicology Forum* 28, no. 1 (2019): 26–44.

Garofalo, Reebee, and Martin Cloonan. *Policing Pop*. Philadelphia, PA: Temple University Press, 2003.

Gilbreth, Chris, and Gerardo Otero. "Democratization in Mexico: The Zapatista Uprising and Civil Society." *Latin American Perspectives* 28, no. 4 (2001): 7–29.

Gillingham, Paul, and Benjamin T. Smith, eds. *Dictablanda: Politics, Work, and Culture in Mexico, 1938–1968*. Durham, NC: Duke University Press, 2014.

Gillingham, Paul, Michael Lettieri, and Benjamin T. Smith, eds. *Journalism, Satire, and Censorship in Mexico*. Albuquerque: University of New Mexico Press, 2018.

Gingerich, Jonathan. "Is Spotify Bad for Democracy? Artificial Intelligence, Cultural Democracy, and Law." *Yale Journal of Law and Technology* 24 (2022): 227–316.

González, Rafael. *60 años del rock mexicano*. Vol. 1, *1956–1979*. Mexico City: Ediciones B, 2016.

———. *60 años del rock mexicano*. Vol. 2, *1980–1989*. Mexico City: Ediciones B, 2016.

———. *60 años del rock mexicano*. Vol. 3, *1990–2016*. Mexico City: Sr González Producciones, 2019.

González-Reimann, Luis, and Eric Zolov. "Digital Resources: *Piedra Rodante* (Mexico's *Rolling Stone* Magazine)." In *Oxford Research Encyclopedia of Latin American History*. New York: Oxford University Press, 2021.

Gracyk, Theodore. *I Wanna Be Me: Rock Music and the Politics of Identity*. Philadelphia, PA: Temple University Press, 2001.
Graeber, David. *Bullshit Jobs: A Theory*. New York: Simon and Schuster, 2018.
———. "Dead Zones of the Imagination: On Violence, Bureaucracy, and Interpretive Labor." *HAU: Journal of Ethnographic Theory* 2, no. 2 (2012): 105–28.
———. *Direct Action: An Ethnography*. Chico, CA: AK Press, 2009.
Graeber, David, and David Wengrow. *The Dawn of Everything: A New History of Humanity*. London: Allen Lane, 2021.
Green, Andrew. "Activist Musicianship, Sound, the 'Other Campaign' and the Limits of Public Space in Mexico City." *Ethnomusicology Forum* 25, no. 3 (2016): 345–66.
———. "Beyond the Crew: Hip-Hop and Professionalization in Mexico City." *Cultural Sociology* 16, no. 1 (2022): 25–44.
Goehr, Lydia. *The Imaginary Museum of Musical Works: An Essay in the Philosophy of Music*. Oxford: Clarendon, 1992.
Gross, Jonathan, and Nick Wilson. "Cultural Democracy: An Ecological and Capabilities Approach." *International Journal of Cultural Policy* 26, no. 3 (2020): 328–43.
Guillén, Arturo. "Mexico, an Example of the Anti-Development Policies of the Washington Consensus." *Estudos Avançados* 26 (2012): 57–76.
Hall, Patricia. ed. *The Oxford Handbook of Music Censorship*. Oxford: Oxford University Press, 2015.
Hall, Stuart. "Encoding/Decoding." In *Media Studies: A Reader*, edited by Sue Thornham, Caroline Bassett, and Paul Marris, 51–61. New York: New York University Press, 2009.
Hall, Stuart, and Tony Jefferson. *Resistance through Rituals: Youth Subcultures in Post-War Britain*. 2nd edition. New York: Routledge, 2006.
Harcup, Tony. "'I'm Doing This to Change the World': Journalism in Alternative and Mainstream Media." *Journalism Studies* 6, no. 3 (2003): 361–74.
Harrison, Klisala. *Music Downtown Eastside: Human Rights and Capability Development through Music in Urban Poverty*. New York: Oxford University Press, 2020.
Harvey, Neil. *The Chiapas Rebellion: The Struggle for Land and Democracy*. Durham, NC: Duke University Press, 1998.
Hay, Colin. "The Winter of Discontent Thirty Years On." *Political Quarterly* 80, no. 4 (2009): 545–52.
Hayton, Jeff. "Crosstown Traffic: Punk Rock, Space and the Porosity of the Berlin Wall in the 1980s." *Contemporary European History* 26, no. 2 (2017): 353–77.
Hebdige, Dick. *Subculture: The Meaning of Style*. New York: Routledge, 1979.

Herbert, Ruth. *Everyday Music Listening: Absorption, Dissociation and Trancing.* New York: Routledge, 2016.

Herzfeld, Michael. *The Social Production of Indifference: Exploring the Symbolic Roots of Western Bureaucracy.* New York: Routledge, 2021.

Hesmondhalgh, David. "Post-Punk's Attempt to Democratise the Music Industry: The Success and Failure of Rough Trade." *Popular Music* 16, no. 3 (1998): 255–74.

Holloway, Carson. *All Shook Up: Music, Passion, and Politics.* Dallas: Spence, 2001.

Holquist, Michael. "Introduction. Corrupt Originals: The Paradox of Censorship." *Publications of the Modern Language Association of America* 109, no. 1 (1994): 14–25.

Holzner, Claudio. "The Poverty of Democracy: Neoliberal Reforms and Political Participation of the Poor in Mexico." *Latin American Politics and Society* 49, no. 2 (2007): 87–122.

Huerta, Arturo. "The Stagnation of the Mexican Economy Is Here to Stay." In *Handbook of Economic Stagnation*, edited by L. Randall Wray and Flavia Dantas, 251–71. Cambridge, MA: Academic, 2022.

Hughes, Sallie. *Newsrooms in Conflict: Journalism and the Democratization of Mexico.* Pittsburgh, PA: University of Pittsburgh Press, 2006.

Hunter Dodsworth, Sian. "Prácticas culturales, memoria e identidad colectiva: El caso de Acapatzingo." MA thesis, Centro de Investigaciones y Estudios Superiores en Antropología Social, 2020.

Ilan, Jonathan. "Digital Street Culture Decoded: Why Criminalizing Drill Music Is Street Illiterate and Counterproductive." *British Journal of Criminology* 60, no. 4 (2020): 994–1013.

Ince, Onur Ulas. *Colonial Capitalism and the Dilemmas of Liberalism.* New York: Oxford University Press, 2018.

Inclán, María. *The Zapatista Movement and Mexico's Democratic Transition: Mobilization, Success, and Survival.* New York: Oxford University Press, 2018.

Jackson, Peter. "The Neoliberal University and Global Immobilities of Theory." In *Area Studies at the Crossroads: Knowledge Production at the Mobility Turn*, edited by Katja Mielke and Anna-Katharina Hornidge, 27–42. New York: Palgrave Macmillan, 2017.

Jenkins, Keith. *Refiguring History: New Thoughts on an Old Discipline.* London: Routledge, 2003.

Joseph, Gilbert, and Jurgen Buchenau. *Mexico's Once and Future Revolution: Social Upheaval and the Challenge of Rule since the Late Nineteenth Century.* Durham, NC: Duke University Press, 2013.

Kaminsky, Graciela, and Alfredo Pereira. "The Debt Crisis: Lessons of the 1980s for the 1990s." *Journal of Development Economics* 50, no. 1 (1996): 1–24.

Karush, Matthew. *Musicians in Transit: Argentina and the Globalization of Popular Music*. Durham, NC: Duke University Press, 2017.

Keightley, Keir. "Reconsidering Rock." In *The Cambridge Companion to Pop and Rock*, edited by Simon Frith, Will Straw, and John Street, 109–42. Cambridge: Cambridge University Press, 2001.

Kirkegaard, Annemette, Helmi Jarviluoma, Jan Sverre Knudsen, and Jonas Otterbeck, eds. *Researching Music Censorship*. Newcastle-upon-Tyne: Cambridge Scholars, 2017.

Korpe, Marie. ed. *Shoot the Singer! Music Censorship Today*. London: Zed Books, 2004.

Kramer, Michael. *The Republic of Rock: Music and Citizenship in the Sixties Counterculture*. Oxford: Oxford University Press, 2013.

Kruse, Holly. "Subcultural Identity in Alternative Music Culture." *Popular Music* 12, no. 1 (1993): 33–41.

Kun, Josh. *Audiotopia: Music, Race, and America*. Berkeley: University of California Press, 2005.

Kun, Josh. "The Aesthetics of *Allá*: Listening Like a Sonidero." In *Audible Empire: Music, Global Politics, Critique*, edited by Ronald Radano and Tejumola Olaniyan, 95–115. Durham, NC: Duke University Press, 2016.

Lamotte, Martin. "Rebels without a Pause: Hip-Hop and Resistance in the City." *International Journal of Urban and Regional Research* 38, no. 2 (2014): 686–94.

Laurell, Asa Cristina. "Three Decades of Neoliberalism in Mexico: The Destruction of Society." *International Journal of Health Services* 45, no. 2 (2015): 246–64.

Lefort, Claude. *Democracy and Political Theory*. Trans. David Macey. Cambridge: Polity, 1988.

Lomnitz, Claudio. *Deep Mexico, Silent Mexico: An Anthropology of Nationalism*. Minneapolis: University of Minnesota Press, 2001.

———. *Exits from the Labyrinth: Culture and Ideology in the Mexican National Space*. Berkeley: University of California Press, 1992.

———. "Modes of Citizenship in Mexico." *Public Culture* 11, no. 1 (1999): 269–93.

López Flamarique, María Teresa. *Alicia en el espejo: Historias del Multiforo Cultural Alicia*. Mexico City: Ediciones Alicia, 2010.

Lunardelli, Laura. *Alternatividad, divino tesoro: El rock argentino en los 90*. Buenos Aires: Editorial Biblos, 2002.

MacLeod, Dag. *Downsizing the State: Privatization and the Limits of Neoliberal Reform in Mexico*. University Park, PA: Penn State University Press, 2004.

Madrid, Alejandro L., ed. *Transnational Encounters: Music and Performance at the US-Mexico Border*. Oxford: Oxford University Press, 2011.

Magaña, Maurice R. *Cartographies of Youth Resistance: Hip-Hop, Punk, and Urban Autonomy in Mexico*. Berkeley: University of California Press, 2020.

Marcial, Rogelio. "Políticas públicas de juventud en México: Discursos, acciones e instituciones." *Ixaya: Revista Universitaria de Desarrollo Social* 3 (2012): 9–49.

Mason, Mark. "Deconstructing History." In *Derrida and the Future of the Liberal Arts: Professions of Faith*, edited by Mary Caputi and Vincent J. Del Casino Jr., 93–121. London: Bloomsbury, 2013.

Massumi, Brian. *Ontopower: War, Powers, and the State of Perception.* Durham, NC: Duke University Press, 2015.

Mattern, Mark. *Acting in Concert: Music, Community, and Political Action.* New Brunswick, NJ: Rutgers University Press, 1998.

Mazzarella, William. *Censorium: Cinema and the Open Edge of Mass Publicity.* Durham, NC: Duke University Press, 2013.

Mbembe, Achille. *Necropolitics.* Durham, NC: Duke University Press, 2019.

Mégret, Frédéric. "Where Does the Critique of International Human Rights Stand? An Exploration in 18 Vignettes." In *New Approaches to International Law*, edited by José María Beneyto and David Kennedy, 3–40. The Hague: TMC Asser, 2012.

Monroy, Katia. "Avándaro y las juventudes en México: Miradas múltiples en torno a un festival." *Revista oficial de historia e interdisciplina* 10 (2019): 115–32.

Monsiváis, Carlos. "Introduction." In *Rock mexicano: Sonidos de la calle*, by José Luis Paredes Pacho, i–xi. Mexico City: Pesebre, 1992.

Moreno-Elizondo, José Rodrigo. "Crisis contracultural y rock en la Ciudad de México: Relaciones de producción, reproducción viva y sociabilidad, 1972–1977." *Historia y sociedad* 38 (2020): 205–28.

Morton, Adam D. "Change within Continuity: The Political Economy of Democratic Transition in Mexico." *New Political Economy* 10, no. 2 (2005): 181–202.

Morton, Timothy. *Dark Ecology: For a Logic of Future Coexistence.* New York: Columbia University Press, 2016.

Munslow, Alun. *The New History.* New York: Routledge, 2016.

Müller, Beate, ed. *Censorship and Cultural Regulation in the Modern Age.* New York: Rodopi, 2004.

Müller, Markus-Michael. *The Punitive City: Privatized Policing and Protection in Neoliberal Mexico.* London: Bloomsbury, 2016.

Nooshin, Laudan. "Whose Liberation? Iranian Popular Music and the Fetishization of Resistance." *Popular Communication* 15, no. 3 (2017): 163–91.

Nuzum, Eric. "Crash into Me, Baby: America's Implicit Music Censorship since 11 September." In *Shoot the Singer! Music Censorship Today*, edited by Marie Korpe, 149–59. London: Zed Books, 2004.

Ocampo, José Antonio. "The Latin American Debt Crisis in Historical Perspective." In *Life after Debt: The Origins and Resolutions of Debt Crisis*, edited by Joseph Stiglitz and Daniel Heymann, 87–115. London: Palgrave Macmillan, 2014.

O'Connor, Alan. "Punk and Globalization: Mexico City and Toronto." In *Communities across Borders*, edited by Paul Kennedy and Victor Roudometof, 159–71. New York: Routledge, 2002.

O'Donnell, Guillermo, and Phillipe C. Schmitter. *Transitions from Authoritarian Rule*. Baltimore: Johns Hopkins University Press, 1986.

Olesen, Thomas. *International Zapatismo: The Construction of Solidarity in the Age of Globalization*. London: Zed Books, 2005.

O'Toole, Gavin. *The Reinvention of Mexico: National Ideology in a Neoliberal Era*. Liverpool: Liverpool University Press, 2010.

Pacini Hernández, Deborah, Héctor Fernández l'Hoeste, and Eric Zolov, eds. *Rockin' las Américas: the Global Politics of Rock in Latin/o America*. Pittsburgh, PA: University of Pittsburgh Press, 2004.

Paley, Dawn Marie. "Cold War, Neoliberal War, and Disappearance: Observations from Mexico." *Latin American Perspectives* 48, no. 1 (2021): 145–62.

Pantoja, Jorge. ed. *Rupestre: El libro*. Mexico City: Ediciones Imposible, 2013.

Paredes Pacho, José Luis. "Fotocopias, grapas y engrudo." In Cortés and González Castillo, *El rock también se escribe*, 40–42.

————. "Un país invisible: Escenarios independientes: autogestión, colectivos, cooperativas, microempresas y cultura alternativa." In *Cultura mexicana: Revisión y prospectiva*, edited by Francisco Toledo, Enrique Florescano, and José Woldenberg, 140–73. Mexico City: Taurus, 2008.

————. *Rock mexicano: Sonidos de la calle*. Mexico City: Pesebre, 1992.

Pareles, Jon. "Rebeldía, genio y represión: 'Rompan todo' el documental que explora el legado del rock latino." *New York Times*, December 25, 2020. https://www.nytimes.com/es/2020/12/25/espanol/cultura/rompan-todo-netflix.html.

Patton, Raymond A. *Punk Crisis: The Global Punk Rock Revolution*. Oxford: Oxford University Press, 2018.

Paz, Octavio. "The Philanthropic Ogre." *Dissent* 26, no. 1 (1979): 43–52.

Pearce, Jenny. "Perverse State Formation and Securitized Democracy in Latin America." *Democratization* 17, no. 2 (2010): 286–306.

Pedelty, Mark. *Musical Ritual in Mexico City: From the Aztec to NAFTA*. Austin: University of Texas Press, 2004.

Pekacz, Jolanta. "Did Rock Smash the Wall? The Role of Rock in Political Transition." *Popular Music* 13, no. 1 (1994): 41–49.

Peñaloza, Patricia. "La subjetividad, interpretación literaria de los hechos." In Cortés and González Castillo, *El rock también se escribe*, 93–97.

Pensado, Jaime, and Enrique C. Ochoa. "Introduction." In *México beyond 1968: Revolutionaries, Radicals, and Repression during the Global Sixties and Subversive Seventies*, edited by Jaime M. Pensado and Enrique C. Ochoa, 3–16. Tucson: University of Arizona Press, 2018.

Pérez Ruiz, Maya Lorena. "¿Cómo Pasó? Reflexiones sobre la reconfiguración del campo cultural en México." *Diario de Campo* 4, no. 1 (2017): 7–38.

Petersen, German, and Fernanda Somunao. "Mexican De-Democratization? Pandemic, Hyper-Presidentialism and Attempts to Rebuild a Dominant Party System." *Revista de Ciencia Política* 41, no. 2 (2021): 353–376.

de la Peza, María. *El rock mexicano: un espacio en disputa*. Mexico City: Tintable, 2014.

Post, Robert. "Censorship and Silencing." In *Censorship and Silencing: Practices of Cultural Regulation*, edited by Robert Post, 1–12. Los Angeles: Getty Research Institute, 1998.

Pynchon, Thomas. *The Crying of Lot 49*. New York: Vintage Classics, 1996.

Quintana, Andrea. "Rompan todo: Las grandes bandas mexicanas ausentes en el nuevo documental de Netflix sobre rock en América Latina." *Pólvora*, December 2, 2020. https://polvora.com.mx/2020/12/02/rompan-todo-trailer-netflix.

Rama, Ángel. *The Lettered City*. Durham, NC: Duke University Press, 1996.

Ramet, Sabrina. *Rocking the State: Rock Music and Politics in Eastern Europe and Russia*. Boulder, CO: Westview, 1994.

Rivera, Raquel, Wayne Marshall, and Deborah Pacini Hernández. eds. *Reggaeton*. Durham, NC: Duke University Press, 2009.

Rivera-Rideau, Petra R. *Remixing Reggaetón: The Cultural Politics of Race in Puerto Rico*. Durham, NC: Duke University Press, 2015.

Riwes Cruz, José Hernández. *Jumping Someone Else's Train REMIX: Una reflexión sobre el revival Post-Punk en la CDMX*. Mexico City: Venas Rotas, 2021.

Robinson, Dylan. *Hungry Listening: Resonant Theory for Indigenous Sound Studies*. Minneapolis: University of Minnesota Press, 2020.

Robinson, Roxy. *Music Festivals and the Politics of Participation*. New York: Routledge, 2016.

Rodgers, William. "Government under Stress: Britain's Winter of Discontent, 1979." *Political Quarterly* 55, no. 2 (1984): 171–79.

Romany, Celina. "Women as Aliens: A Feminist Critique of the Public/Private Distinction in International Human Rights Law." *Harvard Human Rights Journal* 6, no. 6 (1993): 87.

Roura, Víctor. *Apuntes de rock: Por las calles del mundo*. Mexico City: Ediciones Nuevomar, 1985.

Rubin, Jeffrey. "Contextualizing the Regime: What 1938–68 Tells Us about Mexico, Power, and Latin America's Twentieth Century." In *Dictablanda: Politics, Work, and Culture in Mexico, 1938–1968*, edited by Paul Gillingham and Benjamin T. Smith, 379–95. Durham, NC: Duke University Press, 2014.

Rubli, Federico. *Estremécete y rueda: Loco por el rock and roll*. Mexico City: Chiapa Ediciones, 2007.

Rubli, Federico. "Rock en México: Un recuento (Todos éramos William Miller)." In Cortés and González Castillo, *El rock también se escribe*, 13–21.

Ryback, Timothy. *Rock Around the Bloc: A History of Rock Music in Eastern Europe and the Soviet Union*. Oxford: Oxford University Press, 1990.

Salcedo, Benjamin. "El rock no está peleado con el pop ni con nadie." In Cortés and González Castillo, *El rock también se escribe*, 76–80.

Sánchez-Talanquer, Mariano. "Mexico 2019: Personalistic Politics and Neoliberalism from the Left." *Revista de Ciencia Política* 40, no. 2 (2020): 401–30.

Sánchez-Talanquer, Mariano, and Kenneth F. Greene. "Is Mexico Falling into the Authoritarian Trap?" *Journal of Democracy* 32, no.4 (2021): 56–71.

Sanders, Douglas. "Getting Lesbian And Gay Issues on the International Human Rights Agenda." *Human Rights Quarterly* 18 (1996): 67–106.

Scherzinger, Martin. "Double Voices of Musical Censorship after 9/11." In *Music in the Post-9/11 World*, edited by Jonathan Ritter and J. Martin Daughtry, 91–122. London: Routledge, 2007.

Scott, James. *The Art of Not Being Governed: An Anarchist History of Upland Southeast Asia*. New Haven, CT: Yale University Press, 2009.

———. *Seeing Like A State: How Certain Schemes to Improve the Human Condition Have Failed.* New Haven, CT: Yale University Press, 1998.

Segovia, Rafael. "La reforma política: El ejecutivo federal, el PRI y las elecciones de 1973." *Foro internacional* 14, no. 3 (1974): 305–30.

Shefner, Jon, and Julie Stewart. "Neoliberalism, Grievances, and Democratization: An Exploration of the Role of Material Hardships in Shaping Mexico's Democratic Transition." *Journal of World-Systems Research* 17, no. 2 (2011): 353–78.

Sherman, John. "The Mexican 'Miracle' and Its Collapse." In *The Oxford History of Mexico*, edited by William Beezley and Michael Meyer, 575–608. Oxford: Oxford University Press, 2000.

Simonett, Helena, César Burgos Dávila, and David Moreno Candil. "State Censorship and the Controversy Surrounding the Narcocorrido Genre in Mexico." In *Pop—Power—Positions: Globale Beziehungen und populäre Musik*, edited by Anja Brunner and Hannes Liechti, 129–53. Berlin: IASPM D-A-CH, 2020.

Smith, Benjamin. *The Mexican Press and Civil Society, 1940–1976: Stories from the Newsroom, Stories from the Street*. Chapel Hill: University of North Carolina Press, 2018.

Stahl, Matt. *Unfree Masters: Recording Artists and the Politics of Work*. Durham, NC: Duke University Press, 2013.

Stahler-Sholk, Richard. "Resisting Neoliberal Homogenization: The Zapatista Autonomy Movement." *Latin American Perspectives* 34, no. 2 (2007): 48–63.

Stein, Michael Ashley. "Disability Human Rights." In *Nussbaum and Law*, edited by Robin West, 3–49. London: Routledge, 2015.

Straw, Will. "Cultural Scenes." *Loisir et société/Society and Leisure*, 27, no. 2 (2004): 411–22.

———. "Some Things a Scene Might Be: Postface." *Cultural Studies*, 29, no. 3 (2015): 476–85.

Street, John. *Music and Politics*. Cambridge: Polity, 2012.

Sturman, Janet. *The Course of Mexican Music*. New York: Routledge, 2015.

Tatro, Kelley. *Love and Rage: Autonomy in Mexico City's Punk Scene*. Middletown, CT: Wesleyan University Press, 2022.

Tavanti, Marco. *Las Abejas: Pacifist Resistance and Syncretic Identities in a Globalizing Chiapas*. New York: Routledge, 2013.

Taylor, Timothy. "The Commodification of Music at the Dawn of the Era of Mechanical Music." *Ethnomusicology* 51, no. 2 (2007): 281–305.

Tochka, Nick. *Audible States: Socialist Politics and Popular Music in Albania*. New York: Oxford University Press, 2016.

Trevizo, Dolores. *Rural Protest and the Making of Democracy in Mexico, 1968–2000*. University Park: Penn State University Press, 2015.

Undurraga, Tomás. "Neoliberalism in Argentina and Chile: Common Antecedents, Divergent Paths." *Revista de Sociologia e Política* 23, no.5 (2015): 11–34.

Urteaga, Maritza. *Por los territorios de rock: Identidades juveniles y rock mexicano*. Mexico City: NCA, Colección Joven, 1998.

Valenzuela, Francisco. "Rompan Todo y el mito de la censura en el rock." *Revés*, December 21, 2020.

Van der Haar, Gemma. "The Zapatista Uprising and the Struggle for Indigenous Autonomy." *European Review of Latin American and Caribbean Studies* 76 (2004): 99–108.

Various authors. "Declaración de principios para una ley de cultura en México." *Diario de Campo* 4, no. 1 (2017): 123–36.

Vázquez Martín, Eduardo. "La cultura: Espacio de la libertad." Talk given at the Primer Congreso Internacional Cultura y Desarrollo, La Habana, Cuba, 2001.

In *Políticas culturales en la Ciudad de México 1997-2005*, edited by Benjamin González, 23-32. Mexico City: Ediciones del Basurero, 2006.
Vázquez Martín, Eduardo. "Experiencias culturales del primer gobierno democrático de la Ciudad de México." In *Políticas culturales en la Ciudad de México 1997-2005*, edited by Benjamin González, 35-54. Mexico City: Ediciones del Basurero, 2006.
Velasco García, Jorge. *El canto de la tribu*. 2nd edition. Mexico City: CONACULTA, 2013.
Vila, Pablo. "Argentina's 'Rock Nacional': The Struggle for Meaning." *Latin American Music Review / Revista de Música Latinoamericana* 10, no. 1 (1989): 1-28.
wa Mutua, Makau. "The Ideology of Human Rights." *Virginia Journal of International Law* 36 (1995): 589-657.
Wald, Elijah. "Mexico: Drug Ballads and Censorship Today." In *Shoot the Singer! Music Censorship Today*, edited by Marie Korpe, 170-74. London: Zed Books, 2004.
Walker, Louise. *Waking from the Dream: Mexico's Middle Classes after 1968*. Stanford, CA: Stanford University Press, 2013.
Wallis, Ed. "Bittersweet Symphony." *Index on Censorship* 43, no. 1 (2014): 162-65.
Weyland, Kurt. "Neoliberalism and Democracy in Latin America: A Mixed Record." *Latin American Politics and Society* 46, no. 1 (2004): 135-57.
Woodside, Julián. "Carientismos: Cuestionemos las historias oficiales." *Indierocks*, January 4, 2021.
———. "Sobre la festivalización o 'festivalitis' en México: Vive Latino y Corona Capital como manifestaciones contemporáneas de mestizofilia y anglofilia." *Revista argentina de musicología* 21, no. 2 (2020): 107-27.
Zamudio, Francisco. "Los periodistas del rock mexicano y su entorno a partir de la época dorada para los medios especializados: Encuentros y desencuentros." In Cortés and González Castillo, *El rock también se escribe*, 66-75.
Zolov, Eric. "La Onda Chicana: Mexico's Forgotten Rock Subculture." In *Rockin' las Américas: The Global Politics of Rock in Latin/o America*, edited by Deborah Pacini Hernández, Héctor Fernández l'Hoeste, and Eric Zolov, 22-42. Pittsburgh, PA: University of Pittsburgh Press, 2004.
———. "Rebeldismo in the Revolutionary Family: Rock 'n' Roll's Early Challenges to State and Society in Mexico." *Journal of Latin American Cultural Studies* 6, no. 2 (1997): 201-16.
———. *Rebeldes con causa: La contracultura mexicana y la crisis del Estado patriarcal*. Mexico City: Grupo Editorial Norma, 2002.
———. *Refried Elvis: The Rise of the Mexican Counterculture*. Berkeley: University of California Press, 1999.

INDEX

Alatorre, Víctor Manuel, 33–35
Arriola, Mikel, 1–2, 6
Avándaro Festival
   direct experiences of, 33–34
   press scandal relating to the, 1–2, 33
   repression after, 10, 21–22, 27–30, 45, 148–49, 195–96
   narratives about, 31–32, 36–40, 51–52, 93, 172–82

Botellita de Jerez, 100–101, 104, 137, 163
Break It All: The History of Rock in Latin America (Netflix docuseries), 3, 27–28, 30, 40, 45, 50–52, 185
Briseno, Guillermo, 97, 106, 172, 202, 220

Castelazo, Arturo, 33, 42–46, 50, 59, 65, 200
Catana, Rafael, 134–38
censorship
   commerce and, 5, 22–23, 56, 69–71, 75–76
   government and, 4–6, 23, 37
   new censorship theory, 4–5
   self-censorship, 11, 35–36, 73
Chac Mool, 29, 69
civil society, 99–105, 159

ColectivaMente, 182–85
Comite Internacional de la Nueva Canción, 97
communication, 42–44
Competitions of New Values of National Rock, 48–50
Conecte, 22, 31, 58–69, 168–71, 199
Coordinator of Independent Cultural Spaces, 141, 147–51, 161

democratization, 17, 74, 86, 105, 138–40
developmentalism, 36, 178, 199, 239

event security
   accidents and, 70–71, 90, 94
   commoditization and, 87
   privatization and, 10, 23, 78
   protests and, 28, 78, 103–11
   security at Avándaro Festival, 175
   violence and, 20, 47, 87–88, 102

Forum of Alternative Spaces, 147, 161
fresa aesthetics, 22, 54, 68–71

governmentality
   authoritarianism and, 56, 107
   contestations of, 67
   policymaking and, 158–60

governmentality (*continued*)
  poststructuralism and, 9–10, 133
  power and, 126, 182–84

hoyos fonqui, 2, 30–31, 42–44, 50–51, 62, 174

independence
  independent magazines, 91, 170
  in live music scene, 2–3, 62–63, 82–83, 116, 141
  "mainstream" versus "independent," 71–75
  in music production, 22–23, 55–62
  punk and, 64–68
  reification and, 65, 68
Independent Cultural Spaces (ECIs), 25, 148
internationalization, 74

journalists and journalism
  anti-socialism and, 38–40
  disinformation and, 32–33
  education and, 172–78
  government interference and, 35, 40
  journalism and professionalism, 168–70
  journalistic values, 25, 115, 167, 174–76
  music as journalism, 23, 96–100
  musicians as journalists, 2, 14, 140, 166
  neoliberalism and, 167–72
  relationship with OCESA, 79–80, 89–94
  relationship with small venues, 116, 125, 150–51, 166
  support for censorship and, 42–46, 50–51

Los Dug Dug's, 29, 57–60, 93
Los Nakos, 137–39

Malacara Alonso, Antonio, 38, 47–49, 205
Malacara Palacios, Antonio, 31–32, 43, 59–60, 176, 202
Maldita Vecindad y los Hijos del Quinto Patio, 27, 54, 71, 96–99, 103–11
Maná, 13
Medalla Phonos awards, 48
México Canta, 31–34, 41, 43, 199–200
Molotov, 13, 192, 227
Movement of National Regeneration (Morena), 1, 24–25, 112, 114, 128, 142, 151
Multiforo Cultural Alicia, 20, 116–18, 133–38, 147–50, 163–64

Nahuatl, 29, 57, 197, 200, 205
nationalism
  cultural nationalism, 31, 39, 75, 180–81, 191
  ideology and, 105
  nationalization of rock, 188
  rock nacional, 2, 33, 50, 183–84, 187
neoliberalism
  dictatorship and, 17, 194
  ideology and, 18, 39–40
  transition and, 75, 85–86, 127, 171
Network of Independent and Alternative Spaces (RECIA), 147–51, 161
new wave, 41, 55–56, 65, 185
North American Free Trade Agreement, 73–74, 97
Nuevo México, 29, 57, 181, 197, 201, 208

Operator of Entertainment Centers (OCESA), 20, 23, 78

Pájaro Alberto y Sacrosaurio, 29, 57, 135, 171, 230
Panteón Rococó, 27, 99, 109, 123, 173, 226
Party of the Democratic Revolution (PRD), 1, 24, 26, 108, 115, 127, 144
Peace and Love, 33, 45, 93, 181, 197
Pompeyo, Herbe, 53–54, 69, 212
Pop, 20, 32–36, 41, 43, 196, 199
punk, 64–68, 100, 106, 120, 123, 185
Pynchon, Thomas, 139–40

RECIA (Network of Independent and Alternative Spaces), 147–51, 161
Revolutionary Institutional Party (PRI)
  authoritarianism and, 40, 56, 77, 81, 94, 178–79
  clientelism and, 24, 127, 144
  debate relating to, 6–7, 179
  nationalism and, 31, 180
  Revolutionary Family, 10
Rey, Venus, 40–41, 200, 210
right to culture, 141
Rock en la cultura, 30, 145, 197
Rock en tu idioma, 22–23, 54–57, 63

slam, 106–11, 223
social class
  chavos banda and, 54, 67, 102
  fresa aesthetic and, 69
  Malinchismo and, 9
  middle-class rock audiences, 55, 99
  rock journalism and, 32, 45, 49–50
Subcomandante Marcos, 97, 103, 141, 220
Syntoma, 56

Three Souls in My Mind, 31, 134, 196–98
Tinta Blanca, 41, 43, 197, 203

Unique Syndicate of Musical Workers (SUTM), 40–42, 51, 210

Zapatista Army of National Liberation (EZLN), 23, 96

www.ingramcontent.com/pod-product-compliance
Lightning Source LLC
Chambersburg PA
CBHW030533230426
43665CB00010B/871